The Last Deployment

LIVING OUT

Gay and Lesbian Autobiographies

The Last Deployment

How a Gay,
Hammer-Swinging Twentysomething
Survived a Year in Iraq

Bronson Lemer

The University of Wisconsin Press

The University of Wisconsin Press
1930 Monroe Street, 3rd Floor
Madison, Wisconsin 53711-2059

3 Henrietta Street
London WCE 8LU, England

Printed in the United States of America

"The Mustache Race" by Bronson Lemer, copyright © 2006 by Bronson Lemer, is reprinted from *Twentysomething Essays by Twentysomething Writers*, edited by Matt Kellogg and Jillian Quint. Used by permission of Random House Trade Paperbacks, a division of Random House, Inc.

ISBN 978-0-299-28214-1

While some names have been changed, all persons described in the following pages are real, and all events occurred as described.

For my father

"Do you know how long a year takes when it's going away?" Dunbar repeated to Clevinger. "This long." He snapped his fingers. "A second ago you were stepping into college with your lungs full of fresh air. Today you're an old man."

Joseph Heller, *Catch-22*

Contents

Contents

The Last Deployment

Prologue

In a dimly lit restaurant, I stare back at the only man I've ever loved. It's the end of January 2008, and this is the first time I've seen him in seven years. I've come to tell him that I still love him and to resolve some unfinished business I thought we had from when we dated in 2000 and 2001, but looking at him now, I realize that I've probably made a mistake.

We're sitting at a small table in the rear of the restaurant, right off the kitchen. The tablecloths are blood red, and above us a star-shaped light fixture casts a romantic glow over our table. There are wine bottles and take-out containers and appetizers, people talking and laughing and chewing. It is a small restaurant on the outskirts of Boston, with a bowling alley in the basement, and from the staircase I can hear the blunt thuds of bowling pins knocking against each other.

We order a gourmet pizza. The waitress brings us two plates, and my ex-boyfriend—Jeremy—begins talking about Boston. He is, essentially, the same man he was seven years ago. He still has the same sense of humor that comes out during his stories, the same light-hearted air that made me fall in love with him so many years ago. His voice is still pleasant and easy to listen to, and I can remember other times spent listening to him— late-night dinners in greasy restaurants, conversations over coffee at our favorite shop in Moorhead, Minnesota, and his soft, whispering voice late at night. He has less hair now, but his face is essentially the same. There are the same blue eyes that sparkled when he got excited. There is the same wide smile, the one I'd see in my head while I laid awake thinking about him. There are the same rounded cheeks, the same neck and collar bone I used to kiss.

For the past two years, I've been sending Jeremy irregular drunken e-mails about still being in love with him. I rarely got replies. Yet, a few months ago, when one of his replies ended with a casual invitation to visit, it didn't take me long to respond: *How about January?*

When he finishes talking, I clear my throat and, without looking at him, begin the monologue I rehearsed on the bus ride up from New York.

"Well, I wanted to . . . ," I say, but stop mid-sentence.

I want to reach across the table, take his hands in mine, look in those beautiful eyes, and tell him everything he's missed, particularly the long year I spent in Iraq. With vividness I haven't experienced since returning from the war, looking at him I can recall the hot summer of 2003, the begging children who swarmed my platoon's trucks in Baghdad, the scorpions the other soldiers and I caught and released on the Kuwaiti sand, the silly mustaches and even sillier arguments we had for twelve long months, and the men and women we were before all that happened. I want to describe the sand in Iraq, so soft at times that it felt like ash, and how it stuck to our sweat as we kicked our way across that country. I want to tell him how daunting it was being a gay man in the American military, how I'd gotten so used to hiding my sexuality from other men that now, four years after leaving the military, I have a hard time forming a meaningful relationship with another man. Mostly, I want to explain how during that year, my only saving grace—the one thing that helped me get through the war—was thinking of him. I held onto those small memories and replayed them in my head every time I put on that uniform and marched out into that desert. They all come flooding back to me now.

But what doesn't come back, what refuses to resurface, is my love for this man. When we were dating, I loved him like I'd never loved anyone before, and I have yet to love anyone that way since. But now, that love is gone. Something happened to change that.

The candle on the table flickers and casts a shadow of his face onto the wall. From the basement, I hear the dull thud of two objects being forced into one another. Hearing those pins collide and fall onto the waxed wooden floor, I remember what it was like to have two forces at work inside me, knocking against each other, and eventually falling down. I look up at Jeremy and remember the man I was seven years ago. During my early twenties, I defined myself by two things—my sexuality and my service to my country. I was proud of one and ashamed of the other, and it took me a long time to fix because the fear I had about admitting my sexuality to myself stemmed from my association with the military. I hid who I was from different people in my life, thinking I could separate the two parts of my life into nice, even compartments and shift smoothly between them.

But seeing Jeremy now and being reminded of the last seven years, I realize how intertwined those two parts have become. When I think about the first time I kissed him in his dorm room in the fall of 2000, I also remember a dorm room at Fort Carson, Colorado, where I cleaned the dust from the lenses of my gas mask and watched television images of tracer rounds arching over Baghdad as the war began in 2003. When I recall my first day in the army, when I stood by myself in a camouflaged uniform that was too big and boots that weren't shined, I also remember the first time I met other gay men and women, and the nervous energy that pulsated through my body. A trip to an Atlanta strip club with my squad after our deployment to Kosovo blurs into my first drag show where a dramatic queen touched my forearm and winked at me in a way I didn't understand. As much as I try, I can't pry apart those two parts of my life. It took a long year in Iraq to help me understand that.

I entered the Iraqi desert with a mission: to prove to myself—and to others—that I didn't have to choose one or the other; I could be both—a soldier and a gay man.

I returned with so much more.

Olympic Hopefuls

Soldiers are erasing Saddam Hussein from Iraq. They start in Firdos Square on April 9, 2003, helping an ecstatic group of Iraqi citizens topple a twenty-foot statue of Saddam constructed for the ruler's sixty-fifth birthday. The Iraqi men have been throwing shoes at the statue—a great insult in the Arab world. Marines come along, attach a chain to Saddam's ankles, and tug. They pull the statue diagonally. Saddam's erect hand—held out as if he were saluting the moon—swivels from sky to ground. With one last tug the statue tips forward, its legs snapping in half, sending Saddam crashing down to the swarm of Iraqi men waiting below.

The Iraqi citizens pounce on the toppled ruler. They tear the statue apart, first taking a head, dragging it through the streets as children throw shoes and shout in joy. The men offer several swift rib kicks to the statue, which now lies face down in the rubble. Saddam doesn't moan; he lies there and takes it. The soldiers and men find other symbols of Saddam and pull at their seams until the monuments give way, falling like old farmhouse chimneys, backbones no longer strong enough to support the weight of a crumbling country. At billboards, soldiers erase Saddam's image from Iraq as they whitewash them clean, children gleefully wiping away the former leader.

On May 25 we pull up to a soccer stadium in Baghdad and notice a bronze statue of a young boy in soccer garb, one cleated foot holding down a dirty, white, cement soccer ball. The bronze boy has a painted yellow jersey and matching knee-high socks. He stands on a slab of cinder blocks and mortar, facing the soccer stadium, a welcoming symbol of this country's fondness for soccer.

We file from the truck—our weapons in hand—and out onto the parking lot in front of the stadium. I stretch, my back bowing, arms still holding my rifle as I push the weapon into the sky. My body aches from the trip—miles through the half-dark streets of Baghdad, the city still encased in morning light. We've been conducting Task Force Neighborhood missions for almost a week, traveling into the city to repair schools, hospitals, and now soccer stadiums. The city streets look the same, but the people always change.

The missions are more menial than I imagined. The tasks are simple: repair three dozen wooden school desks, build a brick wall at a hospital, rewire the electricity for a fire station. But the people are what drain me. It's a numbers thing—there are always so many more of them than of us. They follow us as we walk around their neighborhoods; millions of eyes are watching us all the time. I can't get past the fact that *I* am the stranger here. I am the one walking into their homes, their schools, down their streets. They *should* be able to watch me, but I still get uneasy seeing them standing on street corners, watching us stretch and grumble about another mission in this miserable place.

Our vehicles have formed a horseshoe in the lot. At the edge of the horseshoe, children and men have started to appear, tan faces with curious eyes. I look over to the entrance of the stadium and notice a herd of U.S. military officers—captains, lieutenants, sergeant majors—talking to an Iraqi man, pointing into the stadium. Next to the officers is the boy, the bronze boy, poised in front of the stadium. He stands ready, his arms folded behind his back, his proud chin up, his eyes a dull, muted gray. His jersey is streaked with white bird shit, yet he remains tall, a survivor against his hardships.

"Lemer!"

Newman, my squad leader, stares at me.

"You and Jones stay with the vehicles for now," he says, before leading the rest of the squad toward the stadium.

"Shit," I say under my breath as I walk back to the truck, deflated from having to do guard duty.

Jones doesn't seem to mind. He sits in the back of the truck and drinks from his canteen. I lean against the tailgate and stare off into the crowd forming at the perimeter. These missions always garner masses of Iraqi citizens—mostly curious kids and men without jobs. For a while the children walk by as if nothing has changed, ignoring us. But soon curiosity strikes, and they look at Jones and me with inquisitive eyes. Most of them are barefoot. Some wander by in loose sandals. They eyeball our weapons. An older boy rides by on his bike, watching us sip water from our canteens. He nearly crashes into a group of men standing at the curb across the street. The boy circles around and makes another pass, again gazing at us, our weapons, the MREs (Meals-Ready-to-Eat) we have in the back of the truck. He doesn't stop. Instead, he turns away and disappears down the road.

The men are jobless. They stand in groups of three or four, some dressed casually in dark slacks and cast-off T-shirts with Coca-Cola slogans. They talk quietly, watching the American troops watching them. Their hungry eyes look out under bushy eyebrows. Now that we've run off their leader, they look to us for guidance, assistance, help. They point off into the distance, as if casting blame on the city itself. Instead of walking up to us, they hold their ground across the street and let the children be the curious ones.

Jones and I watch the military police draw the line. We follow the MPs as they set up police tape around the parking lot, looping it through our vehicles. They are putting up a barrier to separate us from them. They use their weapons to shoo back children, pointing at the boys' bare feet and ushering them behind the line. They direct three women, the only Iraqi women we've seen since we arrived in this country a little over a month ago, to take the long way around our vehicles, now looped together, forming a perimeter of steel truck bodies held together by plastic tape. We stand near the tape, resting on our truck.

Jones reaches into the back of the truck and pulls the box of MREs to the tail of the vehicle. He rifles through it, looking for the good meals: beef teriyaki, chicken Tetrazzini, Salisbury steak. When he finds the right one, he grabs hold of the sides of the package and pulls. I watch the heads of children snap up and look over in our direction. Instantly, the sound of bare feet slapping against concrete bounces off the trucks as the children come running our way.

"Mee-sta, Mee-sta!"

This morning, while loading the truck, we made a sound I'll never forget. It was the sound of rubber soles slapping against steel as we climbed into the truck. It was *our* sound, the sound of sleepy-eyed soldiers going off to "battle," another day of missions in this city. It was the sound of purpose. The sound of work. When Jones pulled apart that MRE, the children made a similar sound, the quick slap of bare feet against cold pavement—the sound of feet on the move.

"Mee-sta, Mee-sta!"

The children come sliding across the parking lot, pushing themselves against the security tape like hockey players shoved against glass. They bump and grind their way into each other, elbowing for a good position. Their small stomachs bump up against the tape, flexing the line to the limit. They push because they know they can; they know we aren't going to hurt them.

Then the hands come out, reaching into our perimeter. They reach for what they don't have. Their dirty fingers wiggle and point in our direction. Their bare toes creep under the line, sliding as far as their bodies will allow. They are closer than either Jones or I would like.

"Mee-sta, Mee-sta! Gimme!" they say, dirty hands making the universal sign for "feed me." They take their thumb and two fingers and move in and out of their mouths like bulimic women trying to purge.

"Mee-sta! Gimme, gimme! Mee-sta!"

I turn to Jones and smile. He's still holding the sides of the MRE. His face is frozen in amazement.

"You brought this on," I say, laughing.

They are all boys, some maybe teenagers. The youngest ones stand in front, their faces smooth and tan. They don't smile. Instead they look at us with the same eyes children use on fathers. The older boys tower over them, reaching. They look like old men, dirty faces with crease lines across their cheeks and dark circles under their eyes. They are more forceful with their questions, yet the young children certainly match their eagerness.

"Mee-sta, Mee-sta!"

They stretch out the "e," drop the "r." For a moment, Jones and I wonder who they are talking to, looking behind us even, as if our neighbors or teachers—men *we* called mister—are standing there. Yet the only thing behind us is the high wall of the stadium.

One of the older boys grabs the security tape, pulls it over his head, and walks toward us.

"Back," I say, pointing my weapon at his feet.

He stops, looks at Jones and his MRE, then at my weapon, my boots, my pockets, the name tag on my chest, the magazine of ammunition I have slapped into my rifle. He slowly raises his eyes to mine. I look into his eyes, seeing the things he desires—food, money, recognition. He looks so old standing barefoot on the pavement. We stay that way for a moment, him looking at what I have, me looking into his sad eyes, his childish face worn down by a country at war. The boy turns nonchalantly, like it's no big deal, as if he's had soldiers point guns at him before, and walks back to the line and the other boys.

I don't like being this way—forceful. I don't like telling people they can't eat. But I must keep these boundaries for my own good and for the good of the men and women in my platoon. I hate to do it, but I need to draw the line. I never used to be like this. I don't remember the last time I was this forceful, and it actually scares me how instinctively I'll point my weapon at anyone who doesn't obey our rules. It's what the uniform has done to me. The uniform has given me power, power that, as a child, I wanted, but now I find myself in this country, pointing M16s at harmless children and shrugging at their eager requests, as if I don't even hear them.

Jones hops off the truck and walks over to where I am standing, a few feet from the vehicle. He knows they are already getting to me and it's only ten o'clock.

Three boys kick a soccer ball down the road. They move around the ball, their skillful bare feet gently tapping it in one direction, then another. They don't smile or laugh. It's as if the act is so common that it no longer holds any pleasure. As they move closer, one boy notices our group. He grabs the ball and walks over to where we are standing.

Jones and I watch the new children approach. We discuss making them do tricks for us. We turn the game on them, asking *them* for something— entertainment.

"Can you do a trick?" I ask the crowd of boys. I first look at the boys down front, the little ones, then over at the kid with the ball. I look them all in the face, all of them except the boy who crossed the line.

"A trick," I say. I move my hands up and down, as if three invisible balls are softly floating between my hands.

For a moment I think they'll understand me. I think that maybe my imaginary juggling has sparked some kind of image in their minds. I wait for acknowledgment that we are all on the same page. I get blank stares and another chorus of "Mee-sta, Mee-sta!"

After five minutes of trying to get the children to do tricks, we give up. We walk back to the truck. The children stay where they are, leaning against the security tape, harder this time, more persistent. They'll stay that way all afternoon, until we feed them or shoo them away.

Roach comes back from inside the stadium. He grabs an MRE and sits on the tailgate. I am now free to go inside. As I walk to the entrance of the stadium, I see the crumbling building towering before me like an old man, fragile at the seams and ready to tumble to the ground. The high, cracked wall cups the field, an opening like a mouth at the center, ushering participants inside.

The bronze boy welcomes me at the entrance. When I walk in the front doors, to my left and right I see offices that have been looted and destroyed; pieces of the building lie across desks, filing cabinets, and tables. Further up the hall I see a door to what I assume is the locker room. At the end of the hall, a white light welcomes visitors out onto the field.

The field isn't in good shape. The grass is brown, with patchy splotches dotting the field. A group of Iraqi men help unearth a pipe near one of the goals, a soldier acting as foreman nearby. Once out on the field I notice the bleachers. A set of stairs on either side of the main corridor leads to the box seats, half of which are missing. From there, steel bleachers stretch out like wings, a wavy steel canopy covering the patrons who used to sit at the very top.

Near the main entrance a dozen Iraqi men talk with three military officers. Other men linger around the field. I notice Rainman staring off at the men working on the field.

"Can you believe that Saddam used to train Olympic athletes here?" Rainman says as I walk up.

He stares out at the field as if he's an archeologist trying to imagine what went on here.

In 2002, when Saddam Hussein announced plans to build a 100,000-seat stadium in Baghdad, the world knew what was coming—Saddam wanted to host the Olympics. Iraq had never been strong in the Olympic Games. In 1960 they won their first and only medal, a bronze in weightlifting. Since then Iraq's participation in the event has been in slow decline. In 1980 they sent forty-three athletes to the games; in 2000 they sent only four.

Yet Saddam was persistent in his desire to host the games, despite his star billing in President George W. Bush's "axis of evil." His son Uday was president of the Iraqi National Olympic Committee. Uday's wrath as leader of Iraqi athletics includes a number of horrible actions, cruelties that might have stemmed from watching his father torture people. He tortured athletes for losing games, sometimes just for fun. He placed athletes in prison for days or even months, beat them with iron bars, and caned the soles of their feet. He screamed at players during the halftimes of soccer matches, sometimes strong-arming coaches into making the changes he suggested. In 1997 the governing body for international soccer sent officials to Baghdad to investigate reports that members of the Iraq national team were imprisoned and had their feet caned. Uday denied the charges and so did the athletes, out of fear. The officials had nothing to hold Uday on.

I can't even fathom these sorts of actions, especially on athletes who are simply playing a game to entertain the masses. I grew up in a house full of brothers who were on the high school wrestling team. I know athletics is about more than just having fun. It is about winning. My brothers' methods of winning were always fair and, to me, ridiculous at the same time. Their torture was self inflicted—senseless liquid diets to slim down before matches, and hours upon hours of weight training and running. But they never complained about an angry coach who beat them after they lost a match or coaches who yelled incisively until they broke down in anger and fear.

I stand watching the Iraqi men pull up the pipe, thinking about Saddam, his sons, my brothers, and I wonder, when did sports become so much like war?

Across the field, I meet Grayson, our platoon leader, at a hole in the wall that spreads along the soccer field. I climb over rock, crushed cinder blocks, and wood, and into another field, similar to the first. This field is slightly smaller, also surrounded by a high wall. However, this field is full of holes. Grayson is smoking a Camel Light. He takes drags from his cigarette and points to another soldier, who's using the Bobcat to fill the holes with dirt. The holes are burrowed into the ground and lined with cement. Three rows of sandbags provide a barrier around each hole. They are spread out across the ground like open graves. I walk to the closest one and kick sand into the darkness.

"Foxholes?" I ask Grayson.

He nods. They *are* foxholes, fighting positions. It is then that I notice an Iraqi teen leaning against the wall. The teen has been helping Grayson fill the holes, and fill in the story behind why this field is littered with what looks like open sores, dark blotches spread across the dusty gravel lot.

Saddam's army used the field to train Iraqi military troops. Athletes turned into soldiers. Grayson points to the far wall. Painted on the wall are targets, white squares on a sunburned orange wall, each with a head-and-shoulders black silhouette like the targets we use back home. The silhouettes are hand painted so each head is a different shape, each body extended to a different point on the wall.

I walk across the field, zigging past each foxhole. When I reach the targets, I run my hand across them. The tips of my fingers fall into the chips and trace the cracks that spider across them. I can't tell if the chips are from bullets or decay. I turn to look back at the foxholes, like a prisoner facing a firing squad, and I imagine the children I saw outside playing soccer on the main field while, one field over, soldiers practice shooting black silhouettes.

Standing there, I realize that there's a disconnect between us and the Iraqi people. We don't know what it's like to live in this kind of fear. We don't understand the troubled mothers who fret over whether their children will return from school, or whether their husbands will find work without being killed in the process. We have yet to fully understand what it means to fear walking the streets of this city or to hear the ricochet of gunfire from the stadium down the street where soldiers now train. Fear flows through this country like water through a hose, and we're the thick thumbs of children pressed up tight against the nozzle, forcing water to fire off in all directions. We just press our bodies into this country and hope the violence subsides.

Before returning to the main field, I inspect one of the foxholes. I poke the sandbags with my rifle. The hole is lined in ragged cement. I want to hop down inside the fighting position, feel what it's like to be these people, these other soldiers. I want to know what it's like to grow up in this country, a soccer ball between my feet, as I kick my way across the city, gunfire exploding like bursts of cheering fans over my head. I want to understand the feeling of becoming a young man here, where my soccer ball is replaced by a gun, and where instead of wandering the city, I seek out targets and release rounds of ammunition from my rifle. Looking up from beside the foxhole, I am immediately aware of how razor thin the line between pleasure and pain is here.

I look up at Grayson, who shakes his head, advising me not to jump into the hole. I feel he fears not only the possibility of IEDs at the bottom of the hole but also the lurking idea that I may actually feel sorry for these people when I lower my body down into a hole long vacated by Iraqi soldiers, and see what they see.

Once, my brother Brandon and I dug a hole. We dug it wide and deep—wide enough to throw a basketball into but not so deep that we couldn't see the bottom. We found our father's hole digger—a long-handled, shovel-like tool he kept in the shed next to the round grain hopper on our family's farm—and we dragged it to the shelterbelt of trees behind our house. With our skinny little arms, we lifted the tool up and slammed the metal pinchers into the dirt. As we worked, it looked like two giant metal fingernails pinching together, scooping up, and moving dirt.

Our goal was to make a trap. We'd seen it on TV. Man builds a hole, wide and deep. He covers the hole with twigs and grass and waits for an unsuspecting animal to discover it and tumble to the bottom, unable to get out. We liked the idea of catching animals this way. We liked how easy it sounded, much easier than chasing after them. More importantly, we wanted the feeling of power that people get when residing over littler things. We wanted to feel that power as we stared at the fox or skunk or cat trapped at the bottom of our hole.

What we didn't think about was what would happen after we caught our fox or skunk or cat. Would we simply keep it trapped while we took weekly trips down to the hole to admire our catch and give each other high fives? How would we release the animal? Or *would* we release the animal? How would we feel if, one day, after a few weeks of admiring our fox/skunk/cat, we walked to the hole and found the animal dead? What would we do then?

We never caught anything in the hole. To regain some sort of power, we tried chasing things toward it—our dog, our sister, even dumber-than-shit sheep. Nothing worked. Instead, years later, Brandon found that power in sports and I found it in the military. I like the power of firing a rifle at silhouetted targets, of throwing a grenade and watching things blow up. Most of all, I like being part of a team. I feel powerful and strong simply by wearing a camouflaged uniform and carrying a weapon.

But with this power comes a price. While the military makes me feel powerful, it also gives me a sense of insecurity—a sense of always being chased. As a gay man, being in the military means keeping silent about my sexuality. Nobody can ask me if I am gay, and I can't tell anyone about myself. Instead, I constantly live with a sense that I'm about to be discovered, taunted, ridiculed, and kicked out. It feels like wolves are always nipping at my heels, occasionally puncturing my pant-leg but never fully sinking their teeth into me. It's a horrible feeling.

And that is the great paradox now. I am torn between two opposing roles. In my role as an American soldier I am the chaser. I am the one in power. I am one of thousands of troops storming into this country, firing our weapons, sweeping through houses, and ushering out Saddam and his supporters in hopes of building a better country. I make people run and hide simply by wearing this uniform. But in my other role—as a gay man—I'm used to always being chased. I am the one who is always running, looking over my shoulder, and hiding wherever I can. I run because I fear getting caught. I don't want to be shamed or hurt or humiliated, and I don't want to fall down a hole and be laughed at by a couple of American boys with God complexes.

So I find myself standing above a foxhole in the middle of Baghdad, feeling both powerful and insecure. I suppose, to an extent, the soldiers who once trained in this field felt the same way.

When I return to the main field the atmosphere has changed from a battlefield into a playground. Several soldiers have changed from desert camouflage uniforms and boots to shorts, T-shirts, and tennis shoes. They are kicking a soccer ball around the field. A group of young Iraqi men stand at one end of the field watching the soldiers fight over control of the ball. They chat with each other while they stretch, preparing for the battle ahead.

This morning Newman made us all take our PT (physical training) uniforms and tennis shoes with us into the city. He mentioned something about a game, but we had no idea what to expect. Most missions don't involve games, and we very rarely have fun in this city. But we obeyed his orders and stuffed our tennis shoes and shorts into our green laundry bags, slung them over our shoulders—next to our rifles—and climbed into the truck.

The bleachers are empty. I stand with a group of soldiers near the main entrance, watching the teams warm up. When all players are ready, the game begins. The United States against Iraq. The soldiers look confused at how simple the Iraqis make it look, zipping past each soldier, tipping the ball from foot to foot with ease. They pass from teammate to teammate, the ball sailing through the legs of the soldiers. The Iraqis spin the troops in circles with their delicate passing. They move down the field before reaching the goal, where their feet make a swift snapping sound as one of them scores.

When the soldiers get the ball back, they have difficulty moving it down the field. They fumble and trip; one soldier even falls over the feet of another and tumbles to the ground. The Iraqis have no difficulty scoring again. The soldiers then try to counter their movements, attempting to block kicks and steal. But the Iraqi men clip past the soldiers, rotating the ball from foot to foot, from man to man.

I am reminded of another soccer game—during my first deployment to Kosovo in 2000. We played soccer once in a neighborhood yard, surrounded by men and children. We took turns going up against the young men of the village, one on one. They were all raggedy teens, toughened by conflict. They kicked a gray ball at us, each time finding a way to move around us as old men and women smiled and clapped from doorways and street corners. We didn't score a single goal that day.

Now I watch the soldiers try to recover against a new opponent. But the troops are down by three and look tired and confused. As the game wears on, the soldiers loosen up. They relax, coming to terms with their inability to work together as a team and their general trouble moving the ball. They laugh whenever an Iraqi kid steals the ball, throwing their hands in the air. They've stopped yelling every time one of their kicks doesn't come close to scoring a goal. They no longer chase the Iraqis down the field. They walk, sweat-soaked T-shirts sticking to their backs.

The parking lot is mostly empty when I exit the stadium and walk to our trucks following the game; the children have taken to begging elsewhere. A few old men linger across the street. A group of women dressed in black glides by. The statue of the soccer player stands idly.

Jones is packing up the truck. I help him load our equipment before noticing a boy watching us. I hop down and walk over to the police tape.

"Hello," I say, waving at the boy. My weapon is slung across my back.

The boy is six or seven years old. His arms and legs are thin, ready to snap right off his body. He wears a white shirt with buttons, small blue shorts, and no shoes. He looks over at Jones, who's holding a blue Iraqi officer's hat, similar to the kind bellboys wear as they pull back hotel doors and escort visitors into lobbies. Jones fiddles with the cap a bit, running it over his fingers, before he notices the boy watching him.

Jones walks over. He turns the hat around in his hands, explaining that an earlier Iraqi kid left the item by our truck. He reaches forward and places the hat on the boy's head.

The hat is too large; the thick fabric devours the boy's head. The boy reaches up, pushing the cap back, and peers out from under the bill. Then, as if instructed, his arm snaps up in a salute.

We laugh, slapping the boy high fives. *Good man*, I say. *Good man*.

Jones goes off to finish loading the truck. I instruct the boy to wait by the security tape as I run over to the tailgate and search inside an MRE box. I find a package of Tootsie Rolls and a chocolate pound cake. I look back at the boy. He's waiting just outside the perimeter line, his body not even touching the tape. I motion for the boy to come here, to the truck, past the security line the MPs have drawn.

The boy steps forward slightly, ducks his head under the security tape, and steps over to the truck. I hand him the candy and pound cake. He holds the packages in his hand, turning them over before looking up at me. Then he's gone, dashing under the tape and out onto the street. As I lift the tailgate closed, I feel good about letting someone cross the line. I've been waiting for some kind of epiphany about why we're in this country. For two months I've been wanting some sort of explanation as to why I had to be plucked from my former life, stripped of an indentity I was just growing into, and placed in this country. I latch the tailgate into place and look up to see the dark blue hat float through the crowd, and I understand why.

I look over at the statue of the soccer player, the one I noticed when we arrived here this morning, and I think back to the scene where Marines pulled a statue of Saddam to the ground. I was in a pizza restaurant at Fort Carson, in Colorado, pretending to be a man but still very much a boy, when that scene played out on a thirteen-inch television mounted at the back of the restaurant. The war had begun and the television was broadcasting coverage 24/7. There were embedded journalists reporting from the desert, riding in tanks, walking next to the soldiers. There were Marines storming the city, pushing their way into Baghdad and never looking back. There were images of Iraqi citizens smiling and howling and weeping, and I wondered if I'd get to see these Iraqis, the ones broadcast so vividly on the screen.

Twenty minutes earlier I'd been talking to an Army reservist who lived in the dorm room next to mine during my sophomore year of college. I hadn't seen the guy in a couple of years. Of all the places in the world, we'd run into each other at this Fort Carson pizza restaurant, two boys headed to different wars. He was headed to Afghanistan; I was headed to Iraq. We were in different circles during college, but he was always next door playing video games with his roommate, instant messaging his girlfriend, watching as I snuck my boyfriend into my dorm room. We were both college students then, but when we ran into one another at the restaurant we were something different. We stood next to each other, dressed in camouflaged uniforms we only used to wear one weekend a month and two weeks in the summer, talking about how we each got there. One minute we were studying for tests, packing beers into backpacks before heading to house parties, and squabbling with our roommates; the next we were cleaning rifles, learning about gas masks and mortar attacks, and getting bombarded by begging children. How did everything change so quickly?

I toss my rifle onto the front seat of the truck before climbing inside. As we make our way out of the stadium parking lot, I watch a crowd of Iraqi people—mostly men and children—walking slowly down a Baghdad alley, headed home at the end of the day. There must be something about the way they move or how the late afternoon sun casts shadows across the street, but watching the people, I can't help but wonder how I even got here.

Last Supper

January 20, 2003: I'm twenty-two and debating growing a beard. I'm sitting in the office of the college newspaper I work for, stroking the three-day growth on my chin. I have to time growing a beard just right, starting after drills this weekend and letting it grow until February's drill weekend, when the National Guard will force me to shave again. Only once did the Guard allow soldiers to grow beards, and that was several years ago, to commemorate North Dakota's one hundredth anniversary, and I don't think they'll make another exception.

I am only six months away from getting out of the Guard, and I'm tired of it all. I'm tired of putting on that uniform and doing field exercises in some cow-shit pasture in southern North Dakota as it dumps rain and snow around me. I'm sick of standing in rank and taking orders, and I would live happy if I never again had to clean another rifle or shine another goddamn combat boot. Generally, I'm tired of being a weekend warrior. But I'll tough it out, for another six months anyway. I made a commitment and I intend to follow through with it.

When my cell phone rings I don't think about answering. It's the middle of the afternoon, and I'm thinking about an upcoming English essay, this week's issue of the school newspaper, and a college photographer I've had a crush on for two years. But when I check my messages and find my squad leader saying, *Pack your bags, we're being deployed*, I let out a loud, sharp *fuck*, and all those thoughts disappear.

I need to report to the armory in Wahpeton, North Dakota, in four days.

I'm probably the last person anyone expected to join the military. But I needed something to get me out of North Dakota, something that would help me figure out who I was, and the army just happened to be at the right place at the right time.

In high school, while my friends were picking up pamphlets from colleges and universities, I brought home several brochures about the Army National Guard. I figured the National Guard would be a good way to ease into the soldiering life. *Army-lite*, I called it, *all the perks but only half the grueling labor.* The brochures sat on my desk for nearly two weeks before I picked them up, looked through them, and called the recruiter. On a summer evening in late August 1997, a recruiter pulled up in front of my parents' house with papers in hand.

I remember most of the details but very little about what I was feeling. My father sat at our dining room table rubbing his hands together as I watched the recruiter cross our front lawn and approach our garage door. He wasn't a big man. He didn't look tough, like the men I'd seen crawling through mud in the commercials, or the Marines cutting up dragons in between episodes of *Growing Pains* and *Saved by the Bell.* He didn't look like my father or my classmate's father, who visited our fifth grade class after he'd returned from Desert Storm. This recruiter didn't look like anyone's father. He looked like someone's older brother, someone you'd ask to buy you beer. He was a young man in his twenties, dressed in an olive green, class A uniform with medals pinned to his chest, holding a briefcase and ringing our doorbell.

My mother welcomed him inside and offered him a seat at our table. He nodded at my father, shook my hand, and sat down. My mother offered him something to drink. She looked nervous; my father looked excited. I sat at the table, numb from all the information and questions that were flying across the table. I simply sat back and let my parents do all the talking. They took turns asking the recruiter questions. The recruiter flipped through some papers and passed a brochure about the Guard across the table to me. It explained how I'd have to attend drills one weekend a month, fifty miles north in Rugby, North Dakota, until I graduated from high school and moved to Fargo to attend college. Then I'd start drilling with an engineer unit in Fargo—the 142nd Engineers. The recruiter also talked about summer camp—annual two-week training sessions where troops train at military instillations across the state and practice their military craft. My father nodded his head and asked the recruiter about deployments. I figured I'd have to help with sandbagging during flooding or provide security during a state emergency, but I thought I'd never leave the United States in my uniform.

The National Guard really only gets deployed during times of war, the recruiter said. I thought about that statement and about what I already knew about our last war—Desert Storm. It was a short war, and if I were to get deployed, I imagined it would be a lot like Desert Storm—brief.

The recruiter talked about the benefits—the G.I. Bill and money for college. I joined the National Guard for the money, and I have no problem admitting that. I didn't join because my father wanted me to or because military service ran in my family. The only family member I knew who served in the military was my middle-aged, beer-gutted, bus-driving uncle. I didn't join out of patriotism or a need to serve my country. I didn't join to provide my five younger siblings with a role model to look up to or to show my friends how noble and strong I was. I joined because I wanted a college education. I am the oldest of six children, and my parents didn't have the money to put all of us through college.

It happened so quickly. This decision, the one concerning my future, went by in a flash. Before I knew it, my father was shaking the recruiter's hand as he walked him to the door. My mother was holding the desk calendar the recruiter had given her—*Here's some shitty calendar with the National Guard logo stamped on it in exchange for your firstborn child*—and she was smiling. I remember looking at her and wondering how so much was decided in such a short time. Did I make this decision or did my parents?

My emotions didn't catch up with me until a few days later. During the following week, I thought a lot about my decision to join the National Guard. I thought about what I was getting myself into and how my friends would react when I told them what I'd done. I thought about how proud my father looked at the end of the table while I was talking to the recruiter. He didn't have to say anything. I knew that he was stepping back and letting me learn my own lessons. He didn't have to tell me that I was making a mistake; if that was the case, he knew I'd figure that out myself.

When I saw the recruiter's car pull up to my high school, I thought about running. I thought about grabbing my school bag and running the two blocks to my house, where I'd lock myself inside my closet and pretend I never shook the recruiter's hand. It was instinct; whenever something hard came along, my mind always told me to run. Mostly, it had to do with being gay in a culture that didn't understand what that meant. I felt it was much easier to run than to face any of my fears—the fear of admitting my sexuality to my family, to my friends, and most importantly, to myself. Instead, I decided to train myself to run long distances, to outrun any obstacle that came my way, to endure. When it came time, I could run for hours and never get tired.

But there was always something else preventing me from running, some other fear that ran parallel to that of admitting my sexuality: the fear of disappointing the people I loved. I thought about how upset my father would be if I didn't join the military. I didn't want to feel the shame of turning back on a decision, of not following through with my commitments. This fear usually won out.

When I opened the door to the recruiter's car and slid into the passenger seat, I felt power surge through me. I knew I was making the right decision.

My transformation from student to soldier starts almost immediately. Outside the campus bookstore, where I've just returned my textbooks, I run into an old friend whom I haven't seen in almost a year. We exchange hellos. I ask him how school is going, and he asks me the same. I don't tell him about the deployment call or that I'd just returned all my books and was headed to the registrar's office to drop all my classes. I don't tell him that I'd been packing the previous night, stuffing uniforms into olive-drab duffle bags, and selecting the CDs I wanted to take on the deployment. I don't tell him that my mother almost cried when I told her the news. Instead, I say nothing. The deployment almost seems like a dream. Everything is happening too quickly for me to even think about what it means. I stare back at him and refuse to accept that my life is about to change.

Another friend stops me in the school courtyard to state that he didn't even know I was a member of the military. The news of the deployment makes me realize the double life I am living. I am a full-time college student and a one-weekend-a-month soldier, and I like it that way. For the past five and a half years I've worked to hide different sides of my life from different people. I hid the military part of my life because I feared that I had made a horrible decision when I joined the National Guard. When I told my boss at the local newspaper where I write obituaries that I was leaving for war at the end of the week, she just looked back at me in amazement, shocked that the man she'd been working with for two years was also a weekend warrior. I felt like a spy who'd been forced to reveal his secret identity.

"I've managed to hide it well," I say.

After I tell my friend that I am a carpenter, a profession I am horrible at, he says, "Like Jesus."

Yes, I think. *Just like Jesus.*

I am an outsider among these men. When I show up for our first formation after the call to duty, I watch the men form the ranks and am flooded with memories of what it's like to be among these guys.

Most of the people in the company are familiar with military deployments. I recognize the looks on other soldiers' faces; it is the same look I'd shared with them a little over three years ago. I was nineteen, a year into my enlistment, and a college freshman when my company was deployed to Kosovo in 2000. I went from writing English essays about animal cruelty and flipping burgers at an A&W to handing out school supplies at underprivileged schools in the former Yugoslavia providence and building bunkers at Camp Bondsteel. I spent seven months not thinking about college exams, beer kegs, or fraternities, but rather how to communicate with the people of Kosovo and how not to let the M249 machine gun bang into my thighs when I carried it around that country.

My fondest memory of Kosovo was our weekly Risk game. Elijah, a new soldier in our company, drew the Risk game board on a white floursack towel and packed the plastic rectangles of game pieces inside his duffle bag. We met weekly to battle over Oceania (all the purple-colored countries), form alliances against one another, and take each other out with the cunning use of strategy. It felt good being a little dictator around the board, playing general as I ordered my men into battle against the enemy. At the end of the deployment, on our last game night, we held a championship game. The winner took home a wooden plaque we'd commissioned a local craftsman to create. We snapped photos, smoked cigars, and laughed at the time we had spent together. I remember these meetings now because this is what I wish being in the military was like. I wish war could be approached with such glee and good humor, as it was those nights in Kosovo. But it's not. War is never as simple as rolling dice, and I don't think I'll ever be as close to a group of men as I was then.

I watch the other men fall into rank, and before joining them, I step back and look at the group. I am on the fringe, watching from the outside but never fully feeling part of the game. They are down-and-dirty type men. They like guns, talking about cars, ogling women in *Maxim Magazine*, spitting chewing tobacco into liter bottles, and reading U.S. Army Field Guides. They are blue-collar workers, men who have grease on their hands and black-and-blue fingernails from the missed swings of a hammer. They are the kind of men who have tiny calendars of topless women under the visors of their trucks, and racks for their guns along their truck's back window. They are drop-everything-for-opening-deer-hunting-weekend men, men like my grandfather, my uncle, my brothers, and my father. I like to go to the theater, study Latin, talk about art, and read Emerson, Hemingway, Thoreau, and Erdrich. I am more interested in academics, the way words form on the page and fall from the tongue, more in tune with music and artistic expression than turkey calls or how a shotgun sounds, but somehow, I find myself among these men.

When I hear the command calling the company to attention, I think about where I am, how I even got here, how I managed to find myself in the second squad of a military platoon about to be informed that we are headed to war. Mostly, I start to think about how I can get myself out of this situation.

The U.S. military has a policy of "don't ask, don't tell," where as long as I don't speak about being gay, nobody can ask me about it, and I can serve my country. During the first three years of my enlistment, I hid who I was in order to fit in, in order not to feel like such an outsider. On drill weekends I sat alone and eavesdropped on conversations about drunken bar fights and angry girlfriends. I listened but never spoke up. Instead, I adopted a silent persona. When people asked about the woman I was living with, I let them assume that I was "shacking up with a female," as they put it, for my own safety and well-being. I never corrected them or told them that we were simply friends. And it worked. I felt a sort of kinship with the men and women who'd shared the Kosovo experience with me.

But eventually, as the years went by, I became sullen and distant. I sat alone, grumbled angrily to myself about the military and my desire to get out. I didn't put much effort into drill weekends because I felt disgruntled at the bad decision I had made to join the Guard, and the people I used to feel comfortable around either left or stopped talking to me altogether. My only salvation was knowing that I could turn the army off like a light switch. At the end of the weekend, when that uniform came off, I went back to being the person I was comfortable being, someone who didn't and couldn't fit in with the army.

Now, three years after the Kosovo deployment, the part of my life I wanted to leave behind was about to become my only life. For five and a half years, I took turns flipping that switch, alternating over and over, and that was about to end.

There are muddy bootprints up and down the hall. As soldiers move about the building, they track the late January melting snow inside, their footprints like stamps of places they've been. The tracks look almost comical, like the black dotted line in the *Family Circus* comic strip that shows were Billy's been in the neighborhood. The muddy prints start at the doors and circle around the maze of hallways. They snake down one hallway, up another, and out across the gym floor. Some trail off; some double back. Some are large and dark, others small and lopsided. They are the footprints of the men and women of Bravo Company of the 142nd Engineers. They are the mark of soldiers on the move, troops preparing for their mission as they haul equipment and luggage through the building's gymnasium and to the back loading dock where it will be placed into trucks and driven to Fort Carson, Colorado.

I am not helping load equipment. I am being punished by mopping up the tracks. This morning I awoke at a quarter after eight, fifteen minutes *after* I was supposed to be standing in formation at an armory sixty miles away. As I dressed in my uniform, found my car keys, and started the drive south, I threw a tantrum of curse words. I cursed my alarm for not waking me, my car for not going fast enough, my parents for letting me join the military, every damn person in my company, and the people who set this deployment in motion. I was frustrated and tired from a week of packing and preparing, and being late only made it worse.

When I arrived at the armory nearly two hours late, I was berated with comments from people thinking I'd run off to Canada. The first sergeant handed me a mop and bucket of water, pointed down the halls, and instructed me to clean up the company's mess. I didn't ask any questions. Instead, I hung my head and went to work.

I lean on the mop and look down the hall at the line of tracks leading to the back door. Swinging the mop left, then right, I make the footprints disappear, wishing everything was this easy to erase. I wish with a flick of my wrist I could wipe away war, conflict, poverty, get rid of all the muddy footprints in the world. Like playing general during Risk, where I'm about to send troops into battle by moving them forward, I wish I had the power to play such a Godlike role. But I am a simple soldier. I don't have the power to change anything, and standing in my camouflaged uniform mopping floors, I can only listen to orders and do what I am told.

I laugh and shrug when other soldiers walk by. They point at me and say things like *Now don't you wish you'd run off to Canada?* I do regret not running away to Canada, but as I lift the mop from the bucket and squeeze out the water, I know that I could never run away from the commitment I made to my country, to this organization. I signed up for this.

When I've finished mopping up the tracks, I find Elijah sitting by himself on the back dock, inventorying the contents of one of our platoon's toolboxes. Elijah is a police officer in Hillsboro, North Dakota. He is short and stocky, with dark hair and glasses. I like talking to him because we both have a fondness for movies and pop culture, even though Elijah leans a little too heavily into the sci-fi realm. His wife, Lisa, used to be a soldier. She was a member of Bravo Company before he was, and when the company was deployed to Kosovo, she asked the company commander to let her husband transfer in so he could spend seven months keeping the peace beside her. She got her wish. Shortly after we returned, she left the company with dreams of raising a family. She was pregnant with their first child.

The dock is littered with different equipment and toolboxes. There are boxes for the power tools and table saws for the carpenters, plumbing kits for the plumbers, ladders for the electricians. Outside, I notice other members of the platoon lining up the trucks. We've spent the last couple of days getting ready, and on Tuesday we'll drive our trucks and equipment down to Fort Carson. I crouch down, grab one of the hammers, and start flipping it into the air, catching it again by the handle.

"I helped move all this crap down here two weeks ago," I say.

In between the semesters, I had helped move my platoon's equipment from an armory in Fargo down to the newly constructed one in Wahpeton. It was an easy job. But during that time there was talk of an upcoming deployment, talk that the United States was going to invade Iraq and force Saddam from the country. I didn't believe in the necessity of another war. I've never felt very political, but when talk of an impending war started to spread, I was strongly against it. It was talk that made me nervous because I was close to having my enlistment expire and kissing the army goodbye, and I didn't want to be forced to stick around just because George W. Bush wanted war.

"Well," Elijah responds, "at least all our equipment is here and not up in Fargo."

He smiles and continues checking off items on his list. He reaches for the hammer in my hand and I give it to him. I help him finish inventorying the toolbox, helping count the tape measures, drill bits, levels, tool belts, and other items. He closes the box, moves to one side, and gestures for me to grab the other handle. We lift and carry it across the bay, placing it in a pile of inventoried and ready-to-load items.

"So," Elijah says as we walk across the bay, "the last rodeo, huh?"

Kosovo was my first rodeo—my first deployment—and as everyone in the platoon knows of my desire to leave the military, they all know that *this* deployment will be my last hurrah.

I nod my head.

"Well, we better make it a good one then."

He slaps me on the shoulder as we walk to the locker room, where the rest of the platoon are emptying their lockers and inventorying their personal belongings. Once there, Newman hands me a packing list and several copies of my orders.

I watch the rest of the company pack their gear. I watch uniforms being stuffed into duffle bags. Some of the younger soldiers are having a hard time packing, and Elijah and Newman are helping them properly stuff their gear in order to save room. I notice brown army-issue T-shirts strewn across the floor, mittens tossed aside. There is some debate as to whether we should take cold-weather items such as scarves and insulated combat boots. Most people want to leave the items behind but Newman tells us to pack nearly everything. *We'll decide what we need and don't need once we're in Fort Carson*, he says. I look around the room at the people I'll be spending this deployment with. I hardly know most of them. They aren't like my friends outside the military. They talk and laugh, help each other check off items on packing lists, and close the padlocks on their stuffed duffle bags. While I've spent the last few years being angry at the military, they were busy forming bonds and friendships. There is camaraderie in watching these men pack. I see it floating around the room but I can't feel it. I'm scared because so much of what goes on in war involves trusting the man standing next to you. Yet how can the United States have an armed force that's based on trust and support if there's also a policy built on secrecy and lies? How can I stand next to these men—packing for war—and feel comfortable among their ranks? I haven't done anything except be myself, and now that decision is coming back to bite me in the ass.

That night, I stand in front of a full-length mirror and take a good, long look at the man staring back. I am still wearing my camouflaged BDU (battle dress uniform) after a long day of packing. My boots are all scuffed up and dull. I look ragged and disheveled, like a different man. But if I squint hard enough, I can still see the man I want to see underneath all this camouflage.

I can still see the teenager wanting to get away, yet now he's gotten all he's wanted out of the military and he wants nothing more than to be free from it. I see the college student who used to go to classes, listen to lectures, and wake up each morning excited about learning a profession he likes instead of pounding nails and measuring two-by-fours. I see a gay man who wants to believe that the military has changed, that in the modern military he can serve next to any other man and not be treated any differently because of whom he sleeps with. And I see a man who's still afraid, even after so many years of putting up his defenses, of thickening his skin so nobody ever knows who he really is.

I start to strip off the uniform piece by piece. The boots fall haphazardly onto the carpet, one slung across the other, the laces tangled together. The shirt and trousers make a pile in the middle of my bedroom floor. I fling aside the beret and the sand-colored T-shirt. Standing there in just my underwear, I am reminded of how it felt during my first year in the National Guard, when I was still new and different. I had yet to build up a dislike for the long weekend drills and the monotonous actions of the military. Both inside and out of the military, I was still finding my legs, figuring out who I wanted to be, where I fit in. Now, years later, I'm nothing but a jaded twenty-something who's angry at the world and the decisions he's made.

I know that once I leave this apartment I won't be coming back the same person, and that scares the shit out of me. *I like who I am*, I think. *I don't need to change, and I don't need some stupid war to tell me who I am.*

In the spring of 2000, we ran in the hills of Camp Bondsteel, Kosovo, almost every day. Usually, we ran as a company—one large formation of soldiers running in four ranks. We all wore the same outfit—gray sweatpants and sweatshirts with ARMY printed boldly across our chests. As we breathed in the mountain air, we trudged up and down the little hills along the road, our shoes dunking into and out of the puddles as we went along. It was a team effort, but if you weren't strong enough to keep up, the platoon would leave you behind, forcing you to motivate yourself to catch up or give in and walk the gravel road home, alone. The stronger runners would leap-frog the weaker runners, kicking up mud as they passed and forcing the weaker runners to fall back to the rear of the formation. Slowly they would drop out of the formation, like pieces of cheese crumbling away from the larger block.

I usually ran somewhere in the middle, not the strongest runner in the platoon but not the weakest either. If I felt particularly motivated, I'd run faster and move to the front of the pack. If I felt lazy and lethargic, I stuck to a steady pace in the middle, content with being average. But I never fell to the back of the formation. I never wanted to feel like I was being left behind.

As the majority of the platoon completed the cool-down exercises after the run, we'd see the weaker runners walking the last hill, looking small and defeated, until they reached the formation and sheepishly snuck into one of the ranks in the rear. The legs of their sweatpants were usually covered in mud; the whole calf area would be brown. They not only took on the mud from their own running, but they also accumulated mud from other runners passing them by. After the exercises, we'd walk back to the wooden SEA (Southeast Asia) huts we called home, shower, and prepare for the day. Rarely did anyone say anything about the weaker runners, but we all thought about them. We all knew who couldn't keep up with the group because we liked to keep tabs on the weakest links.

As I prepare for the deployment, it is this image of the mud-soaked runners that sticks in my mind. I could quit. I could tell someone that I am gay and be discharged from the military. But every time I think about quitting I remember those weaker runners. All I have to do is think about them, their mud-coated sweat suits, their deflated faces, and the silent ridicule we all gave them for not keeping up. It is that fear of failure that keeps me going.

More than anything else, that fear is in the back of my head now. *Keep running*, it says. *Keep running*.

When my friends gather at a local restaurant to bid me farewell, I try not to think about it being my last meal, even though I call it that. Typically, I've thought of "lasts" as times for rejoicing and celebration. I remember my last week in basic training, where I could look forward to no longer having to shovel my meals into my mouth and endure screaming drill sergeants, and I remember our last game of Risk in Kosovo before heading home. The deployment—my last rodeo—will be the final hurdle I'll have to clear, so I try to look at it in a positive way. But when you're going off to a war you have a chance of not returning from, you think about things like last beers, last meals, and last conversations. It's just part of human nature.

My friends are gathered around a long wooden table when I enter the restaurant. I take the only empty chair, the one at the head of the table. It looks like I'm the king at the center of his court. A couple of my friends have brought balloons, an obvious effort to cheer up the occasion. They ask about the past week of preparation, the other people in my company, how my parents are handling everything. I tell them about my mother, how part of me doesn't want her to see me leave because I hate seeing her cry. I tell them about my silent father. It's hard to tell if he feels proud or afraid or what because I have a hard time reading his emotions. I am like him in that way, always able to put on a disguise and cover up how I really feel.

I order a beer, not knowing when I'll be able to drink alcohol again.

"You know," one of my friends says, "we could pretend to kidnap you if you'd like. Take you up to Canada."

"Would I have to ride in the trunk?" I ask, laughing as I flip through the menu.

They've been joking about kidnapping me all week. Each call I've received is filled with ridiculous plans for getting me out of this deployment, any attempt at keeping me free from harm. I don't consider most of the plans—shooting myself in the foot, actually telling them I'm gay—because I knew that being deployed was a possibility when I signed those papers, and I wasn't going to back out now.

"I hear Canada is really nice this time of year," another friend says. "Besides, I love a road trip."

"My parents told me that I have relatives up in the Yukon," I say cheerfully, thinking back to the one time my father mentioned it.

"Well, there you go. You can stay with them."

Until now I've always discarded their foolish ideas of running away from this deployment, but for once I find myself thinking about this latest option. I think about living in the cold, northern Canadian territory, finding work at a library, maybe teaching at an elementary school, or writing for a local newspaper. In the winter, I'd look up at the sky and see the northern lights, and in the summer, I'd stand outside and watch the sky stay lit all night, and I'd be glad to live in a place that doesn't go dark. But I'd have to leave all the people sitting at this table. None of them would want to go with me; they have nothing to run away from. I'd have to leave everything I've come to know and understand, and as I watch my friends chat among themselves, laugh, and listen to my best friend Beka tell one of her rambling stories, I feel sad and thankful at the same time.

I explain to my friends that several people are probably getting married this week—rush weddings to reap the benefit of deployed servicemen. The television news ran several stories, and in this week's newspaper a couple holds hands and smiles, thankful for their time together now. My friend Alicia jumps on the opportunity to propose.

"My grandmother has this really nice chandelier," she says. "And the first child to get married gets it."

I laugh and politely decline her proposal. I don't want to confuse people even more. When the waitress comes to take our orders, I feel an urge to order the most expensive thing on the menu. I remember reading that Timothy McVeigh's last meal before he was executed was a pint of ice cream and a glass of water. I go much grander than that, ordering the largest steak in the restaurant.

At the end of the meal, when my friends have stopped talking about kidnapping me, we pay our bills and drive a few blocks to the only gay bar in town. It is early and the bar is nearly empty. We walk to the back and squeeze into a red and white vinyl booth. The Chinese lanterns above the bar seem to sparkle, and in the adjacent room I hear the thumping of techno music. A couple of drag queens, sipping from glass tumblers, sit near the end of the bar. Two skinny lesbians are trying to get a pack of cigarettes from the vending machine. My friend Ashley wants to dance. My other friends chat with an old drunk at the bar. They order me drink after drink, and soon I am in a comfortable state of bliss, where I don't have to worry about finding my way home. I am among friends, people I care about and people who care about me, and it feels good to be loved. I rest my head on the table and for a few moments imagine what it would be like to never have to leave these people. I imagine that after the bar we'd get in the car and drive north, through Grand Forks, past the U.S.-Canada border, through Winnipeg and Saskatoon, and on to northern Canada. We would drive all night, talking like we did the night we drove to South Dakota to see a concert, when we learned everything about each other and the world was loud and vibrant. Except this time, instead of South Dakota, we'd be in the great wild Yukon. We'd make fun of the guards at the border, exchange our dollars for loonies and toonies (one- and two-dollar Canadian coins), buy beer at a liquor store, and throw the bottles at geese along the marshes. We'd stop at the shadiest Canadian hotel we could find and curl up on one large bed, warm and alive. In the morning we'd wake and repeat that day—just that day—until I couldn't feel that bundle of nerves rolling around in my stomach, until my heart slowed its rapid beating, and until the lump in my throat—the lump that first appeared the day I got that call—disappeared.

But then the heavy reality sets in like cement weighing us down to those vinyl seats. The room is silent. The man at the bar is gone. The jaded queens have fallen off their stools. Ashley is tired of dancing, and everyone wants to go home. Part of me wants to stay here, to hide, because I know that I'm not coming back the same person. But another part of me wants an adventure. As we rise from that booth and stumble to the door, I feel my ghost staying behind, still sitting in that booth as the lights twinkle and the world refuses to change, while my body pushes open the heavy door, feels the cold winter wind, and looks up to see the white peaks of the Yukon's Gray Ridge Mountains.

Snow Bullets

We leave Wahpeton thinking we are heroes. As the sun comes up on January 28, I hoist my rucksack over my shoulder and board the bus headed for Fort Carson. The other soldiers take their places behind the wheels of our trucks or in the vinyl bus seats. They look like statues, all straight-faced and angry from a busy week of preparing and packing, and little sleep. The bus is quiet, funeral quiet, almost too silent.

We leave the parking lot and I immediately see them, the well-wishers and family members along the side of the road. The streets are lined with people as we make our way to the highway. Some hold signs and flags. Children dressed in parkas, scarves, and mittens brave the cold to see off their brothers, sisters, neighbors, mothers, and fathers. A half-dozen senior citizens—veterans who've seen this happen before—sit inside warm Oldsmobiles, honking their horns like geese, proclaiming their support. I don't know what to do, so I just stare back at the people in the streets. I smile at the children, nod to the men outside the welding company on the edge of town who salute as we pass. Some of the women are crying. They wave and hold signs and whip around flags like any red-blooded American would do, but they also wipe away tears and cling to each other. I imagine they realize that the men and women passing before them, the same men and women who used to help sandbag during flooding, who stood guard at the armories after the 9/11 attacks, who were always ready to step up and help their communities, are now stepping up to help their country, and they won't be returning the same. Or maybe they don't. Maybe they think some of us will never return, and the life they are building inside their heads—a life without us—is too much for them to handle. Either way, we leave the city on a high note, thinking that we are invincible, strong, and brave, but also knowing that we can return to the people who love and respect us, the people we leave behind.

Outside the city, a firefighter waves a huge American flag near the highway. His arms are thick and strong, and he waves the flag back and forth as if this deployment is a NASCAR race and he's signaling the start. I put on my headphones and let the Icelandic band Sigur Rós play me out of North Dakota and away from home. I feel nostalgic leaving the place where I was born and raised. I'm uneasy being among people I hardly know, headed to a place I've never been, for a length of time that has yet to be determined. Mostly, I'm confused. All that flag waving made us feel like heroes, like we'd done something brave just by answering the call. It wasn't a bad feeling; it just felt deceptive because I know that the feeling of invincibility I'd felt watching the community wave and salute wouldn't—and couldn't—last.

I stare out the window of the bus as snow-covered fields and fence posts whiz by. We're somewhere in South Dakota, coasting down Interstate 29. The television above my head is playing the movie *We Were Soldiers*, and I watch briefly as Mel Gibson talks to a young soldier about fatherhood. I watch and listen to the advice—much like a child would—because I never had these kinds of talks with my own father. I never had a heart-to-heart conversation about the birds and the bees, about how to trust another man, or what it meant to serve your country. Our hearts never talked in those ways.

My childhood is filled with examples of lessons taught through my father's actions, not his words. I learned to trust by watching him interact with angry neighbors and other ranchers. I learned to love by watching how he treated other living creatures, whether braving North Dakota blizzards just to feed our horses or helping ewes through birth. I learned what it meant to put in a hard day's work by watching the man construct a barbed-wire fence or fix a bailer. There's a silent admiration in watching a man work, and as a child, I was always my father's biggest admirer, even if at the time I didn't fully realize the lesson he was teaching me.

The day I learned about fate I realized that my father was wise beyond his years.

My family used to raise cattle on a small hobby farm. I don't remember how many acres of pasture we owned, but out beyond the hill where I went sledding with my siblings every winter was a patch of prairie along a tiny branch of the Sheyenne River. It was the pasture farthest from our house, and we used to herd cattle out of the pasture and back toward the barn. I remember one trip where my parents loaded my brothers Brandon and Bo, my sister Nikki, and me into our old blue Ford pickup and drove out to the pasture to bring the cattle in.

Brandon and I were six and seven, respectively, old enough to help out on the farm. My father turned to us when he needed the ice chopped from a water tank or help catching our family's sometimes-wild horses. My parents parked the truck on the top of a slope, fifty yards from the river, and Brandon and I got out to help my parents herd the cattle. Below the truck were a dozen short crabapple trees dotting the bank of the stream. My parents had gathered the cattle together and were herding them toward the gate. Brandon and I stood along one side of the herd, the side nearest the river, while Nikki and Bo stayed in the cab of the truck.

I don't remember how it happened, but as my father and mother were ushering the cattle toward home, I noticed the truck slowly inch forward and start to roll down the slope toward the river, with nobody behind the wheel. In my mind I saw what was about to happen. I saw the truck crash into the river, the bumper dipping into the stream and sending my siblings flying from the vehicle. Bo would slowly sink below the water. Nikki would scream and scream until water filled her lungs. At the time I remember the stream being a large gushing river, but in reality it was probably a thin ribbon of dark, murky water. Regardless, as the truck rolled forward I knew that if I didn't do something, somebody would end up injured or, even worse, dead.

So I stepped in front of the truck; I put myself between the truck and river. I childishly thought my body could stop the vehicle from rolling. I saw the truck coming toward me, picking up speed as it rolled down the slope. I saw the eyes of my brother and sister. I heard my father shouting at me to get out of the way, to step aside and let the truck roll. My father knew there was nothing he could do. If fate was going to take his two children then fate would take them. But he knew enough to save my life. He knew that it was better to lose two children than three, even if both scenarios where undesirable. Before the truck could reach me, I listened to my father and stepped aside, letting the truck continue to roll.

I like to believe that my father knew a tree would stop the truck. I like to think that he knew the inner workings of fate, that by stepping in front of that truck I was interrupting my brother and sister's destiny. That truck was *meant* to hit that tree; therefore, my father knew he had to get me out of the way and let destiny run its course. I stepped aside and watched as the truck rolled past me. Ten yards before the river, the truck slammed gently against a tree, causing my brother and sister to start crying.

There was nothing I could have done to stop that truck from rolling. Yet I refused to give up that control. I thought that if I tried harder I could always control the course of my life. If my life was that pickup truck, I wanted to always have control over the direction it was taking, to never let go of that wheel. *I* decided which direction to go. *I* controlled the turns and dealt with the consequences. It's the same feeling gay men and women get when deciding to come out of the closet; they take the wheel and turn their lives in a new direction. I did that when I came out to my friends, and now, I never want to let go of that wheel because I fear what will happen if I do.

When I joined the military, I thought I still had control over my life; I thought I was making the right turn. It wasn't until years later that I realized it had been a wrong turn, and I was staring straight at a no-U-turn sign. I was stuck in an organization that stripped me of control. When I signed that contract, I signed my life over to the U.S. Army, and my fate was in their hands.

The night before I boarded the bus for Fort Carson, I shook my father's hand and gave my crying mother over to him. He knew I'd be all right, that I listened when I was younger and picked up on the things he'd taught me. And I knew that he couldn't always protect me. He wouldn't always be there to pull me out of the way. He didn't say anything, and he didn't really have to. He looked at me in a way that said he was proud of me, nodded, and turned to escort my mother out of the armory.

We pull into Sioux City, Iowa, as the sun sets. On the outskirts of the city we find an old brick armory, where we're scheduled to relax and eat. I walk into the building and sit down at one of the half-dozen long tables set up in the gymnasium. Across the table is Hackman, one of the new soldiers in my platoon. I got to know him a little on the ride down because we were both sitting at the front of the bus. He looks so young, still a kid with a pudgy baby face. He reaches into his pocket and pulls out a pack of playing cards.

"Wanna play a game?" he asks. He takes the cards from the cardboard box and shuffles them between his small hands.

"What game?" I ask.

"War."

I laugh at the irony of playing War while headed to war. Hackman is silent as he deals out the cards, puts his hand together, and starts the game.

He gets into it, flipping his queens over my jacks, his tens over my twos. I'm losing at War and for now, I'm alright with that.

"Call me Bobby," he says as he looks up between hands.

I nod as he lays an ace atop my queen.

After dinner, as we load the bus bound for our hotel, I notice a pair of black combat boots dangling from a power line above the parking lot. I point at the boots and nudge Elijah.

"What's with the boots?" I ask.

"You've never seen that before?" Elijah replies. He then explains that soldiers will toss a pair of boots over power lines for three occasions: once they've completed basic training, when a soldier leaves one post for another, or when a soldier gets out of the military. Oftentimes, the troops will paint the boots orange or yellow to make them stand out. *Shoefetti*, they call it.

I watch boots swing in the breeze and fantasize about the time I'll get to toss my boots over a power line. I get this grand idea of painting the boots bright pink and gathering my friends for a sort of shoe-festooning ceremony, where I'll gladly fling the boots over a power line and then proceed to the Red River, where I'll dump everything in military camouflage into the water and watch the gear sink into the muck. If nothing else, I get by just thinking about the day I'll be able free myself from this organization.

It will be the day I reclaim control of my fate.

When we arrive at Fort Carson on January 30, we are eager for a warm bed and place to settle down. The journey to Fort Carson had spoiled us. We spent three days on the road, traveling from Wahpeton to Fort Carson military base, outside Colorado Springs, Colorado. Along the way, we stopped in Sioux City and North Platte, Nebraska, where we refueled both our trucks and our bodies. We slept in queen-sized hotel beds, ate fancy buffet dinners and continental hotel-lobby breakfasts, and nursed hangovers on reclined bus seats.

We walk into maintenance bay 8142 with great anticipation. We expect beds, clean sheets, showers to wash away the days of traveling. Instead, we see an open room filled with cots, troops from Headquarters Company lined up across the bay. They look like flood victims forced from their homes, people in transit. The building used to house military Hummers, two-and-a-half-ton trucks, and maintenance equipment needed for repairing vehicles. Base personnel wiped oil from the floor, rolled barrels of gasoline and grease elsewhere, and moved trucks and equipment away to allow us to sleep. Each soldier has a five-foot living space between his cot and the next. Duffle bags and gear are stuffed below the cots; pictures and children's drawings hang above the cots near the walls. The line of green cots stretches down the entire bay and across the hall into two other bays.

Grayson leads Second Platoon—thirty-five soldiers—to the rear of the building. Here, we set up camp, unpacking our gear, settling into our new home. We construct a wall with our camouflaged ponchos and hang it from the rafters, curtaining off a section of the bay. Relics of our former lives appear out of duffle bags. First come pictures of loved ones—wives, children, parents. Then come things to take our minds off the deployment. A couple of soldiers pull out huge black binders full of CDs. I notice books being pulled from bags. Elijah takes out his Risk set, and I smile, fondly thinking back to Kosovo.

Once unpacked, we lie on our cots, resting and laughing at the circumstances we are in. Our cots are so close we could reach over and lock arms right now, forming a human chain stretching across the bay—links in a military defense force. But we don't; we're not that comfortable with each other yet.

We spend the next couple of days attending briefings and prepping for the deployment. We receive the small pox vaccination and spend hours scratching our armpits like gorillas. I watch the scab on my arm form and eventually fall off. I start reading Joseph Heller's *Catch-22* and become as paranoid as Yossarian. When Yossarian states that even his lymph nodes are out to get him, I feel my own lymph nodes, then check myself into sick call, believing (like Yossarian) that I have cancer. I find out that the swelling is just a side effect of the small pox vaccination.

We relax around our bay or walk to the convenience store at the top of the hill for beer and junk food. Most of the time we sit around our bay awaiting orders. Bobby and I play another few games of War. Others break out the Risk board and battle over continents. Rumors swirl around the building. The bay is alive with an uncomfortable buzz, whispers of possible deployment locations, possible assignments, possible threats. We want to know where we are going; we want to know our future. The buzzing gets louder as the rumors are passed from soldier to soldier. Someone brings in a newspaper, and Newman reads out loud a story about Turkey letting U.S. troops into the country in preparation for an Iraq invasion. When he finishes the article he looks up to find all eyes on him. We listen because we want answers, but in the end all we have to hold on to are rumors.

Sitting in a waiting room at Fort Carson, this is what I imagine: The desert is gray. The sand is dull and colorless. It is the clichéd desert of movie sets and television shows, and it is gray because it is a place I've never been, never set foot on, never touched. In the dream the desert is the same as the one in the movie *Three Kings*, except there's no color and George Clooney isn't kicking ass across the sand.

I am driving an army truck across this gray desert as members of my platoon sit in the back. The sand has pushed itself up against an abandoned truck, charred black by a roadside bomb and now lying lonely in the ditch. I stare at the truck as we pass, before forcing myself to shake the image from my mind. Across the field the children are faceless. They gleefully kick a ball across the sand. They seem to be having a good time, and I want to pull over and play soccer with them, but I can't. I must move forward with the mission.

Women covered in black sheets walk by with buckets on their heads. There are chickens and goats, even a donkey pulling a cart as a teenage boy whips the animal, forcing it forward. I look at the men in the back of the truck. We have guns and are pointing them out the side of the truck, ready for an attack, or to put that poor donkey out of his misery. It is summer in the desert and we are all hot.

Suddenly, a car swerves into my lane and heads straight for our truck. I crank the wheel to the right, expecting to crash through the rusted side rail and down into the ditch. I swerve just in time to miss the car, but as I steer the truck toward the ditch a rocket-propelled grenade strikes the windshield, splitting the truck like an axe to firewood. Before we get a look at the bastard in the car or even flash our weapons, the truck explodes—straight out. We spin into the ditch and fall open, bursting into flames. There is no time to scream, no time to run, no place to go. Debris shoots into the bright blue sky and there's a brief meteor shower. The children stop moving their legs and start craning their necks, one by one, to watch the spectacle before them. They scatter like pigeons as the crumbs of debris float down onto their field.

The dream cuts to St. Cecelia's Catholic Church, where in a creaky old pew an old woman leans over and whispers to her neighbor what everyone already knows: *They had to identify him by his teeth.*

"Lee-mer?"

I blink hard to shake away the daydream. A specialist is standing before me, frowning into a chart. I rise from my chair and follow her out of the room. I look back at the soldiers waiting in the green chairs along the wall.

They're all staring at the large-screen television across the room. I get a glance of the screen and watch a CNN news clip of the space shuttle *Columbia* exploding and falling down to earth, and I realize what inspired my crazy daydream.

I follow the specialist through a small room crammed with three desks and three busy specialists typing on computers, and across the hall to the examination room. A tall, broad-shouldered man stands in the corner, almost completely out of sight behind the door, writing something inside a folder. The blinds are up and two large windows cast dull rays of light onto a waiting dentist's chair. Nothing scares me more than military dentists.

I sit without being instructed. The clear plastic sheet covering the chair slides against my cargo pants, and I feel the cold, hard surface of the plastic rub against my neck as I settle in. *Get it over with.*

The doctor shuffles over without saying a word. For him I'm just another GI with horrible teeth, needing an inspection before I go to war. This is just one in a number of stations that I must go through today, each with different military personnel waiting to mark an OK on my list, making me deployable to Kuwait, Afghanistan, Qatar, Germany, or Iraq. To them we all look the same—young kids with bad teeth and acne, impatient and nervous. The doctors' callused faces are indifferent to our situation; there is little need for either of us to acknowledge the other. I ignore him the same way he ignores me.

I recline, grip the hard plastic armrest, and try to relax. I think about both my daydream and the *Columbia* explosion. What were the astronauts thinking? So much of their fate was entrusted to the shuttle that took them into space but couldn't deliver them home. They had to let go. They had to have faith in NASA and their mission. And, I have a hard time accepting the fact that I need to let go as well.

Now, I want out of a future I foresee. My mind goes wild with the possibility of tragedy, the possibility of a fate I have no control over. I could be picked off by a renegade sniper. A roadside bomb could explode under the truck I'm riding in or a spiraling missile could melt the flesh and muscle clean off my bones. I know what must be done—I must put my life in the hands of others. I have to trust these men and women who surround me now and let others take control—be it a dentist, a squad leader, a bus driver, a young lieutenant, a naïve president, or other soldiers. I have to learn to accept that I may die from circumstances beyond my control. It's a hard thing to accept. How do you come to terms with your own possible death? In your mind, how do you prepare for the fact that you were simply in the wrong place, at the wrong time, among the wrong people?

I'm so wrapped up in the image of my daydream, I don't even hear the dentist instruct me to open up until the instruments are dangling above my lips.

"Specialist, open please."

I drop my jaw, opening to the unknown.

You can't help but wonder how you got yourself into this mess.

At the rifle range on Fort Carson, you watch fat snowflakes fall to the ground and feel the cold night surround you. You're at the range for a night-firing drill. It has been snowing all day—the coldest day since you set foot in Colorado—and the snowflakes hit you at an angle, pelting you in the face. The snow reminds you of home, how you drove fifty miles north to Rugby, North Dakota, one weekend a month for ten months, to drill with a water purification unit. You remember those drives like they're home movies of your youth. You remember how liberating it felt to coast through rolling hills at 5 a.m., when everything was dark and silent. You remember that barbed-wired fence with cowboy boots on the posts and the names of all the small towns along the highway. In the winter there was a sort of magic about that dark landscape, lit up by a blanket of snow. The road dipped down into valley after valley, across crusted-over rivers, and past cold prairie pastures. It was the best part of drill weekend—the calm before the storm—when you prepared yourself for the day. It was a time when you had control over your destiny; you drove yourself to those drills, and you were happy about the direction your life was taking.

You also remember that night you came out to your best friend. You remember driving your parents' car through the nighttime streets of Fargo, how the streetlights cast dark and looming shadows around the vehicle. You remember a woman walking her dog, the song playing on the radio, the glow of the Burger King sign as you parked below the neon light and told your best friend you are gay. You felt relieved because you could finally live your life the way you wanted.

Now, you look up at the mountains towering over you, large and looming like gods, and you feel small, so you step a little closer to the soldier in front of you, and realize that everyone around you is doing the same thing, huddling together for warmth. You start to understand the magnitude of this war: how big war can be and how small you can become. You try to shake the feeling away, the feeling that war is days away, but you can't. You look around and realize both the eeriness and tranquility of firing rifles at night in the snow. It feels like the beginning of the end, and you remember a recurring dream from your childhood involving a train, millions of spinning clocks, and people screaming about the end of the world. The dreams woke you at night and sent you running for your parents' room like a little girl. Strangely enough, you get that same feeling now but realize there's no place to run.

I read somewhere that a lot of Vietnam veterans believed there was a bullet with their name on it. If the bullet didn't take them out during the war it was bound to do so eventually. To an extent, I believe this is true for everyone.

I try not to think about when my bullet will finally hit me and lodge itself deep inside my skull or rip through a tendon. But on February 9, after nearly a week in Fort Carson, we get some answers, and that bullet starts to inch a little bit closer.

Anticipation and fear hang over the bay like thick fog as we wait to hear the news. We don't talk much. We sit around our bay thinking about the announcement before climbing out of the fog and walking across the building, to Charlie Company's bay, where a circle of military brass— lieutenants, majors, sergeant majors—stand welcoming soldiers. We silently drift into the bay, filling the sleeping area with men and women full of questions. We make nervous chatter, shifting from right foot to left in anticipation. Most people just stare at their boots. I watch married men twist their rings around their fingers. The fear, doubt, and anxiety show in our cheeks, our downcast eyes, our furrowed brows. We are a bay full of worry and wonder.

I look around and notice the walls coated with memories—pictures of young children playing outside, photographs of beautiful women smiling into cameras, group shots of friends crowded around a table with glasses of alcohol in hand. It feels like I've stepped into someone's living room. Except here, instead of overstuffed armchairs, armoires, and hutches, we have green cots covered with sleeping bags, cardboard-box tables, and crudely made clotheslines hung with wet uniforms.

At the center of the bay, a sergeant major asks for our attention.

"Troops, we've gathered you here to relay the news," the tired-looking sergeant major says. He looks around the room at the men and women staring back at him. He doesn't beat around the bush. Instead, he gets right into telling us what we've been waiting to hear.

"The 142nd will be attached to the Fourth Infantry Division in Turkey, in support of a possible war against Iraq." He pauses briefly. "Your mission may involve a number of different things including building a prisoners' camp and helping build up military bases across the country."

The sergeant major continues by explaining how proud he is of all the troops. He commends us for deploying so quickly and putting our lives on hold to defend our country. He finishes by thanking us for our service thus far. For the past week we've heard about the United States' desire to enter Iraq from both Kuwait and Turkey, and of Turkey's resistance to letting us do that. The sergeant major does give us some news we can use—a place and a mission. It helps me visualize what's going to happen, and I feel better knowing where I'm headed.

After the briefing, Grayson gets the keys to a five-ton truck and thirty of us pile into the back for a trip into Colorado Springs. We drive to a steak house, where we stand around the lobby opening peanut shells and taking pictures. We're wearing civilian clothes. We aren't all green, black, and brown, and I'm glad we're not all camouflaged anymore. As I watch the line of people follow a waitress across the restaurant to a large table near the back, I think, *We can finally stand out as individuals.*

At the end of the meal, Trangsrud, a young guy who looks like he'd rather be at a grunge concert than firing a rifle, is feeling particularly bold. He has dark, bushy eyebrows, which he raises as he leans into the table.

"Should I ask the waitress for her number?" he asks the group of guys at our end of the table.

Trangsrud smiles and looks around. He looks different in this restaurant, cocky and confident, almost brave. It's a side of him I don't see when he's in the camouflaged uniform; it's a side I identify with because I feel he also doesn't fit in with the army.

"Why?" I ask, laughing. "You're never going to call her."

The rest of the men return volley, saying that even if Trangsrud did get her phone number he could never see her again. But the comments do nothing but act as bait for Trangsrud's challenge. It doesn't matter if he'll call her or not. What matters is the challenge—the mission.

"I'm going to do it," he says.

Trangsrud pushes back his chair and gets up from the table. He's dressed in all black with safety pins lining the collar of his shirt. He's the kind of kid you'd see at a Marilyn Manson concert—baggy pants, black fingernail polish, thick laced-up boots. He's probably the only soldier among us who actually wears his combat boots when he's not playing soldier.

He's the kind of guy who wears eyeliner and actually looks good in it. He walks up to the waitress, who is standing near the bar. They talk briefly, and when she turns her back to grab a cocktail napkin, Trangsrud looks over at us and raises his bushy eyebrows. He comes back to the table holding a folded napkin in his hand.

The rest of the night continues in a similar fashion. For once I get to see these men and women outside of the military. I get to see who they really are. The three women in the platoon order vodka tonics and talk about their boyfriends. The young guys talk about drinking and getting laid. The restaurant makes me realize that these people aren't just numbers, like the military makes us feel, but real people. They are people who like to laugh and have a good time, something that is sometimes hard to do in uniform.

I look around the table at the people in my platoon as they finish their meals, and I'm reminded of sitting among another group of soldiers at the beginning of September 1997, when I signed my life over to the military.

I sat at a table in a restaurant across the street from the MEPS (Military Entrance Processing Station) in Fargo and wondered how the six other soldiers around me felt about joining the military. That afternoon we went through a series of medical examinations and briefings before we were each escorted into a small room and asked to raise our hands up next to our heads—palm out. We were then told to recite an oath to "support and defend the Constitution of the United States against all enemies, foreign and domestic." My arm went numb, my knees wobbled, and my toes itched to get out of that room. The light slanted through the closed blinds as I stood in that dark room, and I felt both alone and alive at the same time. I knew other men and women had stood there before me, reciting the same oath I did, and that others would come after me, but I also felt alone—out of my element—like I was getting into something much bigger than myself.

Now, at night, when I hear the breathing of the young soldiers in the bay, I am reminded of the uneven breath coming from my seventeen-year-old lips that day, the gasping sound of a mouth that couldn't suck in enough air.

As we leave the steak house and walk to our truck, snowflakes cover our tracks. I watch the men and women pull themselves into the back of the vehicle and I realize that I can't entirely be myself among these people. I can never show them who I really am, like they are doing now. I could never ask another guy for his phone number in front of them, especially now, as we're getting ready for war. I'd be shunned; I wouldn't make it through the deployment. The best I can do is to continue putting on the mask, the one I've been using for years to hide who I really am. I don't like it, but I have no other choice. I settle into the cold, hard seat in the back of the truck, and the harsh realization that I can never really be myself.

Grayson turns the key and gets nothing. After several attempts, Grayson gets out of the cab and walks to the back of the truck.

"She wouldn't start."

"So now what?" someone asks.

"We wait," Grayson says. "I guess we'll have to call for a jump."

Grayson walks back toward the restaurant. While he makes the call, the rest of us make our way into a karaoke bar next door to the steakhouse. We've already had a few drinks with dinner and are laughing about the absurd Japanese decorations as we walk up to the bar. A few of the guys are still jabbing Trangsrud about getting a phone number. We shake the snow off our shoulders and pull up stools at the bar.

The place is nearly empty. We notice a Japanese couple behind the bar taking orders and a young woman waiting tables. We fill the place while we wait for our jump. Once we've settled in and ordered drinks, someone passes around a book full of karaoke titles. I shake my head, refusing to sing, even after Trangsrud tries to get me to. But there is something about their pleading that makes me reconsider. I take their offer to be a sign, an initiation of sorts, a gesture that I don't have to be an outsider if I don't want to.

After a couple of drinks, I get the courage to sing. I settle on the Beatles song "Let It Be," an entirely fitting tribute to my situation. I don't know if it is the alcohol or just the general good spirit around the room, but it seems like the entire platoon is singing along as I belt out the words. I hold the microphone close to my mouth, my lips finding the right words without the prompter, and I watch as the men and women around me sing along. I watch their mouths move in unison. I think part of my fear of this deployment is being an outsider among these people. But over karaoke and beer I forget about the impending war. I forget about my nightmares about dying and the newsclip of the space shuttle explosion being played over and over. I forget about guns and bullets and firing ranges and everything military related. Instead, I relish a warm Friday night, where every one of my worries can be drowned by another beer and another karaoke song. I relax knowing that I can now put at least some trust in these men and women.

Back at Fort Carson, we stumble into the bay, half drunk from sake, beer, and karaoke. We fall into our cots and drift into a deep, contented sleep. We have a mission, a purpose, something to look forward to. In the morning, we are so close to each other that we can reach over and slap the face of the soldier next to us, and feel the swift snap of fingers against our skin, almost as if we are slapping ourselves.

We spend the first week of February rushing to get ready for war. By the middle of the month, we still haven't heard whether Turkey will let us in their country, and instead of shipping out, we spend our days doing field drills on the hills behind the maintenance bay we call home.

The southern edge of Fort Carson is covered in rolling hills and prairie. The land is used for various activities, from land navigation exercises to mock gun battles and field activities. I wait as half the platoon piles into the open back of a two-and-a-half-ton truck before lifting the heavy tailgate, latching the chain in place, and climbing into the cab. Lieutenant Burns sits next to me, his Kevlar helmet already on his head as he peers out the window. He looks like a brainy turtle—hard on the outside but all soft and slow on the inside. We simply call him the LT, and like most enlisted men we make fun of his college-educated naïveté about the world.

I'm driving to the back section of the hills, where the rest of our platoon is already waiting to take part in a number of field exercises including a GPS class, a basic combat class, and a course on how to build a wire barrier. It has been snowing all morning and the white powder covers the land, masking the normally gray hills in a clean sheet.

I turn onto a gravel trail. The melting slush fills the potholes in the road, hiding them as the truck's wheels dip down into the holes. We're bouncing along the road and I hear people in the back of the truck curse my name. I try to control each turn, taking my time to make it down the road and safely out into the field where the rest of the platoon waits. I come to a one-way sign and turn to the LT.

"Is this road a one way?" I ask.

As I've gotten to know the LT over the past month, I've become more and more uncomfortable going into this deployment with him as our leader. He shrugs and tells me to keep going, and I realize what kind of man I've turned my life over to. I've finally started to accept that my life is in the hands of people like the LT, men and women who'll lead soldiers into battle. The platoon looks up to the LT for leadership, but I've found myself trusting less and less in his judgment. He's socially inept and unable to make a decision, and I feel that if I follow his advice, I'll never make it through this deployment alive.

The LT points to the left, and I turn down a narrow road. The road runs along the valley between two buttes, and as we make our way down the path, I look up at the small hills on both sides of the path. The LT says that the staging area is just ahead. I pull the truck out of the valley, and as we approach the clearing, I see a snowball come flying at us from the left. I look out in front of the truck and notice a half-dozen soldiers with snowballs jump out from behind a bush and block the road. I have driven straight into an ambush.

My first instinct is to run, to whip the truck around and hightail it out of the valley. Instead, I listen to what I'm being told. The LT takes the mock ambush seriously. He tells me to pull the truck off the path and to turn around. I immediately snap into action, listening to the LT like I used to listen to my father, imagining what I would do if this were a real ambush, with real attackers and real ammunition. As I whip the truck around, I notice two soldiers running down the hill, their arms lobbing snowballs at the truck. I hear a couple of people in the back of the truck yell as they're pelted with snow. I try to drive away, back the way we came, but the ambushers have us surrounded. The group blocking the road has caught up with us and is now chucking snowballs at the cab. I watch as a snowball hits the passenger side window and splatters against the glass. If that snowball had been a bullet it would have pierced the LT's skull, killing him instantly.

When the snowballs cease, I stop in the grass and turn off the engine. I feel a little defeated as I climb down from the truck. I've killed the fifteen men and women in my platoon. The troops in the back are already shaking the snow from their coats and climbing down into the field. The ambushers—the other half of our platoon—are laughing and explaining how perfectly the ambush was executed. They tell us how they had scouts on the top of the hills, and when I drove the truck out of the valley, they had us surrounded. We had no place to go.

We all have a good time laughing at the mock attack. For most of the platoon, the attack helped them relieve stress and enjoy being out in the snow. But for me, the attack was a sign of what is to come. It helped me realize what I was getting myself into. Even when I had control—control over my own life as well as the lives of the fifteen soldiers in the back of the truck—there was nothing I could do but accept our fate. We were doomed the moment we left that valley; our fate was death by snowball.

I like to think that the attack also helped me prepare for this war. But in reality, I know nothing about war. All I know is what I've seen in Hollywood movies—soldiers storming beaches and charging across deserts as oil fires blaze behind them—or what I've read in books like *Catch-22*. That isn't war. It's the dramatized vision of what we imagine war to be. We imagine a war where Vietcong soldiers live in ant tunnels and snipe American boys from jungle trees. We imagine wars to be like the ones in *We Were Soldiers* and *Saving Private Ryan*, where tanks rumble through European cities, and soldiers rescue each other from frightful deaths. All the thoughts of impending doom and tragedy that have been running through my head are fueled by these images of war. But no two wars are alike. I have no way of knowing what to expect, no way of knowing what to prepare for, and that frightens me even more.

Even Pawns Have Nice Legs

I stand next to them, but not among them. They stand rigid—black boot next to black boot—in formation on the pavement outside our barracks, listening to Captain Roar ramble on about the training and how he still hasn't heard when they'll be leaving. They are dressed in their camouflaged uniforms and slick black berets, hands cupped together behind their backs. They look dignified and hard like matching pawns poised along the front lines of battle.

These pawns are all I've known for the last month. We've trained together, slept in the same giant maintenance bay, eaten together, and partied together on our weekend passes. Some—like Newman, Elijah, and Lake—I've known for years; they were with me when we went to Kosovo three years ago. They talk at great length about their wives, their children, their mortgage payments, how the National Guard has changed. Others are new to the unit, young and naïve. They come back to base drunk from a night of dancing and pass out on their cots. We have a hard time waking them in the morning.

I've always felt uneasy standing next to these men and women. After returning from Kosovo and telling my friends that I was gay, I started to dread drill weekends with the National Guard. I loathed those weekends like I loathed trips to the dentist. My female friends called it my own male version of PMS because I became grumpy and angry at the thought of putting on that uniform, even if it was only for a weekend. Mostly, I fear what will happen when the soldiers in my platoon figure out what I am hiding.

But these men and women are all I have now.

It is lightly raining now and the boots around me become slick and dark. Yet my boots refuse to change. I've had dreams that start like this. I'll be standing among these men and women, dressed exactly like them, but not. My boots will be a different color—sometimes pink, sometimes baby blue, sometimes pea-shit green—but always different, like they're cut from a different cloth. However, I'll be the only person who notices. Nobody seems to see how much I stick out, how different I am. During inspections, the LT will look me over like he does everyone else. He'll ask me the same questions. He'll look at me with the same stern expression on his face. I'll look back at him like all the other soldiers, and wonder, *Why doesn't anyone else see how out of place I am here?*

Lake is far too arrogant for his own good.

Right now, he stands shivering in the doorway of a closed café. The February wind collects under his shirt, blowing the fabric away from his skin like an inflating balloon. The wind moves on, and the fabric falls back against his chest. Earlier this evening, his shirt was three buttons open, revealing his tan Native American skin to the women crowded around the bar. He always wears his shirts this way when he goes out dancing, but now as he shivers against the night breeze, the shirt is buttoned to his chin, his collar popped up to cover his exposed neck.

Standing next to Lake, I smell the musky scent of his cologne and his sweet alcoholic breath. I step out from under the awning and look up and down the street. There are seven of us standing in T-shirts and short sleeves under the awning. Nobody has brought along a coat, and we huddle together for warmth, waiting for our ride. We're on a weekend pass and have just spent the night drinking and dancing in a half-dozen clubs in downtown Colorado Springs. Across from us, men and women are emptying out of the clubs, filling the icy sidewalks. The street is crowded with young people who have places to go—all-night diners and warm apartment-beds. I look back at Trangsrud, who has retracted his arms from the short sleeves of his black T-shirt, making himself appear armless, and realize how much we stick out. We have no place to go; home is 942 miles away.

I pull my arms out of the sleeves and hug my sides with my cold hands. I sigh, looking up and down the street before stepping back into the huddle.

When King and Tuna pull up with the van, we rush to get inside.

"Where have you guys been?" Lake asks as he slides open the van door.

King turns around in the driver's seat and smiles at us. "We went to the strip club," he says.

King reminds me of someone's younger brother—not necessarily *my* younger brother but somebody's. He's hopeful, enthusiastic, and full of energy and drive. He's like a messy puppy—dirty and clumsy, but also endearing and charming, in his own sloppy way. Yet King also comes across as mature for his age, more thoughtful than you'd imagine a man talking about strip clubs could be. I often see him with a book and can tell that he's at least interested in something other than military jobs and grunt labor.

Tuna is a little more reserved. He's married and the father of two young children. He's the same age as I am and was a student back home. I can tell that he's been hardened by marriage and children. He's wiser than other soldiers his age. He's the perfect counterpart to King—the Skipper to King's Gilligan.

King is giddy with excitement as he tells the rest of the van about his night. February has been filled with stories like this, men operating out of lust. Every Monday morning men come back with more tales about strip clubs and bars. I quietly listen to descriptions of lap dances and how girls flung themselves around metal poles. There are descriptions of beautiful waitresses and sexy bartenders. Trangsrud never calls the waitress from the steak house. Lake makes moves on a female security guard at the gates of the base, yet fails to get her phone number. Once, when we drove away from the gates, Grayson shook his head at Lake and said, "You could've had that, man, you could have had that."

When we get back to the hotel room we sit around drinking and watching *Good Morning, Vietnam.* Robin Williams's character is trying to befriend Vietnamese women. I think about my own attempts at making a connection to the men in my platoon. I've tried to adapt to my surroundings, to take on some of the traits of these men. When I went to South Korea for two weeks with the National Guard in 1999, I remember stopping at a number of bars and strip clubs outside the military bases. While the other men bought drinks and talked with the women who slid up next to them, I buried my nose in a newspaper, nervous and out of place, afraid to talk to anyone. The other guys yelled at me for ignoring the women, for reading the newspaper, for just generally being a nervous fool. I was eighteen, gay, and in over my head. I didn't know what else to do.

What I learned to do was adapt, to change my skin to fit in with the men around me. When we returned from Kosovo in 2000, we spent a week in Fort Benning, Georgia. One night my squad decided to go to a strip club. I was then nineteen and hardened from eight months of keeping the peace in a war-torn country, so when I showed another man's ID to the bouncer outside the club, the bouncer just handed it back and let me pass. I looked like all the other young soldiers. I appeared older than I really was, something the military had done to me, and I think the bouncer could tell. I sat among the men, like I was no different, and watched the women dance around silver poles.

Now, I'm surrounded by seven other men, in a hotel suite living room no bigger than my old apartment bedroom, and I think that this is what it's like to fit in. Some people say that military units function like families. When you're living closely with thirty-some other men you can't help but bond like family does. Like any typical family, members start to take on roles. Squad leaders alternately become mothers and fathers, asking soldiers in their squad if they have all their gear for the upcoming mission and punishing them with push-ups if they do not. The man standing next to you becomes your brother, the woman your sister. There is always the rebellious teenager who refuses to take orders, and the slow cousin who simply can't comprehend what the lieutenants say.

I look around the room and think for a second that we are a family, all camped out around a room like children on Christmas night. King is asleep on the floor to the left of the bed, Tuna on the right. Someone has passed out on the chair, and a couple of people are sleeping on the carpet at the foot of the bed. Only Lake is absent, sleeping alone on the king-sized bed in the next room, because he paid for that luxury himself.

I've never referred to the members of my platoon as family. Instead, I've compared them to a kindergarten class. Many members of my platoon are young kids, men in their early- to mid-twenties, college students who are more used to holding a beer can than a rifle. We're men who've been raised on Chris Farley movies, WWF wrestling, Zubaz, and grunge music. We are men still trying to figure out who we are, most of us confused at the new responsibilities that come with wearing the military uniform. Mostly, we think we don't have to change, that like stubborn kindergarteners who refuse to learn, we don't need to accept the responsibilities that have been placed in front of us. We're living in limbo between a past we can't return to and a future we refuse to accept.

In the morning, Lake comes out of his room and stands stretching in the doorway. He rubs his eyes and looks around at the rest of us still waking from the night.

"Jesus Christ," he says plugging his nose. "It smells like eight people slept in here last night."

We continue to prepare for a deployment to an unknown destination. We conduct a number of field exercises in the snow. We return to the rifle range. We do a land navigation course in the foothills and joke about getting lost in the desert. Mostly, we get anxious about leaving Fort Carson and actually doing something productive. The lack of activity during the day drives us into gossiping. As the days progress with no orders saying we're headed to Turkey, the rumor mill again grinds. Newman overhears Captain Roar talking about a newspaper back home reporting we'll be in Fort Carson for six months. Trangsrud says that he talked with a soldier in the Triple Nickel who said that if we don't deploy to Turkey we'll head to Kuwait like everyone else. One rumor even says that in three weeks we'll find out our fate—going overseas or going home.

I've dreaded this deployment from the day I got that call to duty, but now, after wasting nearly a month in Colorado, there's part of me that wants a war, a small sliver of my mind that wants to be a part of something momentous. I want a war that will justify so many people being uprooted from their lives and thrust into action. I *need* this war to happen.

One afternoon I watch Fredricks admire the diamond engagement ring he's bought for his girlfriend. Fredricks is new to the platoon, but he fits in like he's always belonged. He was a college student at North Dakota State University before we left. He has a blonde girlfriend he admires and constantly talks about. He tells off-color, tasteless jokes like the rest of the men in the platoon—jokes about dead babies and prostitutes. But he can also be witty and charming, and I'm instantly drawn to how personable the guy is, how comfortable I feel around him. When he smiles his perfect country boy smile—wide and white—he makes you almost forget you're in the army, cleaning your rifle, or that you're angry about the uncertainty of your mission. It all just seems to melt away.

I watch Fredricks pick up the black box, flip open the top, and stare into the million eyes of the diamond, almost mesmerized by it. I imagine that he is thinking about his girlfriend every time he smiles, or what she'll say when he pops the question after she drives down to see him. I smile because he is smiling, and watch as he stuffs the ring back inside his duffle bag.

Fredricks isn't the only person holding onto the past and thinking about the future. Elijah is having a hard time being away from his wife, who is due with their first child. One afternoon, while waiting around our bay, he sits down next to me on my cot. I close *Catch-22* and look over at him.

"You alright?"

"Yeah, I think so," he says. He rubs his hands together and looks down at his boots.

We get into the details of the deployment, our frustrations about being at the military's mercy, and the latest rumors buzzing around the bay. Finally, I ask him about Lisa, his wife, and I know I've hit a nerve. He's hunched over on my cot, his head cupped in his hands. He looks over at me and I see tears in his eyes.

"I just want to be there for the birth," he says. "I don't care where I have to go or for how long, but all I want is to be back for the birth. That's all I want."

We've all been feeling the stress of being away from home. The battalion has started giving us the weekends off, and several of the wives, girlfriends, and family members have started carpooling down to Colorado Springs. Fredricks's girlfriend is coming down this weekend, and Newman and Grayson's wives have talked about riding together to come down to see their men.

While some of the soldiers reminisce about wives and girlfriends back home, we single men go into bars and clubs and wash away our loneliness with alcohol. Lake and I go to bars in downtown Colorado Springs to discuss military promotions. We're both specialists, and since we don't have girlfriends or wives to fret over, in between rounds of drinks we talk about passed-over promotions and missed opportunities to become sergeants. Lake has been passed up for a promotion a couple of times now, and I passed up the opportunity to attend sergeant training because I knew I was getting out of the army. We both hold to the notion that in the military there are always far too many chiefs trying to take charge. Sometimes, Lake likes to argue, it's better to just sit back and let everything work itself out. It's a sort of "Let it be" mentality that we've adopted and call our own. We call it "The Specialist's Creed."

"But it will never happen," Lake says before taking a swig from his beer. "That's the irony of this situation. Those clowns we call the leadership will never step aside and let the situation play out. They'll continue to fuck things up for all of us."

On February 28, after nearly a month in Fort Carson, I sit in our bay and watch the men around me. Fredricks is holding his jewelry box and grinning ear to ear. Ivy, a Gulf War veteran who works in construction back home, is telling stories about the kangaroo rats he saw his first time over in the desert. Some of the men are napping; others are playing cards. Trangsrud is listening to music on his Discman and bobbing his head to the beat. Tuna is writing a letter with a pen that says *Daddy* on the side. Newman sits in one corner reading from a newspaper. They all have different means of coping with this deployment, different ways of taking their minds off the situation, and my way of dealing with all this is to watch them.

Newman looks up from his newspaper and announces to the group that Mr. Rogers has died.

"He was a sniper in Vietnam, you know," Newman says.

I've heard this tall tale before and know it isn't true. Mr. Rogers never served in Vietnam. Sometime over the years someone started the rumor that Mr. Rogers was in the Navy SEALS and had a number of confirmed kills. But I knew Mr. Rogers wasn't a vet and never served in the military. I'd looked it up the first time I heard it.

I shake my head and laugh. This is how rumors get started.

I fondly remember reenacting scenes from the television show *Tour of Duty* on my grandparents' small farm. My youngest aunt, Wendy, was more like an older sibling than an aunt, and when my parents dropped my two brothers, my sister, and me off at my grandparents' house, we'd spend hours watching episodes taped from television and casting our own private Vietnam in the backyard.

Wendy played the young lieutenant and led us into the patch of woods behind the house. We pretended to hear gunfire off in the distance, and every now and then we'd twist around as if the Vietcong were in those trees trying to pick us off. We even took prisoners, usually my brother Bo and my sister. Wendy put them inside the tiny shed at the edge of the woods, as if they'd been captured by the Vietcong, and then she led a recon mission to rescue them.

My brothers and I were typical American boys. We liked destruction, violence, guns, and blowing things up. We liked getting dirty, playing dirty, and pretending to go to war. Wendy was a tomboy who, like my sister, took pleasure in hanging out with the boys. She didn't have dolls or tea sets. She was one of the boys during those summers on the farm, pretending to be an American soldier traipsing through a Vietnam jungle that looked a lot like a farmyard shelterbelt. She managed to fit in right alongside us.

But as boys turn into men they lose interest in destruction, warfare, and violence, or at least I did. I grew out of these things and eventually forgot about *Tour of Duty*. I became fascinated by much more than just action. When I joined the military I found myself among the boys again, men who *didn't* grow out of these childhood obsessions, and I didn't really know what to do.

At the end of February I find myself standing on the demolition range in the foothills of Fort Carson, helping my platoon put together Bangalore torpedoes. And I am again fascinated with destruction.

Standing in the snow, members of the platoon hold four metal fence posts and enough C4 plastic explosive to blow a dog house to bits. We're combat engineers and the Bangalore torpedo can be our best friend. The torpedo is used to clear obstacles. We're putting together a "field-expedient" version of the torpedo by filling the concave portion of a fence post with C4. I watch as Lake and Newman put one of the two torpedoes together. Once the task is completed we stick the torpedoes into the concertina wire fence—our obstacle—and watch as the demolition sergeant sticks the charge into the C4. As he uncoils the detonation wire, he looks over and hands me the spool.

Watching the construction of the torpedo, I realize how completely sheltered my life has been up to this point. I never get to do these kinds of things outside of the military, so I find myself excited when the sergeant hands me the spool of wire and points up the hill. It is my chance to prove that I belong among these men, that I fit in here even though everything about my life outside the military says I do not.

The rest of the platoon marches up the bunker at the top of the hill. I follow them, unwinding the wire and watching as the cord falls into the snow. Once at the top, I crouch behind the bunker and, with the help of the demolition sergeant, attach the detonator to the end of the wire. I feel the detonator in my hand, the metal cold against my skin. I think about all the times I felt like an outsider among these people, how worthless and uneasy I've been wearing this uniform. I run my fingers around the pin at the side of the detonator, and when the sergeant counts me down, I pull the pin with my index finger and hear the explosion at the bottom of the hill. As I rise from behind the bunker, I get an odd feeling in my stomach, a strange and eerie sensation of enjoying pulling that pin a little too much.

When the war begins on March 19, I am alone, watching *American Idol* on a three-inch television screen. It was the announcement from President Bush two days earlier that sent shivers through my body. Bush gave Saddam Hussein and his sons forty-eight hours to leave Iraq. Since then, I'd been waiting to hear Bush announce that the U.S. military was launching missiles at key locations around Baghdad. They were the words I'd wanted to hear.

Sitting in silence, watching the missiles light up the Baghdad sky, I realize that I am on deck—waiting—for a war I never thought I'd be a part of. Somehow, after a month and half at Fort Carson, after days of waiting and preparing, after speeches from Captain Roar and other military officers about the importance of our upcoming mission, I've become fond of the idea of war. I've started to believe we could do some good in Iraq. We are needed in that country—to run off their hypocritical leader and to restore peace and order to a country in conflict. We are going to give this country back to the people.

All I can think about now is how I am standing in a carpeted room in Fort Carson, Colorado, doing nothing while a war is springing to life half a world away. I am missing it; I am missing my war.

I start to pace my room and wonder where my roommates are. Earlier today we'd suffered through a series of long classes on military procedures and equipment information. At the end of the day, the sergeants quizzed us on what we'd learned. The final question was: "How many trucks are there on a military post and what is inside them?" The question refers to the use of "masthead trucks" at the top of flagpoles. If a military post is overrun, the legend goes, the commanding officer is supposed to climb to the top of the post commander's flagpole and retrieve a singular masthead truck, which contains a match, a razor, and a bullet. The officer is supposed to use the razor to cut apart the flag, and the match to burn the flag. Finally, the officer must dig up a gun buried at the base of the flagpole, place the bullet inside the gun, and send that round through his brain and out the back of his skull.

As I listened to one of the battalion sergeants explain the answer, all I could think about was 9/11, how terrorists had attacked our country. I knew better than to think we were headed to Iraq simply to give the Iraqi people a better life. I knew there was something else in our motives, something more private and justifiable. I'd heard early critics of the war on terror describe the United States as a bully, but I didn't see us as bullies. We were doing what had to be done. We had to regain what was taken from us on 9/11—our dignity.

I lie down to sleep but my mind is racing with images of war. In my head, I dream up this scenario of what I'll be doing this summer, this grand adventure in the Arabian Desert. I imagine sand dunes and camels, turbans, machine guns, oil fires, and sun, lots of hours under the hot, beating sun. I also start to imagine a future where I'll return to North Dakota a worn, war veteran, where I'll bump into old high school classmates who'll ask me what I did over the summer. I'll look blankly at them and say, *I rode a camel across an oilfield in the Iraqi desert. What did you do?*

The men fall in love with the war every morning over breakfast.

In between bites of scrambled eggs and sausage, they watch the news reports for the latest information on the war. They point at the screen when the missiles fall on Saddam's palaces. They stare at the screens filled with images from the "shock and awe" campaign, their mouths open and their eyes glazed over. They sit silently as smoke billows out of Baghdad and sigh loudly when fourteen American casualties are announced. They boo and curse at the footage of antiwar protests in Chicago and Washington, D.C., and cheer at the children jumping on Dixie Chicks CDs.

One morning I watch from the second-story window of our barracks while a few members of my platoon conduct drills with their gas masks. They take turns timing each other, seeing how long it takes them to put on their masks, starting when the timer yells *GAS! GAS! GAS!* and ending when the soldiers are pumping their arms in the air, signifying that they're done. They train us to don and seal our gas masks in eight seconds. We used to do whole weekend drills on gas masks. We'd put them on and run around the building. We'd run laps, take our weapons apart, even put them on at night and walk around the training camp. Now, I watch the soldiers dotting the grass below the windows, their gas masks strapped to the sides of their right thighs, their left arms twitching like a gunslinger's before a showdown. The timer yells *GAS! GAS! GAS!*, and the solders rip open their carriers and struggle to get the masks to their faces. They look like beekeepers once the masks are donned, a dozen zombie beekeepers wandering the barracks courtyard.

The men's enthusiasm quickly reaches home. We take turns calling our friends and family back in North Dakota. When I call my mother to tell her that my battalion is leaving for Kuwait in a couple of weeks, she breaks down and starts bawling. Once she hears those words fall from my mouth—*Mom, we're finally leaving the States*—she lets loose. I stand in the hallway of our barracks, where three phones have been installed, and listen to her sob violently into the phone. Next to me, Viv, one of the new members of the platoon, is telling one of his buddies about being deployed.

"Dude, can you believe it?" he says. "I'm going to war. Me. Out of all of us, I'm the one going to Kuwait. How far out is that, man?"

He spoke with a kind of enthusiasm most of the battalion felt for finally having a mission.

Mostly, I share the men's desire to be a part of the war. I gaze starry-eyed at the television as missiles are launched over Baghdad. I like the way the red and green tracer rounds light up the night sky. When the battalion issues sand-colored camouflaged boonie hats, I too place mine on my head and stand before a mirror, commenting at how renegade the cap looks. I imagine slap-dashed camouflage makeup across my face. I imagine a machete and my rifle, jungle vines hanging from the trees. I am Rambo or Charles Bronson, ready and angry.

But there is still something holding me back from fully trusting these men, from entirely fitting in among them. It could be that while the men are falling for the war, I am also falling for the men.

In uniform, the men all look the same. But outside that uniform, when they shed their camouflaged skin and turn into civilians again, I fall for them like I did a gray-eyed photographer during college or the British men I met in London pubs. Particularly, I've fallen for Fredricks and his good-ol'-boy smile.

After classes and training one day, we go down to the base bowling alley for bowling, pool, and beer. I'm not much of a bowler, and the pool tables are all occupied, so I belly up to the bar, order a beer, and sit down before a video-game machine. Fredricks sits down next to me and smiles.

"Not a bowler, huh?" he says, his awe-shucks dimples catching the little light in the bar.

"Nope," I say.

The bar is dark and crowded. Across the chipped-up tables, near the back of the bar, the DJ is setting up karaoke equipment. Fredricks and I talk about his girlfriend, his family, and his classes. He eventually taps the video-game machine in front of us and asks what I'd like to play. We settle for some matching game, and for a few minutes we sit in silence, drinking our beers and playing the game. I watch him smile every time he gets something wrong or the way his eyebrows bunch up when he can't figure out the game. Behind us a woman has stepped up to the karaoke microphone. She announces that the next song is for all the soldiers in the bar tonight. The bar erupts with people cheering. The song is "Love Is a Battlefield" and the woman is perfectly in tune.

As the liquor takes affect, I lower the wall I've managed to keep up during the deployment. Fredricks leans against the bar and watches the woman sing. I watch him. I feel entirely comfortable in his presence. I mouth the words to the song— *We are strong*—looking between the woman who sings and Fredricks, as if I'm the translator passing the words from her to him.

For a moment I just want to blurt out everything. A week ago, Grayson nearly outed me in front of the entire platoon. We were packing our gear, and I was talking about my best friend. Grayson looked at me and said, "Oh, I always thought you were gay." I looked back at him and wondered what to do. If I told him I was gay, I would probably face the ridicule of the platoon for the entire deployment, and I just couldn't handle that. So I lied. I said, "No. I'm not gay. Why would you ever think that?"

But now, watching Fredricks sing along to the song, I have this great desire to confide in him. I have nobody else to confide in, and it's killing me to keep so much bottled up. I want to show him the picture of our lives together, the one that's been forming in my mind. I see us sitting at the bar, as if this moment were a movie I am watching in a theater. I see myself—visibly distraught and half drunk—spilling my entire story to Fredricks. I see Fredricks smile and nod his head as he listens to my story. I see myself explain the difficulty of not being myself during this deployment, how I started this deployment a naïve but self-respecting man, and now I don't even recognize the man I've become. The bar scene fades out and we cut to years later, where I'm living the life I want to live, and Fredricks is standing next to me as we buy a house, shop for groceries, pick out wine, choose a wooden crib.

But then reality grabs my shirt and shakes me violently. I look over at Fredricks. I open my mouth but I don't say a word. I can't. Men just don't do that in bars on military bases. I remain silent while in the background a woman compares love to a battlefield.

I'm not strong, even though the Pat Benatar wannabe made me feel otherwise.

What I realized, that night in the bar, was that it wasn't Fredricks I was longing after. I didn't really imagine a future with Fredricks, although at the time I liked to think I did. Fredricks was simply a stand-in for Jeremy, and ever since we got deployed I've wondered what went wrong between us. So in March I decide to send him an e-mail.

I sit down at the computer. I start by describing the men I'm with, our nights of drinking out in Colorado Springs, and the days we've spent preparing at Fort Carson. But before long the e-mail turns from simple descriptions of events and people into heartfelt feelings. I'm scared, and for the first time during the deployment, I admit it to someone else. I try to explain all the feelings I've had over the last two months, how I've been thinking about him ever since I left North Dakota, and how I've wished for someone to confide in. Mostly, I ramble on about our relationship and how we never really had closure. My relationship with him was my first, and only *real*, one with another man, and after a year we simply decided to call it quits. He'd moved on—to graduate school in southern Minnesota—and I wasn't ready to move with him. But for the last three years, I've been thinking about what would have happened between us.

Then, at the end of the e-mail, I type three words that surprise me: I LOVE YOU. I want him to know that even though I didn't say it much during our relationship, I did love him. And if I didn't return from this deployment I wanted him to know that. I stare at the computer screen for a few minutes and wonder if I really mean it. Do I love him or just the memory of him? I LOVE YOU. It's typed out right there in Times New Roman, so it must be true.

I check my e-mail several times over the next couple of weeks, hoping that I'll get an e-mail back from him, something along the line of *I love you, too*, or simply *I used to love you, too*, but nothing ever arrives.

Lake is crass, opinionated, and foolhardy, and that's exactly why I like him. We're a week away from leaving for Kuwait, and he's standing outside our barracks, smoking a cigarette, and joking about re-enlisting in the army.

We all know Lake has no intention of re-enlisting. Lake, like me, is tired of playing the part of weekend warrior. For the last couple of months, we've all listened to his rants about the absurdity of our leadership and the ridiculous circumstances we've found ourselves in.

"The only way I'll re-up," he says, taking a long drag from his cigarette and blowing smoke rings into the night, "is if somebody from our battalion gets killed in Iraq. That's the only way."

I stare back at him, unsure if I should laugh or not. I let Lake's comment sink in and wonder if his statement will actually come true.

"For every person killed, I'll re-up for one year," Lake says, smiling. "If the LT is killed, I'll re-up for six."

Lake goes on about seeing someone die in Iraq, and I wonder if he really means that, if he has this odd fascination with death, or, as I suspect is the case, he talks about death and seeing someone die as a means of coping with his own fears about the war. Even though he wouldn't admit it, I think Lake fears the worst about the deployment, and this is his way of being prepared.

For the past three days we've been receiving briefings on our upcoming mission to Kuwait, and we're almost prepared to leave. We've divided our time between packing and a disguised form of celebrating. The hours of packing are interrupted with a medical briefing or a last-minute trip to the firing range or some field exercise on how to read a compass. At the end of the day, we celebrate with cans of beer and cigars because we are finally leaving, and our mission is about to begin.

On April 7 we sit in Fort Carson's auditorium waiting for our farewell ceremony. Some colonel will get on stage and tell us that even though we haven't the faintest idea what we'll be doing once we get to Kuwait, we are still needed—our presence is critical to the military's mission.

To my right, Rainman is telling a story about the past weekend. Rainman is an old navy seaman who joined Bravo Company shortly before we left. He is short and stout, and wears a bushy, sand-colored mustache under his nose. We've nicknamed him Rainman because he walks like the Dustin Hoffman character in the movie.

"So I was out shopping with my wife this weekend," Rainman says, leaning over from my right. His wife is one of the more frequent visitors to Fort Carson. She's been here almost every weekend. Every Friday we release Rainman from our grasps—the tangled mess we call military brotherhood—and back into the arms of his wife. "We're in Target and she takes me over to the pantyhose display and asks, 'Which kind do you want?'"

Lake laughs. He's sitting in the row behind us. "Well, well, well. The truth finally comes out," he says.

Rainman laughs along with us.

"No, no. I guess she was at some family support meeting and they were preparing care packages to send to us. One of the items on the list of things we *supposedly* needed was pantyhose."

I notice the look on Lake's face, trying to figure this out.

"It's because of the sand fleas," Newman says, leaning in from Rainman's right. "My wife did the same damn thing. Like we're supposed to know what shade of pantyhose goes best with combat boots and dog tags."

"My grandmother sent me pantyhose in her last package," Elijah says. "There they were, tucked neatly between a jar of Planter's peanuts and a tube of Colgate."

"I mean, can you imagine," Lake says, "some stupid-ass lieutenant briefing his troops before a battle and saying, 'Okay men, all you have to do is gently pull it over your legs covering any exposed skin, as it is pertinent to success in this battle'?"

Rainman doubles over, folding his head between his legs as laughter echoes against the auditorium walls. The image of soldiers on the front lines of battle sitting in silence as they roll the pantyhose up over their thighs strikes us all as funny, and we join Rainman in a bout of joy. These are the same men who've been fascinated by war, the ones who helped build Bangalore torpedoes and gawked at the CNN images of Baghdad burning. They are now laughing like a group of women after church, giggling about runs in their stockings.

"So anyway," Rainman continues, regaining his composure, "I was going to buy some but all they had were control tops and I don't want that much control."

Our laughter bounces off the wall, off the chairs, and off the soldiers themselves.

"Wait a second," I say. "What the hell makes you think pantyhose are going to keep these things from chewing on our legs? I mean there has to be some other way. What if I'm killed? I don't want my mother finding out I spent my last days making sure my legs looked great in a pair of L'eggs pantyhose."

We've been at war for nineteen days, and every day the newspaper releases a record of the number of troops killed in the war. This morning the paper reported that seventy-two U.S. troops had been killed since the war began. Our laughter, the hearty eruptions bursting from our throats, is simply covering up the fear that buries itself in our stomach.

"Well, they feed off of dead skin," Newman says. "You don't cover them up, you take that risk."

It seems simple. I've been covering up this entire deployment. This camouflaged uniform is just a mask—a disguise—that turns me into a different person. When I look in the mirror, I don't see the man who left North Dakota more than two months ago. Instead, I see a chameleon, some-one who shifts colors to blend in with his surroundings. He's different; he's more violent and greedy; he no longer thinks of peace but rather of vengeance. And he protects himself from his surroundings by putting up a wall—a shell—so no one can see his true self.

I zone out for most of the ceremony. I am too busy thinking about the man I've become. Inside I've roared and howled and fought against the circumstances I am in. I don't want to take on the responsibilities this deployment has given me. Mostly, I don't want to become one of *them*— these military men I used to try to separate myself from. Yet what I've realized is that I've become exactly that. I've let myself be consumed by the lifestyle of a soldier. I don't have this *other* life I can return to after taking off the uniform. When I am done playing soldier at five o'clock, I am stuck with the same group of men and women I've just spent the day with; there is no room to lead a double life.

After the ceremony we wait in the lobby. The buses, which will take us back to our packing, are on their way. Over the next few days we'll make our final preparations. We'll eat our last decent meals, drink our last cans of beer. We'll celebrate and joke. The few women in our platoon will tease the men for buying black pantyhose, because *only sluts wear black*. Regardless we'll stuff them deep into our bags, hoping that the fleas aren't as bad as they say and that we'll never have to retrieve them.

And I'll settle into the fact that's I'm alone on this deployment, even with so many people around.

A week after arriving at Fort Carson, we got lost on the city streets of Colorado Springs. We weren't worried about where we were going. We just needed to find a Laundromat. Any Laundromat would do.

We loaded a two-and-a-half-ton truck with soldiers and dirty laundry, and took to navigating the streets of an unfamiliar city. I sat near the back of the truck and watched the store signs and streetlights whiz by. I noticed familiar signs—McDonald's, Barnes and Noble, Best Buy—and realized we were not far from home. But the signs soon became unfamiliar. A jewelry store with a bright, shiny diamond on the sign. A bank. A small, run-down grocery store. A hometown café with a pig over the front door. After nearly thirty minutes, we pulled into a parking lot. I looked out the back of the truck and saw a tiny unnamed Laundromat across the street.

"Is this the ghetto?" King asked. "Where the hell are we?"

Rainman ambled out of the truck, released the chains from the tailgate, and lowered it, allowing us to climb down.

"It's the first one we found," Rainman said as he looked over the building. "It'll have to do."

We grabbed our laundry bags and made our way toward the building. I looked around and noticed that the street was in rough shape. In fact, the whole neighborhood was in rough shape. The houses were small and squat, pushed together along a dirty street block. Some of the houses looked abandoned. From the front porch of one house, a dog barked as we walked by. I quickly realized we were in the poorest part of town.

"Ghetto Joe's," King said softly as he pushed open the door.

Inside, about twenty beat-up washing machines lined the back wall and formed two lines down the middle of the room. The outside wall was lined with dryers. The Laundromat was nearly empty aside from an old woman near the back and a middle-aged man loading jeans into a dryer. Outside I heard children playing in the distance and that dog barking his heart out.

I quickly began my laundry routine, sorting and stuffing. As I stuffed a load into one of the machines, I heard my name from across the room. I looked over and saw Roach talking to the man who was loading jeans into a dryer. Roach is in his thirties, with gray hairs at his temples. He's very business-minded yet amicable, easy to talk to. He's also new to the unit, so he's still humble and approachable, unlike some of the older guys in the platoon.

I walked across the room, and Roach introduced me to Roger, a man who looked to be in his late thirties, gray hair poking from the old cap he wore. He shook my hand firmly and asked if I wanted to play chess.

"Yeah, I'll play," I said.

As Roach made his way over to one of the washers, Roger began setting up the game. I watched his thick hands—clean and tan—handle each piece. He seemed to place the pieces in just the right spot. I noticed the intensity with which he set up the game, as if the setup were more important than the game itself.

"He said you're at Fort Carson," Roger said. "How long have you been there?"

"About a week," I said. I explained our situation. I told him about our rapid deployment, how close I was to getting out of the military, and how close I was to graduating from college and moving on with my life. I also told him about the uncertainty of our mission, something that gets Roger thinking.

"What do you think of Fort Carson?" he asked.

"They don't really seem prepared for us," I said. "We're living in a maintenance bay . . . on cots."

I noticed a smile creep across Roger's face. He nodded, as if he understood. I was immediately drawn to his eyes. They were dark blue—inviting and warm. They softened the hardness of the rest of his face.

"Well, that's the military for you."

Roger released the knight he'd been holding and captured one of my pawns. He lifted the pawn off to the side of the board and laid it down on the Formica countertop.

"Have you ever been in the military?"

"No," he said. "It's complicated, but I could never do that to myself. I could never let the government have that much control over my life."

He lifted his eyes from the board and looked me straight in the eyes. I noticed the dark circles, his thin lips, and his high cheek bones.

"What do you mean?"

I watched his strong fingers grip a rook and move it forward. His moves were well calculated and quick. He never thought too long about a certain move or second-guessed his actions. He reminded me of my father in that way. Yet, what threw me about Roger was the mystery of what he said. There was something cryptic and spooky about his words.

"Let me ask you this," Roger said. "How do you feel about being a minion in the army?"

I watched his knight take another one of my pawns. We were silent for a few minutes. Behind me, the washing machines spun their final cycle. Inside the machines, my uniforms were being spun around in circles—controlled.

"I mean no disrespect," he explained. "I just don't trust our government. I just can't let my life be run by them. That's why I threw away my driver's license and burned my Social Security card. I removed the license plates from my car. I live a truly free life. Nobody controls me."

I didn't know what to say. I listened respectfully and watched as Roger's fingers tossed one of my pawns from palm to palm. I felt a little uneasy standing across from him. Part of me wanted to simply walk away, but that was what I always did when I didn't like what I heard. For the first time, I stood and listened to what was being said to me.

"I just want to understand, you know?" Roger said. He'd returned his attention back to the game. "I want to understand why the government feels they can use people like that."

The game finished when Roger's queen took my king. I knew early on that I couldn't win that game. All I could do was put up my best defense until that simply wasn't enough.

Roger thanked me for the game and shook my hand after he'd gathered up the pieces.

"Good luck," he said.

He looked me squarely in the eyes. I could tell he felt sorry for me and for what the government was making me do. It almost seemed that in my eyes he could see what the future held for me, what this deployment had in store. I wanted to ask him what he saw, if he saw me returning from this deployment the same person. But, sadly, I already knew the answer.

Roger gathered up his laundry and left the Laundromat. I returned to my washer and moved my uniforms over to the dryer. The LT and Grayson took a truck to a nearby burger restaurant and came back with half-pound burgers and fries. Roach and I sat on the plastic lawn chairs outside the building, each holding a giant burger, and watched the sun sink lower in the sky.

"When do you figure they'll tell us where we're headed?" I asked Roach.

"Who knows," Roach said. "I figure we'll be stuck in this town for quite a while."

"What makes you say that?"

"Turkey's never going to let us in. It just won't happen."

I remember feeling the warmth of sitting in the sun outside that Laundromat. As I took another bite from my burger, I watched a couple of kids throw a ball against the side of the building. They were waiting for their mothers to finish their laundry and take them home.

"What happens if they let us into Turkey?" I asked.

"Well, then we're in trouble."

Roach leaned back in his chair, gripped his burger with both his hands, and took a big bite from the middle. Grayson and Newman stood near the street with their hands on their hips and their backs turned to us. The setting sun shone on their faces, and pink rays of light snuck through their arms and cast shadows onto the sidewalk behind them. A little girl rode by on a bicycle, red and blue streamers waving from her handlebars. Inside, I heard the gentle sound of water filling a washing machine and I felt at ease. Then suddenly the machine began its washing cycle and sent the world spinning on its head.

Click, Click, Click

Inside a large white tent at Camp Wolf, just outside Kuwait City, young men and women push ammunition into steel M16 magazines. The bullets go *click, click, click* against the metal plate above the magazine's spring. Each bullet hits the next, staggering left then right, left then right, like a steel zipper. Young hands rapidly push the bullets into place. They must load thirty bronze-colored bullets into every magazine until each has four of them fully loaded, enough firepower to get them across the desert. As thumbs push the blunt end of each bullet against the already placed rounds, the tent is filled with the sound of bullets hitting bullets, the *click, click, click* like a desert lullaby.

Click, click, click, click, click.

Someone is playing an Elton John record on their boom box. As the troops recline on stuffed duffle bags, some resting their thumbs in between loadings, the music reminds them of home. It has the sweet, slow rhythm of a lazy Sunday afternoon, and if they were to close their eyes some of them would picture themselves back in sunny parlors, sipping ice-cold beer and watching children play on the lawn. Some would smell apple pie and the earthy scent of mud and grass clippings, and in between Elton John's lyrics they'd also hear the gentle laughter of children having fun.

If they try hard enough, some of them will be able to drown out the sounds just beyond their tent—the rush of air being sucked into airplane propellers on the Kuwait Airport runway or generators motoring along as they provide power for dozens of tents. Some may even forget they are in Kuwait.

Click, click, click, click, click.

Most of the soldiers know very little about Kuwait. They were too young to have participated the first time the United States was over here in 1990. Most of them were still in elementary school. They know nothing about oil and Saddam and the dozens of military camps that cropped up across the desert after the Americans pushed the Iraqis out of Kuwait. Camp New York. Camp Virginia. Camp Pennsylvania. These are places to remind the troops of home, but they will always feel foreign to traveling soldiers. Camp Doha. Camp Fox. Camp Arifjan. Camp Spearhead. Who would ever call these places home?

Click, click, click, click, click.

They stand in line under the towering floodlights. They're covered from head to toe in camouflage and gear. Their skin is black, green, and brown, so much so that they can hardly tell each other apart. Their weapons are slung behind their backs so the muzzles point at the ground behind their right boots. Loaded ammunition magazines stick out from their breast pockets, within reach. They listen to a corporal explain the coming day's activities as the sun peeks over the airport runway. Rays of sunlight throw themselves toward the soldiers, temporarily blinding them. Sand blows into their eyes and sticks to their sweaty faces. As the troops turn to gather their bags, nine buses pull up beside the white canvas tents.

They have ammunition. They have weapons. All the military needs to do now is point them in the right direction.

The Mustache Race

The curtains are the color of blueberries. It's difficult not to notice them. They sway hypnotically with the warm air rushing into the bus, and because it is hot, all eyes are on the undersized windows. The air cycles in, pushing the curtains back and forth in a game of tug-of-war. It's as if the curtains sense the nearby turmoil, and through their constant shifting, they help the wind communicate with us. *This breeze will be the last gentle thing to hit your face.* Swoosh. *There's nothing gentle about war.* Swoosh.

We are in Kuwait and it's hot—miserably hot. At four o'clock this morning we moved from a cramped tent in Camp Wolf to a cramped bus headed for Camp New York, one of several U.S. military posts scattered throughout the Kuwaiti desert.

Sweat drips from our brows, splashing onto the seats in front of us, our chins, our weapons, our BDUs. This is my first big sweat during the deployment and will certainly not be my last.

Jones looks exhausted. His head, like everyone else's, is covered with a shell of Kevlar, and he rests it on the seat in front of him. His weapon points awkwardly toward his boots. At nineteen, he is the youngest member of our company. I can only imagine the things running through his mind: *Why Iraq? What's happening back home? What if I need to kill a man? What if I'm killed? How does my mustache look?*

My father has a mustache. For as long as I can remember, he's had one, a row of straight dark hairs piled on top of each other like lumber. When I was a kid, he'd come in from outside—the cold midwestern wind blowing another snowstorm across the Dakotas—and there'd be ice hanging in shiny, clear strands below his nose, coating the bristly hairs. In the basement, as he removed his snow boots and the plastic bread bags that kept his feet dry, my father slowly warmed, sitting on that green vinyl chair placed awkwardly among the furnace, deep freeze, tools, and other amenities that cluttered the unfinished basement. My brother and I watched from the stairs as the ice on his mustache thawed, and the slick, dark slash of hair under his nose reappeared. We wondered when our own lumber pile of hair would sprout.

Like many young boys, I wanted to be like my father. I wanted a mustache. However, I often romanticized my mustache, thinning it out and curling it, like Peter Sellers's in the *Pink Panther* series, or growing it dark and thick, letting it sag like Wyatt Earp's.

Every now and then, as if he wanted to create this huge surprise, my father shaved it off, paying little regard to what people said. My mother thought its absence made him look younger. But for me, it made him look strange, deformed, or deranged. It seemed as if his mustache had walked right off his face, leaving a blurry substitute to the thick hairs that complemented his rugged appearance. My father's mustache was like a crooked nose or dimpled chin—strangely alluring and somehow oddly appropriate.

I have no idea which direction we are headed. I don't even know if we are still in Kuwait. This is what I do know: We are on a well-paved highway; there is garbage everywhere; and we all look like wet seals, drenched in sweat, with long, confused faces. Not only do the few people we see along the road look unpleasant and sad, but everyone on this tiny bus senses the misery and lets it consume them.

My face is damp from sweat, my eyes stinging. My head hurts from the helmet, and my muscles ache from traveling. Yet my ass hurts the most. The half-inch cheap cushion between me and the iron seat provides little relief.

The blueberry curtains are proving to be more harmful than helpful. They get in the way of the air, but if we pull them aside, the Kuwait sun comes down on us with vengeance. So we just sweat.

Kuwait is all sand. The country, with the occasional clump of trees or cluster of gray, windowless homes, looks like nothing more than a giant sandbox. In fact, that's what we began calling it—the Sandbox. We first heard the term from some sergeant in Fort Carson before flying over, yet we refused to believe it. He'd say, "When you're over in the Sandbox, you'll understand the importance of cleanliness" or "You better clean your gas mask daily, because once you're in the Sandbox, that thing will fill up in seconds. And if your gas mask is full of sand, it's going to be hard fitting your head in."

This sandbox is nothing like the sandbox I had when I was a kid. My parents created three sandboxes on our farm—one for my brother, one for my sister, and one for me. Each was made out of an old tractor tire and positioned throughout our farmstead. Thinking back, playing in my childhood sandbox—making those roads and cities, filling up my Tonka dump truck with load after load of sand, or creating houses out of packed, wet sand in the shape of a bucket or a cup—was simply preparation for what I was going to do over here.

I turn away from the window and the endless desert. The bus is loud—not from talking but from driving down the road, windows wide open and the old Marcopolo bus engine coughing up years of sand as it goes along. We are quiet. Rainman sits next to me, his hands cupped in his lap, his forehead dripping, and his expression blank. He stares at his boots. We sit in the back, on the long seat that stretches across the entire bus. The seat is raised slightly, and Rainman is in the middle, as if at the head of a grand table, staring at his boots, which stick awkwardly out into the aisle.

"We were just at an airport. Why couldn't we have just taken a helicopter there?" he says without looking up. His cheeks are flushed, and there are bags drooping under his eyes. Anyone could gather from his face that we'd been traveling for days.

"You forget. This is the army," I respond.

"Well, it would have been a hell of a lot quicker than this shit. Where the hell are we?"

I scan the rest of the bus, looking for an answer. Rogers is reading a magazine—*Newsweek*—that he brought with him from the States. Beaming on the cover is Jessica Lynch. When I heard the story of her rescue in Iraq I stored it in the back of my head, along with thoughts about home, friends, and family. Stories like that only make heading to war more painful, and pushing them out of your mind is the best solution.

Roach and King are both asleep, resting on their rucksacks, piled like bags of coal next to them. Roach is softly snoring. Viv is anxious or has to pee, I can't tell which. He keeps shifting around in his seat, alternately looking out the window and watching the rest of us. The curtains don't seem to have the same calming effect on him as they do on me. Everyone looks on edge. Even Johnson's whistling, which drifts quietly around the bus, has little calming effect.

The driver seems like the only completely calm person on the bus. He's a Kuwait native. He wears a long, white robe and a deep blue scarf wrapped around his head. The only visible part of his face is his eyes, dark and darting. He fits in here in a completely different way than we do. We are camouflaged with the land. He is camouflaged with the people. Our new desert camouflaged uniforms are the perfect shade of nothingness, which is exactly what the U.S. military is going for. *Get in and make it look like we aren't even there.* The driver's white robe is clean and pure: the color of peace, surrender.

It's something the military forces upon people. The Kuwait natives surrender to our neediness. We need them—to drive our troops to outlaying posts, to find the land mines, to translate the words, to pump away our waste. But do they need us? What benefit do we bring to these people?

I notice Jones looking up, almost as if to answer my unspoken questions. With his forefinger and thumb he gently smoothes the fine hairs above his lip.

Have you ever grown a mustache?" Jones asked me one morning.

He was standing by the mirror. We'd been packing, and there was a sense of excitement as we stuffed DCUs (desert camouflage uniforms), boots, and gear into the olive-drab duffle bags. It's like sifting through the remains of a tornado, separating the useful from the useless.

"What do you mean grown? Like petunias?" I replied, looking up at him.

It seemed odd to talk about a mustache as something you grow. It was as if we were two old women comparing gardens, one asking the other if she'd ever had success growing Blue Hubbard hybrid winter squash.

"Yeah, grow. How else would you say it?"

I didn't know. I doubted I could grow a mustache or a garden, so I had nothing to say.

"Do you think I'll need these?" I asked, holding up a pair of mittens with fur on the cuffs.

"It's the desert, not the Arctic."

Earlier that morning we'd been told that we were headed for Kuwait. After being strung along for two months, we were finally headed somewhere. Now it was time to sort out the stuff we needed from the stuff we could leave behind, with our families, our friends, and our country.

Jones and I had been roommates ever since they moved us into the barracks. He married before we left, one of several rush weddings to reap the benefits married couples receive, such as extra money for your wife. I'd met his wife once, the day before we left. They were headed to the courthouse following formation. During the family time the following day, they sat in the corner of the auditorium, enjoying each other's company and their new titles—husband and wife. In between talking with my parents, I watched them. They talked as if they were the only people in the room, ignoring everyone else and the upcoming goodbyes.

"I've always wanted to grow one, but I know Maria wouldn't even look at me if I did. So I was thinking of starting one now."

Maria had flown down to Colorado three days earlier. Now, with Maria gone, and not knowing the next time he'd see her, Jones was looking to experiment.

For me, growing a mustache always seemed like a right of passage from boyhood to manhood. Having a mustache meant you were a man. You'd finally proved that you were meant for manly ordeals. Most of the guys in our company had smooth upper lips, including myself.

I had never grown a mustache. I didn't want Jones to know that. The mustache simply didn't fit in with our generation. Having a mustache was like rolling your jeans, a fad that eventually faded with time.

Yet we were days away from heading overseas, to a war that required boys to become men.

"I'll tell you what, we can both try growing mustaches," I said. "It could be a race. Whoever grows the best mustache wins."

"Oh, a challenge then? You're on."

Jones reached over the boots, uniforms, canteens, flashlights, shampoo, suspenders, gas masks, and other equipment littering our floor. We shook on it, agreeing to begin the next day. Our belongings began to separate into piles and among those piles we started a competition, hoping, I thought, that a pile of hair under our noses would help disguise the fear on our faces.

Suddenly, the reason we're in Kuwait makes sense and everything is silent. A calm engulfs the bus. The whistling has stopped. The bus has cured itself of its cough, and the wind is still, unwavering. It simply ceases to exist.

This is our equivalent to riding into battle, six beat-up Marcopolo buses charging across the desert. It isn't gallant. It isn't elegant. We aren't the cavalry, the infantry, or the artillery forces. We don't have the tanks, the guns. We're engineers. We have hammers and wire strippers and monkey wrenches. For us, cruising across the desert in beat-up buses is as grand as it gets.

We have turned off the paved highway onto a thin, dirt road. The countryside opens up into a field of nothingness, sand for miles upon miles. The six buses form a line, like ducklings, making their way down this sand trail to their home—our new home.

Roach and King are awake now; the bumpy dirt road is simply too rough for sleep. Everyone is surveying the land, peeking out from behind the curtains to get a glimpse of what is in store for us.

Abruptly, the bus jerks to the left, forming its own trail through the sand. I look back and notice that it is barely a trail at all. It's simply a slightly more traveled line of sand than the one we are currently on. There really isn't a road, and the buses, instead of following one another across the desert, spread out, side by side, racing across the sand. Six tiny Marcopolo buses are cruising across the Kuwaiti desert. The race has begun.

Rogers puts down the magazine and glances over as two buses glide past us on the left. I pull back the curtain, getting a glimpse of another soldier peeking beyond his curtains as another bus passes us on the right. We've been traveling for about three days, shifting from one post to the next, and this is the first real excitement of the trip.

The land doesn't stretch on for too long before we see signs of military life. An old trailer-bed lies wasted and empty in the sand. Other vehicles are left abandoned along the road—an old five-ton truck, tireless and half covered in sand; a broken-down Hummer. I wonder if anything lives in this desert.

Rainman jabs me with his elbow. "Look at Johnson."

Johnson is two seats in front of us, his back to the aisle, looking down toward his waist. He has a Coke bottle and is peeing into it. When he finishes, he turns to the rest of us, a smug grin on his face as if he's accomplished something no one else could. We give him looks of disgust, knowing that we would do the same thing if we had to.

"What? I had to go. Who knows where this damn base is!"

Five minutes later, the bus slows and we stop. I glance out the window as soldiers exit the other five buses. Some just stand around, hands over their eyes, looking into the desert, surveying the land. Others stretch, arms jutting straight into the sky, chest bowed out, welcoming the new environment. About fifty yards away, a line of soldiers forms, their backs to the buses, as they urinate into the desert. *This is now our territory. We claim this for the United States of America.*

We eventually climb back into the buses and continue the trek to our next home. We don't know where this base is. We're racing toward an unknown place, an invisible target. I imagine the American camps strategically hidden in the Kuwaiti desert, with secret routes and unmarked paths. There will be no maps, no signs—only a handful of obedient bus drivers who know where the bases are, and they aren't telling anyone. By frantically racing toward these unmarked places, the drivers are distracting us, taking our minds off the fact that we are riding into war. Instead, we're filled with excitement at the possibility of winning a race to an unknown (and possibly secret) place.

We come to a sign, the first sign I've seen out here. It points us toward Camp New York to the right. The buses file down to one line again, our bus bringing up the rear. I look up at the bus driver with disappointment. Yet the race isn't finished.

We pass along a narrow stretch of road, between a small patch of brush and an even smaller sand dune, before the land opens up again. We spread out, each bus taking its own path, separating into its own lane for the final leg.

After a while we pass a line of Abram tanks. They are lined up, like they would be in a military handbook. They're stopped, silent and beautiful, like geese waiting in a marsh, fuel cans, rucksacks, and gear dangling from their boxy bodies. Soldiers poke their heads out the tops of the tanks. Their faces are dark, covered in sand, dirt, and sweat. I wonder how long they've been in Kuwait. How long have they been in the sun, the rays licking their faces? How long has the wind been whipping up the sand and pelting it against their brows? How long will it be before we wear those same bitter, worn faces, and what will it take to get there?

I sense we are close. If nothing else, I imagine the rough terrain is the military's last attempt at diverting people away from their secret bases. Each time we hit a bump, sending us toward the ceiling, I look over at Rainman, who gives me this look. *How does a helicopter sound now?*

Nothing can explain the relief at seeing Camp New York. We follow the other buses through a gate and onto a base that looks almost abandoned. Coming to a halt, the driver—our savior, our guardian—looks into the mirror above his head. With his eyes, he says to us, *We're here.*

Three days after Jones and I shake hands, we're on a plane headed for Kuwait. I splash water on my face and lift my head to the tiny restroom mirror. The weak light barely catches the whiskers poking through below my nose. I turn my head, left then right, trying to cast some light on the few hairs on my upper lip. Laughing, I exit the small bathroom, noticing the people lined up down the aisle. How long was I in there examining my new mustache?

Newark looks so large. Glancing at the city that lies below, I realize that this city, foreign to me because I've never been here, will be the last

American city I'll set foot in for quite a while. The seat-belt light comes on, and the pilot explains that we're landing soon. We need fuel.

They don't even give us a gate or anything. We exit the plane onto the tarmac of the Newark International Airport. We stand in a circle, stretching, smoking, joking, taking in the last American air for a long time.

"So Lemer, does this count?" Elijah asks.

Elijah and I argue about what countries and states we've visited. When counting, I don't consider countries where I've only been in the airport. For Elijah, the airports count.

"No, of course not," I say. "How can it? It's only the airport."

"So you wouldn't even say that you've been to New Jersey after this?"

"No."

It's almost a game. He argues with me just to argue, and I comply because I have nothing better to do.

"Why not?"

"It's not real."

"Well, neither is your mustache."

That gets everyone laughing. I smile, laughing along, rocking from my toes to my heels, thumbs tucked inside my new BDU pants. I somehow imagine the camouflage spreading from my pants up onto my face, covering the blood rushing to my cheeks. I turn to look at the plane, pretending that the remark doesn't hurt a little. Jones is standing by the plane with Roach. His mustache looks so much better than mine. At nineteen, he can grow a better mustache than I can at twenty-two. Jealous and embarrassed, I walk back toward the plane.

Once the plane is loaded, fueled, and ready to go, the flight attendant announces that our next stop will be Milan.

"That's in Italy," she adds with a sense of excitement.

Elijah looks over at me and raises an eyebrow. He knows I've always wanted to go to Italy.

All Sand and Stars

The thing about Kuwait is that it's all sand and stars, and we're stuck somewhere in between.

I wake to the sound of somebody snoring. I sit up, wipe the sleep from my eyes, and look around. The tent is midnight black, dark, and full of shadows. Across the wooden floor I see bodies laid out like corpses in a mass grave.

As I stand a layer of sand slides off my uniform and sprinkles onto the floor, bouncing around like miniature marbles. I brush the remaining sand from my sleeve, and look around at the motionless men, trying to figure out what time it is or even what day. It was ten in the morning when we arrived at Camp New York. It was a Saturday and we were tired from traveling—from Fort Carson to Kuwait City, then into the desert. I remember hitting this floor pretty hard, and even though the plywood offered no cushioning, I slept soundly through the afternoon.

Across the tent I see an opening, a rectangle of deep blue with a couple of low-hanging stars, and I walk toward it, thinking, *This could be home.*

Tuna is sitting outside eating diced peaches from an MRE sleeve. He looks disheveled. His uniform is a collection of wrinkles and salt stains. Particles of sand stick to the inside crook of his arm. His face is wet with sweat, and I notice the tiny particles of sand that have wedged their way into the corner of his eye and up along his hairline. He looks like he's just crawled out of a bomb shelter.

"Woke up hungry," he says, pointing at an open box of MREs with his spoon.

I grab an MRE from the box and sit down next to him. He offers me his canteen, and I pour water into the heating sleeve.

"What time is it?"

"Three in the morning," he says between bites. "And all is silent in Camp New York."

Above us a blanket of stars spreads across the sky, shining down on us and all this sand. I look out across the land and watch the wind whip the particles into a fury. Four Porta-Johns are lined up across from our tent, and behind them a concertina wire barrier runs like a river in both directions. On the other side of the wire, the wind plays with the sand in an empty lot, and beyond that, off at the edge of camp, a single floodlight shines down on a guard tower poised at the top of a berm, an observation point peering out into the desert.

The sand covers everything, and oddly enough I am reminded of the snow-covered North Dakota prairie, where I could look out across the land and see white for miles. Here, even at night, I see sand piled upon sand, extending beyond sight.

The camp looks almost magical in the early morning hours, quiet and motionless, lit by a million stars, only the wind keeping things moving. I feel the cool night collecting around me, taking me in, and I think that maybe this wouldn't be so bad; maybe Kuwait will be more like home than I realized. Tuna and I sit in silence eating our MREs and thinking about the tranquility of the night. After a few minutes he looks over at me, notices my pathetic attempt at a mustache, and says, "I see you haven't given up."

"It's a race," I say.

"How do you know who wins?"

I set down my MRE and smile back at him.

"When somebody says 'Nice mustache' and means it."

I started running for candy.

When I was a child, my parents would take me to the track behind our local high school for children's running competitions. The competitions were hosted by Hershey's chocolate company, and since I have a really big sweet tooth, the events were an easy sell for my parents. They told me that at the end of every tournament the organizers and coaches handed out candy. *Jackpot.*

Eventually, I grew to love running because it was such a solitary sport. Unlike basketball or football, I didn't have to be part of a team and I didn't have to rely on others. I didn't have to spend time sitting on the bench, dreaming about playing or fetching water bottles for the exhausted players coming off the field. I only needed my own two lungs and the skinny little legs that took me around the track. It was perfect. There was nobody to blame but myself.

But that all changed when I became part of a relay team in junior high school. I was particularly strong at sprinting the 100-meter dash, and my coach asked me to anchor the 4 x 100-meter relay race at the regional track competition. If I did it, I couldn't be on my own. I would have to rely on others and others would have to rely on me; there would be three other runners counting on me to run the last 100 meters and cross the finish line in first place. Plus, I would be forced to work together with the other runners during training. We would have to practice handing off the relay baton over and over until we each knew how to hold our hand so the baton could easily be placed in our grip and what to do once our fingers were firmly wrapped around it. It would take us all summer. I eventually agreed to be on the team, but only because I was the anchor, the final runner in the race, and the thrill of crossing the finish line first motivated me all summer long.

It took every ounce of me to learn how to work together with my team. I wasn't used to running with others. Everything had to be timed just right, otherwise we could risk dropping the baton and being disqualified from the race. I knew that, because I dropped the baton a lot. But in the end, it all paid off. We came in second place and advanced to the state competition, where we placed first in our heat. It was the only time in my life I've ever crossed a finish line first. I remember busting the white, plastic tape with my scrawny junior high chest, and feeling overjoyed as I stood on the podium, proud to be part of a team. It was a great moment, something I rubbed in my brother Brandon's face every chance I got.

I've been thinking about that relay team lately, only because I'm once again being forced to be a part of a team. Since coming out, I've gotten used to being on my own. I've gotten used to not fitting in with these men and not sharing information about my personal life because I'm not allowed to talk about being gay. But now I'm forced to live with these other men like I've never had to before. As much as I want to believe that I can get through this deployment on my own, I have to accept that I'm going to have to let down my guard a little bit. If I don't gain their trust and friendship, this will be a long deployment.

Keep running, I have to tell myself. *Keep running*.

We are forty-five miles from the Kuwait–Iraq border. The higher-ups want our battalion to move into Iraq in six to nine days, but we must first wait for our equipment—the trucks and Hummers that will take us over the border. It is April 14, and the weather is already unbearable; during the day we've taken to sitting shirtless inside the concrete bunker near our tent, waiting for the unforgiving sun to set. In the early evenings, just before the sun goes down, we climb atop the bunker and gaze out across the desert, watching as the orange ball sinks into the land, gobbled up by the sand . . . like everything else.

I settle onto the roof of the bunker, thankful to be just a little farther from the sand. In the desert there is no escaping the sand. I find it everywhere—up the sleeve of my uniform, pasted to the inside of my thigh, stuck to my scalp, coating the firing pin of my M16, and inside my sleeping bag, making rubbing up against the fabric feel like my whole body is being dragged along fine sandpaper.

"I don't know if I can take another day like this," Trangsrud says, staring off at the setting sun.

Beside him Elijah is drinking from a canteen, and at the end of the bunker Tuna is finishing a letter to his wife. For the last week we've met atop this bunker to philosophize about the war and complain about the weather. It's our own desert version of gossiping over coffee.

"I stayed inside the bunker all day," Tuna says, looking up from his letter. "The damn thing was packed. Couldn't fit another person inside without making it just as bad as out in the sun."

When we arrived at Camp New York in the middle of the day, the place seemed nearly abandoned. Few soldiers wandered the grounds. While a good portion of the troops had moved north into Iraq, the people who remained had learned to stay hidden during the day. When the sun began to set, everyone came outside to enjoy the air dropping from triple-digit temperatures to more bearable conditions and to celebrate the sun's disappearance.

Beside the bunker, three guys from Charlie Company are tossing around a football and goofing around. Others are taking down the laundry they've laid out on the tent ropes to dry in the midday sun. At the end of our tent, a group of soldiers from our platoon is lounging around in folding canvas chairs they've purchased from the PX (Post Exchange, a commissary), smoking, joking, and playing cards.

"You know," Elijah says as the sun's final rays turn the tents red, yellow, and orange, "these tents look familiar."

He points at the tents behind us, the ones next to our large, circus-style, white tent, where the officers and Headquarters Company sleep.

"I think this is where that soldier threw that grenade at those officers. I recognize the tents from the pictures."

When we were at Fort Carson, we heard about the soldiers waiting in the Kuwaiti desert, poised on the border to a country we were ready to invade. On a weekend pass, I watched *MTV News* reporter Gideon Yago talk with soldiers waiting out here in the sand, on the "launching pad," and I couldn't help but wonder how it felt to be waiting so close to war. We heard about the soldiers struggling with the stress of such a situation, and saw the photos printed in *Newsweek* and *Time* when a soldier threw a grenade inside the tent of his fellow comrades, killing two officers.

I look closely at the tents and remember the pictures from the magazine, but I can't tell the difference. All the tents look the same to me. And that seems to be the theme in the desert—everything looks the same. The tents look the same, the bases look the same, the sand looks the same as it covers everything and everyone. Even the soldiers look the same as they traipse around with their light-weight desert boots and pathetic, scratchy mustaches.

"How long do you think we'll be here?" Trangsrud asks Elijah.

Tuna and I turn from the sun to look at Elijah, who's shaking his head. He brushes the sand from his pant-leg, sighs, and peers out at the setting sun.

"Who knows," he says. "We may be here a while. Waiting."

When the sun finally sets, Elijah, Trangsrud, and Tuna climb down from the bunker, leaving me alone to stare up into the early evening sky. I lie back and focus my attention on the emerging stars. A nearly full moon takes shape, almost winking at me as the light disappears from the sky; its shape becomes more visible as I wait for the sky to fill with stars. The night sky makes me nostalgic and romantic, and I start remembering everything that brought me here to this desert, every turn I fought against, every excuse I tried to use to get myself out of this situation. As the stars multiply and the moon grows brighter, I feel small and insignificant, like I did back in Fort Carson. I'm just another soldier sitting on the "launching pad," and as much as I want this place to feel like home, it's far from it.

But when I see the constellations, I am transported back. When I was a kid, we lived on a farm five miles from our tiny hometown, where the stars were magnified by the absence of city lights. My father used to work nights for an ice-cream warehouse in town, and on the Fourth of July we'd wait until he came home at two in the morning to set off our fireworks. Earlier in the evening, my brother Brandon and I used to climb atop our farm-house, lie on the roof, and watch our neighbors set off theirs, observing the shapes and colors but also contemplating the stars that twinkled between the flashes. Our father had taught us how to pick out the Big Dipper in the night sky. He told us to look for the brightest star—Polaris—and trace a line down to the corner of the Big Dipper's cup. He then drew the shape of the cup with his finger, pointing out the handle. That was the only constellation we knew, and every Fourth of July we'd try and find it.

I easily find the Big Dipper above Kuwait. I also find Orion and the two bright stars Betelgeuse and Rigel that make up Orion's right fist and left foot. On our second night at Camp New York, after another day of sleeping through the afternoon as our bodies adjusted to a new schedule, I walked with Rainman and Roach to the telephone trailer and stood in line to call my mother. I overheard another soldier describing the night sky, how bright the stars are when there isn't anything to block them out. I gathered that he was talking to his wife when he said, "As long as we can see the same stars, we aren't that far away."

I think about this now as I look into the sky, and I am a child again. It is the beginning of July, and Brandon and I are pointing out stars while lying on the roof of our house. I hear my father's truck coming down the gravel road, a cloud of dust drifting over the twinkling stars, and I climb down off the roof, excited.

Let the fireworks begin!

Lake stands above me wearing goggles and holding his weapon. He points at the deep blue opening we call a door. Across the wooden floor I see bodies laid out like corpses, a few of them rising and wandering out the door, weapons in hand.

As I stand, a layer of sand slides off my uniform and sprinkles onto the floor. It is early morning, and ten of us are headed to port to retrieve our equipment. The military has strung us along for three days, telling us to be ready to leave in a flash. All we've been doing is waiting, and that is about to change. I watch Jones and King rise from the floor, gather their gear, and walk toward the door, like zombies beckoned to another world. I brush the remaining sand from my sleeve, grab my goggles, helmet, and weapon, and walk toward the blue, thinking, *This could certainly be purgatory.*

I walk across the sand to a two-and-a-half-ton truck with an open back. We load a couple of boxes of water and three boxes of MREs, and climb atop the boxes, the cool morning air blowing sand into our faces. The stars aren't as bright this morning. I look up to see a few clouds drifting across the sky, blocking out my memory of home.

When the truck pulls out of the gate, we all almost simultaneously lower our goggles from our helmets to cover our eyes. A couple of the guys have brought scarves to cover their noses and mouths; as ten men riding in the back of a truck with weapons gripped in their palms and scarves over their faces, we look like thieves. We speed back the way we entered the desert, kicking up dust and sand. We move toward the sun as if it's a beacon drawing us closer. We zip past piles of garbage and abandoned trucks, half-swallowed by sand. Near the highway, a group of women wave despite the fact that we look like bandits, and we wave back, happy with our celebrity status. At a checkpoint along the highway, Kuwaiti soldiers shout our praises as we pass through their gates, and we smile and nod back at them as if we're all together in the cause.

Racing across the sand, I am amazed at how calming it feels to be riding in a truck across the desert. There is something soothing about the way the sand rises up from our tire tracks, creating a cloud of dust that collects around us, swallowing us into the sand. Coming back later in the day and again being consumed by the sand, I realize that the sand is sending us a message. I steer the truck I'm driving across the sand, but at times the dust becomes so thick I lose sight of the truck in front of me. Instead of slowing down, I push through the dust, trusting in the sand and hoping for the best. We're being welcomed into this place, not only by the women and soldiers along the road but also by the sand itself.

It's as if the sand is saying, *We'd love to keep you here.*

I wake to the windiest day in Kuwaiti history—*our* Kuwaiti history anyway. I sit up, wipe the sleep from my eyes, and look around. The tent is pitch black, darker than usual. The winds are shaking the tent, causing a few people to shift and stir. I hear the rain sharply pelting the canvas. Across the wooden floor I see bodies laid out, again like corpses, a few of them sitting up as if they're rising from the grave, listening to the wind and rain.

I shake the sand from my sleeping bag. The wind whips up again, and I hear the LT whimper. I look over and see that two boxes of water have fallen from their stack near the door and landed on top of him. I smile a little bit and try to go back to sleep.

In the morning, the wind is still going strong. I stick my head out the tent door. I should be able to see the chow hall from here, but instead I see a curtain of moving sand, whirling and whipping its way across the desert. I sigh because I have guard duty today; I have to stand outside enduring this sandstorm all day. No need to brush the sand from my sleeves; it will just find its way back. I grab my goggles, helmet, and weapon, and walk toward the closed curtain door.

It seems odd that engineers should have to guard the front gate, but so many people have moved forward into Iraq that there aren't enough troops left to keep this base running. Plus, in the army, everyone does guard duty.

I sit in the back of a truck on my way to Camp New York's front gate with the fifteen other soldiers from our battalion. The gate is a double-lane entrance into the post with a guard shack on one side and cement barriers making vehicles swerve left, then right, to get past the gate. I gaze out beyond, into the rest of Kuwait. I see sand and nothing else. I can make out the faint haze of the sun still rising before us, but beyond that all I see is a tan curtain of sand.

Our job is to check in and search all vehicles coming onto the post. I am in charge of the check-in sheet, taking ID badges from the Kuwaiti civilians entering post and checking them against the record of names and occupations in the binder. The vehicles start to appear out of the cloud of dust and sand, rolling up to the gate nonchalantly, as if the sandstorm poses no threat to them. I stand in the wind and sand, watching these vehicles appear out of thin air. I peer through my goggles, first at the badges, then the Iraqi faces, most of which are covered with scarves to block out the sand. Another soldier searches the vehicle. Once the vehicle has been checked in and searched, a third soldier must ride with the Kuwaitis as their escort, just to make sure they don't run amok and start doing wheelies around the post or steal the underwear the female soldiers have laid out in the sun to dry.

As the day wears on, I become more comfortable in the sandstorm. At first I can feel every sand particle hit me, piercing my uniform like tiny needles. The wind seems to be torturing me with its insistent bombardment. But the wind forgets where I come from. I'm an American boy from the Midwest, from North Dakota, a state known for its snowstorms and harsh winters, and I'm used to the brutality of weather. I'm used to the way wind can make a man feel lonely; how gusts can make everything invisible; how wind can turn you blind, drive you crazy. I know the effects of wind that can wrap around a man, spinning him into confusion because everything looks the same. In North Dakota, winters are white. But as I'm now finding out, winters in Kuwait are tan and sandy, and just as deadly.

At the end of the day, we catch a ride in a truck back to our tent. Across the truck from me, the only woman in our group starts to describe her day.

She was tasked as an escort and spent the day riding around with Kuwaiti truck drivers.

"I was in this truck with three other guys, squeezed into the end, riding to the chow hall," she says. "At one point one of the guys starts licking his finger."

She laughs and tries to brush away the sand from her cheek. She looks like a raccoon—two ovals around her eyes where her goggles used to be and the rest of her face black, covered in sand and dirt.

"He's twisting a ring on his finger, licking, trying to loosen it," she says. "He does this for about twenty minutes before the ring finally slides off. Then . . ."

She pauses and looks around the truck.

"Then he gives the ring to me, along with a carton of juice, an apple, and Kuwaiti money."

As the female soldier told her story, I couldn't help but notice how, in her story, she seemed comfortable around the Kuwaiti truck drivers. I've always been fascinated and a little scared by other cultures, and listening to this female soldier tell the story of her day, I am reminded of my interactions with the local people during my first deployment to Kosovo and the apprehension I've always held on to.

Before we ever left the base in Kosovo, we'd been exposed to the variety of local people who worked there. Of these people, we had the most interactions with the women who worked in the laundry tent. The military commissioned women from the nearby villages to do the soldiers' laundry. Every week we'd haul a green sack full of dirty clothes to a tiny canvas tent next to the chow hall on Camp Bondsteel. Inside the tent were several women of various ages. There were shy younger women in their late teens, middle-aged women who chatted and snickered like the women who worked at the craft store in my home town, and an older woman who seemed in charge of them all. We'd dump our clothes out before them, and they'd check off the items on a list, ripping off a duplicate of the list, handing it to us, and telling us to come back in a couple of days.

I was nineteen during my first deployment and afraid of women speaking foreign tongues. Every time I dumped out my laundry I felt like I was dumping out something about myself, something I didn't want revealed. I didn't like the way they looked at me, the way they looked at my clothes, or the way they snickered and said something foreign, as if they were saying, *Look at this scared little boy. Barely strong enough to hold up a rifle. Now he's begging us to clean his clothes. Poor boy. Poor, poor boy.*

When I'd come back to pick up my clothes, while other soldiers in my platoon attempted to chat and flirt with the women, I'd just hold out my laundry list and wait for them to hand back my clothes, thankful to have the items back in my possession. It was as if there were a line drawn between us and them, and as much as my mind desired interaction, my body always slowly backed away.

The female soldier holds up the ring from the Kuwaiti truck driver. The copper band barely shines in the darkness of the bed of the truck, but I see the smile on her face, the satisfaction of knowing her job here in Kuwait is appreciated.

"Really nice people?" someone asks.

Riding back to our tent, it is this question that keeps playing in my mind.

We're teaching Viv to play pinochle. He's a little high-strung. He joined our platoon before we left on the deployment, and people in the platoon have since been confused and mystified by the guy. He used to be a student and worked part-time as a waiter at a Mexican restaurant. He has a girlfriend named Pam, whom he constantly talks about, and buddies back in North Dakota, whom he called on the day we heard we were headed to Kuwait. I stood next to him when he said to his friends, "Can you imagine, man? Me of all people. Me."

In a lot of respects, Viv is like the rest of the young guys in the platoon — Tuna, Trangsrud, King, Jones. But what sets him apart is his odd behavior and general naïveté. He often has a smile spread across his face, and when you ask him what he's smiling about he'll just nod and say nothing. He is young and a little innocent, and he often asks stupid questions, sometimes because he simply doesn't know the answer, other times just to be funny. After a meeting where Newman stressed the importance of not eating inside the tent because the desert is full of rats, Viv asked, "What kind of diseases do rats carry?"

"Hepatitis, Viv," Newman replied. "Hepatitis."

Elijah is dealing out the cards and describing the game to Viv. Viv nods, accepts his cards, and starts to order them in his hand according to Elijah's directions. Around us the rest of the platoon is relaxing on cots. The Rolling Stones song "Angie" drifts around the tent, and outside I hear the wind and sand dancing to the rhythm and bumping up against the canvas walls. Fly and Cole have started calling each other Battlesnakes, a variation of the "Battle Buddy" term we learned in basic training, and I hear them address each other that way now. The term was supposed to be a means of camaraderie and brotherhood; no man should be left alone in battle. But Cole and Fly have turned it into a humorous label, and every time they address one another they use this new variation. It helps lighten the mood.

Rainman comes into the tent and tells us that a bunch of women are sun-tanning over at pad eighteen.

"If anyone comes looking for me that's where I'll be," he jokes.

I used to dread days like this because I figured sooner or later, while I was sitting around getting comfortable with the men in my platoon, I'd let slip that I was gay and be ridiculed for the rest of the deployment. But I really haven't had a problem getting close to these men *and* still keeping my distance. They are a bunch of jokers and if I did accidentally tell them I was gay, I could always brush it off. Once, while sitting outside our tent, Lake stated that he was going to be gay until he got back home. King chimed in with his support, saying what a good idea it was. I just laughed and shook my head. Something about the desert makes these straight guys think they are gay. I think it may be the sun.

"Diamonds," Elijah says, "go with spades. Clubs with hearts."

Elijah looks up at Viv to see if he understands the rules of the game. Viv starts singing "Lucy in the Sky with Diamonds," and the rest of us just shake our heads. We've gotten used to this.

"Do you understand?" Elijah asks.

Viv nods.

"What's wild?" Viv asks.

"You mean trump," I say. "In pinochle it's called trump."

"Yeah. What's wild?"

I just shake my head. I feel like I'm teaching one of my toddler cousins.

I learned how to play pinochle from my father. My father's family used to have a tournament during the holidays. We all got together in my grandparent's house—my grandparents, their seven children, spouses, and grandchildren. The adults divided up into pairs and seated themselves at three different tables throughout the house. They played a tournament round of pinochle, switching tables between rounds until a pair was declared champions. I often watched from the corner, wondering why the game got my uncles so excited, why my grandfather grinned when a game was going his way, or what it meant when my father folded his cards into a single pile and played off the top, a confident look plastered on his face.

Viv and Elijah are in a bidding war. While I wait for the war to settle, I watch Trangsrud do his laundry with our new cement mixer. One day, while relaxing in the shade, Grayson dragged a brand-new cement mixer over to the end of our tent. He loaded the mixer with his sand-crusted uniforms, poured powdered laundry detergent into the mixer, and loaded it with the water he'd been warming in the sun. Then he turned on the mixer, and we had our own field-modified washing machine. Ever since then life around camp has been getting better. We used to sleep on the wooden floor, where the desert rats could run across our ankles, but a few days ago Rainman came riding over to the tent atop a Hummer full of cots. I half-expected everyone to come running from the tent, eager for a little luxury in the desert. Rainman began handing out cots to everyone in the platoon. It was reminiscent of a Christmas scene—Rainman was our Santa, delivering cots to all the good boys and girls.

Eventually, Elijah tires of playing pinochle with Viv, and the game ends. I walk outside, where most of the platoon are sitting in canvas chairs under the camouflaged netting we've put up to block out the sun. They've taken out the Rolling Stones CD and replaced it with Jack Johnson. Everyone is a little tired from the sun and from packing. We've been working on preparing for our move into Iraq by loading up the trucks and trailers with our equipment. We spend an hour out in the sun before we're forced to retreat back inside the tent, where we drink lukewarm water from plastic bottles and wipe away our sweat. Cole and King are slumped in their chairs, their heads tipped back, trying to look at the stars through the netting. Yet the stars aren't really out tonight; they're blocked out by clouds and dust. I sit down in one of the chairs, tip my own head back, and listen to the music floating out into the desert night. I start to think about home. We've managed to make Kuwait seem like a home away from home. We have music, cold Coca-Cola from the PX, and playing cards to keep us occupied (and to remind me of home). A few nights ago, someone in Headquarters Company even acquired a karaoke machine and had a sing-along outside the tents, complete with cases of "near beer." I felt so at ease singing karaoke with these men and women, like they were my friends. It has taken me two weeks to become acclimated to this place, where sand and wind and stars prevail, but I think I've finally gotten used to Kuwait.

I no longer need the stars to tell me just how close I am to home.

I always wondered, Jeremy, why you even liked me. I was just another confused college kid, goofy and awkward, fresh off the farm. I wasn't anything special. I certainly didn't feel different, especially on drill weekends, when I put on a matching uniform and joined the other men and women at the armory north of town. I looked like them, talked, walked, and shit like them, and eventually I even became them, and it was all because of this uniform.

Did you ever see me in my uniform? I like to think that you did, so then you understood why I was so miserable those drill weekends. I like to imagine you lying in bed, watching as I stepped into the camouflaged pants, as I tucked the mud-colored T-shirt inside and cinched up the belt. In my dreams, you were there to button up the blouse, to smooth out the sleeves, to run your fingers across the name stitched on my chest. You were always there when I walked out that door, and you were there when I returned, when I kicked my boots off and tossed my beret aside just to kiss you. But in reality, I don't remember this ever happening. If you saw my uniform, it was probably hanging in my closet or tossed on the floor after another long weekend of blending in.

Then again, maybe it's better that you didn't see me in my uniform. I wouldn't want you to see me looking like all the other boys, acting like them just to fit in. Everything about my civilian life told me that I was different. Outside the military, I wanted to stand out. I wanted to be unique. But when I put on this uniform I am reminded that I am nothing special. I am just like thousands of other men and women. Nothing more.

And this is what I struggle with now. I used to tell myself that I was different, and you were there to reaffirm these ideas. But now, I can see that I'm nothing more than a name, another pair of hands able enough to hold a weapon and march into another country, ready to fight.

I hear Jones getting ready before I even open my eyes. We have guard duty tonight. I look at my watch. It is April 22, a quarter to midnight.

Jones and I stumble from the tent, groggy from a couple of hours of sleep. I sling my M16 across my back and walk to the motor-pool lot behind our tents. As I walk, I look up at the night sky, bright with a canopy of stars.

Our job is to guard the motor pool where our equipment is waiting for us to move it north into Iraq. Just beyond our tent, beyond the Porta-Johns and concertina wire barrier, our vehicles and trailers are lined up under a couple of looming floodlights. We must patrol the lot from midnight until 6 a.m., making sure nobody tries to take our equipment or run off with one of our Hummers.

Jones and I are almost the same soldier—we both have sarcastic attitudes about the military. At the beginning of our shift, as a way to mock the act of guard duty, we come up with a ridiculous plan to interrogate every single person on their way to the Porta-Johns by asking for ID cards. It's just one of the ways we like to make fun of the army. Beyond our dislike for the army, we have similar tales of basic training and AIT (Advanced Individual Training). We both know when to be silent, when to sit back and let the "chiefs" run the show. We even look alike, with our ragged mustaches under our noses. We haven't declared a mustache winner, although I've nearly conceded to him and his superior 'stache.

During the first two hours of our shift, we brief each other on our entire life histories as we walk around the motor pool. We share stories about being geeks in high school and attending college parties our freshman years. We talk about the dropouts from basic training and stories from advanced training in Gulfport, Mississippi. He tells me how he met his wife in the military and how they sat in a golf cart in the middle of the course, talking for hours; how they've even talked about having their wedding ceremony on a golf course and riding around in carts during their reception. I've gotten so used to keeping quiet about my sexuality that I forgot that it was possible for me to make friends. I've forgotten how easy it was to talk to the other soldiers, and as the night wears on I enjoy getting to know Jones. I also realize that I don't have to run this race alone. Actually, I *can't* run this race alone. If I want to survive this deployment I'm going to have to get to know these men.

Guard duty always creeps by slowly unless you have something to do. Two hours into our shift, we notice a plump desert mouse dart between two generators situated at the edge of the motor pool.

"Hey," Jones says, taking off his cap. "Let's try and catch it."

We take turns trying to rush the mouse from its hiding place. Jones stands atop the generators, waiting to drop his cap on the creature when it comes darting out of its hole. I do my part by kicking the generator and trying to scare the mouse out. We take turns in each role, before finally giving up. Around 4 a.m. I notice a series of wires running around the sand in our motor pool. The wires look like communication wires abandoned by soldiers who came before us. They are spread out across the lot, most half-covered by sand and running in every direction. I point them out to Jones and we each take a wire, following it like a finger would a subway line. My line cuts across the sand and under a Hummer. I follow the wire farther, under a few more vehicles and trailers. Eventually, I lose the wire beneath one of our bulldozers and pick up another wire going in the opposite direction.

It's easy to get caught up in following the wires. We follow them for nearly two hours, barely noticing the sun about to peek over the sand horizon behind us. At the end of our shift we go to the chow hall for breakfast before passing out on our cots. I dream about the sand and stars, how in between the night sky and the endless desert, we're left to wander, often chasing a wire with no end. I dream that other soldiers are doing the same thing on guard duty at night. I imagine what it looks like to see us from above, as if we are mice maneuvering a maze. You'd see thousands of young men and women, tiny, identical-looking dots aimlessly wandering around the sand, all looking down at their boots as they walk wherever a wire directs them. They don't look up or forward or even behind. They just follow the wires out into the silent desert, some of them never to return.

Wolves

Bobby has the perfect poker face—demure, innocent, emotionless. He doesn't give anything away with his pale brown eyes, his cherublike face, his thin lips. Words tumble from his mouth in a monotone like bricks slowly falling from a wall. He's still a boy; baby fat clings to his young face. Yet when you look at him, he stares back with those sad eyes, and you instantly feel cold, as if you are looking at an old man who's spent his entire life holding everything in.

During our last week in Kuwait, we switch from pinochle to poker. We shuffle cards around a makeshift table—two MRE boxes—and wait to move north into Iraq. We spend our days sitting on stuffed duffel bags, betting on flushes and pairs of brooding queens, and our nights lying on green army cots pretending to sleep. We lie awake at night wondering who, and what, awaits us.

As much as Bobby's face is made for playing poker, his fingers never touch the cards. Instead he sits on his cot playing his Game Boy, his fingers swiftly pushing the buttons as he stares into the tiny screen. Occasionally, he looks up at the troops around him, sometimes over at the table where I am playing cards, before turning his attention back to his game. In between hands of cards, I watch his fingers move. His fingers and thumbs are in full motion, forcing the black buttons down into the blue plastic Game Boy shell. His feet are firmly planted on the dusty wood floor, boot next to boot. But his face, that wonderfully naïve face, never changes. He never cringes at the thought of his game ending. He never yells when he loses or smiles when the game goes his way. He remains stone-faced through all the fun.

Bobby is reserved to the point of being somewhat suspicious. I look at him and wonder where he came from, who he really is, why he never speaks. While I was able to gather information from most of the other men in my platoon, Bobby remains a mystery, an enigma. He never reveals anything about his life back home. His quietness makes me wonder if he even *had* a life before the army, if he had career ambitions, desires, crushes on girls. With little to go on, I recast Bobby's past, placing him at a lonely gas pump along a North Dakota highway, staring off into the tall wheat fields before someone yells *dumbass*, forcing him back to work.

But Bobby's family is what puzzles me the most. I imagine an alcoholic stepfather who pushed him out the door when he turned eighteen, a man who always called him *boy* or *fuck-up* but never *son* or *champ* or, God forbid, *Bobby*. I see a loyal housewife, Bobby's mother, whose two failed marriages left her with no love for Bobby. And maybe because of all this, Bobby finds himself with a future he has no idea what to do with; a future with the army is his only option.

Bobby is the only person in our platoon I refer to by his or her first name. In a way, I feel a need to protect him, to call him by his first name like his father never did, or his mother had a hard time doing, because I know he has real emotions—real desires, real hopes, and, most importantly, real fears.

On May 1—the night before we're scheduled to leave Kuwait—Bobby and I lie on our cots, staring at the white canvas tent above our heads. My cot meets Bobby's at the center of the tent, our heads inches apart. Around us the platoon is packing gear. Troops stuff equipment, uniforms, boots, and other necessities into olive-drab bags while chatting about our upcoming move into Iraq. We are leaving Camp New York in the morning and traveling 480 miles north to Anaconda Army Airfield near Balad.

King runs around the tent shirtless, his dog tags slapping his chest as he jumps on cots, hooting and hollering. Lake is telling jokes to whomever will listen. Cole is farting on people. Rogers is walking around the tent with a cardboard sign reading IRAQ OR BUST around his neck. They are men eager to leave, excited to reach beyond the tent they've been living in for almost three weeks.

"Bronson," Bobby says.

He doesn't move from his cot, get up, or even turn his head toward me. He continues to stare up at the ceiling like he's trying to see the stars beyond the canvas.

"Yeah?" I reply.

"You alright?"

Staring at the ceiling of the tent, listening to Rogers and King laugh, I become aware of the similarities between the army and the circus. Both organizations travel from location to location, pitching tents in a clearing, a city park, the desert. These tents are the same, white canvas stretched over wooden support rafters and propped up with poles. There are no windows and no doors, per se. Instead, the doors are curtains, so from outside the tent the ringleader can pull back the flap and reveal the freaks inside, men dressed in camouflaged trousers and scuffed-up boots, dog tags dangling over bare chests, as they make jokes and laugh. These people—these clowns—are us, and this is our show.

Yet somehow these men don't make me feel the same way circus performers do.

"Yeah, I'm fine," I lie. "Are you?"

"Yeah, I'm alright."

I hear him breathing, the slow, steady in and out of air. Around us the platoon settles into cots. King calms down; Lake becomes silent.

A few minutes pass before Bobby speaks again.

"You excited?"

I don't feel excited, mainly because we live in a constant state of the unknown, from day to day relying on information passed down by our squad leaders, getting only what we need to know *now*. We don't get concrete details, plans, or descriptions about where we'll be in two months or even two weeks. It leaves us with a sense of disconnect, an uneasiness about our own lives. We might not show it on the outside, anxieties making us run around like clowns, but we're all uneasy inside.

"Yeah. I can't help but feel this is a little exciting."

"You bet it is," Bobby says.

I want to look over at Bobby and see if he means what he's saying. I want to see if he's smiling about the possibility of coming upon conflict, of shooting his rifle, of killing a man. But I stay in my cot, looking up at the tent.

There's another pause, and for a moment the tent seems quiet, as if everyone is thinking about the mission. I hear the breathing of sixty men, and as I tilt my head to the left, and look down the line of soldiers lying on cots, I see their lungs expand and deflate, almost in unison, each man thinking the same thing: *What lies ahead?*

The clowns are quiet because they have realized that they are being watched. Captain Roar steps into the tent, nonchalantly brushing aside the curtain door. Captain Roar doesn't live in tents like these; he lives across the common area that separated the white circus tents we've been living in from the air-conditioned green military tents the officers and Headquarters Company live in.

He walks around, asking soldiers if they are ready for the trip into Iraq, joking with the young lieutenants. Bobby and I sit up and watch him as he laughs at his own jokes. He makes one trip around our cots before ducking back out the curtain door.

When he is gone, Bobby and I again lie down on our cots, as if Captain Roar's visit was the equivalent of being tucked in, and we're now ready for sleep. Then Bobby asks the question I've been waiting for.

"Bronson, are you scared?"

Am I scared? I've been betting on straight flushes and pairs of kings for the past two weeks, trying to take my mind off this question, but whatever I do I can't help but feel this question in the back of my mind, like a song I'll never forget. There it is ringing through my head when I shuffle the deck of cards between my fingers and thumbs. There it is spelled out in the sand as if a scorpion has read my mind and etched the question into the ground outside our tent. And when I sit down and think about my friends and family back home, it feels like the question is buzzing around the tent like a rumor that floats from soldier to soldier. The question is everywhere because everyone refuses to ask it.

"I don't know, Bobby," I say from my cot. "I really don't know."

Bobby leans up on one elbow and looks over at me.

"Well, it's alright," he says as a rare grin spreads across his face. "I'll take care of you."

When we were in our early teens, Brandon and I spent several summer nights sleeping in our pup tent out behind our family's farmhouse. We pitched the tent just off the back door. We made sure we were close enough to the house in case we needed to use the bathroom or ransack the kitchen for snacks, but also far enough away, so when we told stories our parents wouldn't yell at us to stop scaring each other with wild tales of headless ghouls and monsters. We lay in that tent during the early evening hours and talked about our day. My brother was a year younger than I, and years later, during high school, he would outgrow me. We fought over who was bigger and stronger, and he always won. But during those years on the farm, when he was twelve and I was thirteen, we shared everything—a tent, a bedroom, even a double bed with springs that poked out of the mattress like steel worms. It seemed like we were equals.

It was a tent for two: a square of green vinyl propped up in the middle by a pole in the front and a pole in the rear of the tent. We had a tiny window in the back with a flap that exposed a mesh screen to the North Dakota night. I liked to open that window and look out past the clothesline, past the giant willow tree, to the shelterbelt of trees gently swaying at the edge of our farmstead. I sat with my face pressed against that mesh screen and felt small and insignificant. Brandon and I zipped open the two triangles that made up our front door and rolled the canvas fabric up, exposing the mesh screen, so the air blew through our tent at night. I felt so tiny inside that tent, but as long as I had my brother there and the gentle breeze whispering in my ear, I slept like a little boy, content and at home.

Our father had a cautionary tale he liked to tell over and over. He reminded my brother and me of the coyotes beyond our farm. He sat us down and explained the differences between coyotes and wolves, talking like an expert about the animals that howled just beyond the shelterbelt of our farm.

"You wouldn't find wolves up here," our father said. "Those sounds you hear at night, those are coyotes."

We didn't know the difference, but we still believed him. He was right, of course; gray wolves don't typically live in central North Dakota. But coyotes are plentiful in the upper Midwest. They like to roam the sparse prairie, finding their way into farms where they kill livestock, sheep, and smaller dogs. My brothers, sister, and I came home from school once to find our dog Cha-Cha dead, killed by a coyote, my father said. The beast also killed four of our ducks and injured Lassie, our other dog. My father had to raise a shotgun to Lassie's head and pull the trigger before the bus brought us home.

When the sun set and the sky grew dark, my brother and I closed the flaps to our tent, bundled up into our sleeping bags, and told ghost stories. Late into the night we scared each other until we heard the sound of coyotes howling off in the distance. From beyond the shelterbelt surrounding our farm, we heard the throaty sound drifting into our tent, silencing us. We looked at each other, checked the zipper on the tent door, and tried to sleep through the night, hoping the animals didn't move beyond the shelterbelt and pounce upon our tent.

Waking Bobby is like waking a baby: you hate to do it but it must be done. *It's time to leave*, you must say. *It's time to be fed on warfare and greed.*

I wake Bobby at 4 a.m. We rise from our cots, pack our sleeping bags, and fold our cots into the shape of logs. I help Bobby shoulder his bag, holding back the curtain door as we exit and walk toward the line of trucks.

A line of seventy-one military vehicles awaits us outside the tent. We're moving almost all our trucks into Iraq—Hummers, two-and-a-half-ton trucks, five-ton dump trucks, flatbed trailers carrying bulldozers, scrapers, and cranes. They are all here, lined up and ready to go. Floodlights pour generous light over the trucks, and for a moment it looks like a movie set, as troops load duffel bags into shiny trucks, light bouncing off the cheek-bones and teeth, faces like ceramic masks.

I help Bobby lift his bag into the back of a two-and-a-half-ton truck, before climbing aboard, next to the bags. The truck is built to carry soldiers, with benches that fold down from the sides, so troops can ride comfortably into battle. The railing along the side also serves as support for tired backs. However, there will be no time for rest on this trip. I'm riding with seven other soldiers in the back of the truck, packed in next to twenty-five boxes of MREs, twelve boxes of bottled water, our bags, and our cots. We line the luggage and boxes along the bed of the truck and sit on top of a layer of packages, everyone leaning against bags and each other in the center of the bed so we can see out the sides. I lean my weapon on the bench, pointing the muzzle out between the wooden slats. I look over at Bobby as he does the same thing. We both look back at the silent tents, now vacant, sad white peaks poking out of the sand.

"This is it," I say, looking over at him.

He lifts his head and looks over at me, his baby face peering out from under his Kevlar helmet.

"Yeah, man," he says in monotone. "This is it."

As Rogers climbs into the back of the truck, he fumbles over our bags and us until he reaches the front of the bed. He places his M249 machine gun on top of the cab, rests his elbow next to his weapon, and thrusts his hip against the back of the cab. He's our lookout for the trip, while the rest of us watch from the sides. I look up at the canvas tarp covering half of the truck. A wooden beam stretches from side rail to side rail, the tarp rolled over the beam, shading the back half of the bed, so Rogers can watch for possible threats up front. We're shielded from the sun above, but unprotected from the elements that may come at us from the sides.

I lift my weapon slightly, touching the muzzle of the gun against one of the razor blades jutting out of the concertina wire strapped to the outside of the truck. Concertina wire is a soldier's best friend. The wire is used as a barrier, to prevent intruders from grabbing what isn't theirs. We use it around our tents, around the motor pool, around any place that needs protecting. To build a concertina wire obstacle you grab a roll of wire, which lies flat in a coil, and "bounce" out the coil, until the roll expands like an accordion. Once you've "bounced" out three lines of wire, you create a pyramid, placing one line on top of the other two, and secure the obstacle with wire ties.

We had missed the ground war, but we had our own war—a war against the needy. We knew there were women and children with eager hands that wanted to reach into our trucks and steal whatever was easy to grab. So, we counteracted the actions of the needy by tying rolls of concertina wire to the outside of the side rails, like interlocking rings spread on both sides of the troop carrier. Anyone who tried to reach into our truck risked slicing his or her arm open just for a bottle of water.

When everyone is loaded into the trucks, the convoy of vehicles moves toward the gate. The tents are illuminated by the rising sun, now peeking over the sand. Morning is coming and we are going, and in the early morning hours, we watch the white tents fade away as we leave Camp New York and move across the Kuwaiti desert, bound for Iraq.

It takes us two hours to reach the Kuwait–Iraq border. The hours pass with little activity, few signs of any kind of life. It is still early and the sun is like a mirage off on the horizon, rays of red and orange clouded by a light haze. For a moment, I think Bobby is asleep, and I wonder how anyone can sleep now. I want to poke him, but before I do, he shifts over, leans his elbow on a box of MREs, and looks around the truck. I catch his eye and nod at him, thanking him for not sleeping.

Breakfast today is an MRE. We open a box of MREs and reach inside, pulling out brown bags of prepackaged food. I grab menu 23: chicken with Cavatelli, a fig bar, wheat snack bread, pound cake, cheese spread, and grape powdered beverage. We trade for various items, like we're back in elementary school swapping the items in the lunches our parents prepared.

"I can't eat this wheat bread," I say, holding the package above my head. "Any takers?"

I find none. We create a pile of items nobody wants to eat: three packages of wheat snack bread, two packets of peanut butter, and, of course, Charms, the square version of LifeSavers.

My back aches from leaning on an MRE box, and I wish I were driving the truck into Iraq, rather than riding in the back. But then we see the people watching us pass. When we reach the border, men and children rush the convoy, standing next to the road as we kick sand up into their faces. From the road we see their one-room stone houses off in the distance, walls sealed with mud, and roofs made from palm branches and sticks. I notice a man hoeing a ravished garden near his house; his head barely lifts to acknowledge us as our convoy of trucks waves at him with a cloud of dust.

Half-naked children run up to the road, bare feet making tracks in the sand as their eyes find the boxes of MREs in the back of the truck. They ask for food, pointing at their mouths or their round little stomachs. One boy lifts his shirt to show the troops his tan stomach, patting his abs in an effort to get food. A little girl in braids, red ribbons tied into her hair, stands by the road holding an entire unopened MRE, clutching the package of food to her chest. She's already gotten to previous troops.

I stop chewing my crackers when a boy's eyes find mine. The child's eyes hollow me out, burrowing deep into my mind. His lips are closed as he does all the talking with those sad eyes. *Mee-sta, please.* In the back of the truck, a look of guilt spreads across everyone's faces. We all come to the same realization at once.

Here we are swapping pound cakes for jalapeño cheese, wishing for the "good" MREs, when children, stringy and shy, are forced to beg. The Iraqis we see are so poor, farming or herding animals to make a living, their children collecting the dust of passing Americans while we sit back in our trucks and thank God we have our twenty-four boxes of MREs.

I wave at a little girl on the side of the road, her brother clinging to her leg. When she sees me looking at her she gives me a thumbs up, smiling as she thrusts her arm out at the soldiers. I want to believe she's happy to see us here, in her country, but in reality she only pays attention to me because she knows I have food. A group of young boys stops their soccer game to wave at us, and when they see us eating, they stop thinking about scoring goals and start thinking about scoring food. Our chewing mouths start their racing, hands jutting up into the sky in hopes that food will land in the open palms.

I watch it all from the reclined comfort of the truck. Then, impulsively, I reach into the pile of unwanted food items and toss the packages into the crowds of children, like candy at a parade. The food bounces off their heads, hits their arms, and falls to the ground; a half-dozen children fight for a package of crackers or Charms. We drive on, leaving them scurrying like dogs. Outside a town, three women stand along the road, as if they've been standing there all day. When we approach they flash us peace signs with both hands. They cheer as we pass. One of the women holds a small American flag and waves it as we glide by. She smiles weakly, and I see the joy in her face, and I believe that we are in Iraq for a reason and that Iraqis like these women are the proof.

But there are also miles when nobody greets our passing convoy. Instead, the sand stretches over small dunes and whips up into our faces. Off in the distance, squat bungalows pop up out of the earth like corn, each home surrounded by a cluster of palm trees and children who either don't notice us passing or are sick of seeing traveling soldiers.

Bobby is silent through most of this. He takes it all in the way he takes everything in, absorbing the environment, the people, the neediness, and holding it tight, keeping everything close to his chest. I want him to react, to reach out and shout at the injustice of it all, but he doesn't. He watches from the truck as the hands reach up and beg for his attention.

In the afternoon we come to a river, and dip down into the valley to meet a bridge. On the other side of the bridge, an old man stands by the side of the road in a long, white robe. Three small, wooden crates piled with shoes and sandals lie at his feet. Bobby notices the man and points to him. The man notices Bobby and walks toward our truck.

"Look," Bobby says to me, "an Iraqi shoe salesman."

He laughs shyly like he's not sure if the man is funny-comical or funny-sad. I watch Bobby's face, his eyes taking in the man and his situation. He watches the man until he's out of sight, then turns back to the position he was in, staring off into the desert.

"I swear," he says while looking out at the sand, "he wanted my boots."

Around 11:30 p.m., we pull into Checkpoint 8, our stop for the night. We pull the trucks into the military compound, past the lines of concertina wire surrounding the facility, and line the vehicles up so the spaces between the vehicles look like aisles in a grocery store. It's dark, and we're tired from traveling all day. We don't have tents to sleep in. Instead, we pull out our cots and assemble them wherever there is room. Bobby and Elijah set up their cots on the ground between the trucks. Rogers and King curl up on the luggage. I grab my cot and climb onto the top of the truck. From here, I see the dark night stretch into the desert, a wall encircling our trucks, moonlight bouncing off the razor wire, and soldiers busying themselves with creating a place to sleep. I set up my cot on top of the cab, my weight slightly denting the hood, and watch everyone settle in for the night. We're scattered over the sand like drunks who've decided to sleep wherever they fall. I pull out my sleeping bag and climb into the folds of the camouflaged fabric. I lie on my back, looking at the few stars that dot the sky before drifting off to sleep.

I am awakened by the sound of barking dogs. I hear the faint howls, first above my head, the distant cries of lonely animals drifting into the canyons between the trucks. The noise echoes off the vehicles and climbs into the night sky. Then the howling stops. I hear the animals creep around the checkpoint. Then I hear the low moan again, this time to my right. The howls shift location, now coming from beyond my feet. It's as if the dogs are circling the compound, pacing the ground before taking their prey. The howls get stronger, closer. Then I hear the barking on all sides, as if they're just beyond where the trucks are parked. I stare into the night sky and wait for the howling to stop, thinking about how the howling sounds so much like North Dakota coyotes. Ten minutes pass before the barking eventually settles and I drift back to sleep. But later I find myself dreaming about the dogs. I dream that they've broken into the compound, black-haired and bare-toothed, drool foaming at their mouths, their eyes red and fierce. I hear them coming toward us, running through the aisles between the trucks, tearing at the soldiers that sleep below. There are no tents to shield us, no barriers between us and the beasts. They sink their teeth into our uniforms. They take an arm, a leg, someone's foot, whatever they can grab, pulling until we scream, as they drag us off into the cool desert night.

In the morning we wash up quickly, eager to get back on the road. I climb down from the top of the truck and pour water over my face, the water splashing recklessly into the sand between the trucks. Bobby stands next to me, brushing his teeth.

"You hear those dogs last night?" he asks after spitting into the dirt.

"Yeah," I say. "Damn things wouldn't leave us alone."

We prepare the trucks, packing our cots and sleeping bags. I climb into the back of the truck, taking the same position I was in the day before. Outside Checkpoint 8, we pull the vehicles to the side of the road to make final preparations before our day-long trip further into Iraq. An old man is steering a wooden cart down the road toward us. The cart, full of sticks and branches that reach out like hands ready to grab onto people or soldiers passing by, is being pulled by a gray donkey. In the ditch, a young boy rides a white donkey up next to our truck. Lake walks up to the boy, his weapon in one hand as he pats the mule with the other.

"Bobby," Lake yells, waving Bobby over to him. "Come take my picture."

Bobby goes to Lake, takes his camera, and sets up the photo. Lake stands next to the mule, his rifle propped against the inside of his elbow and pointed into the morning sky. The boy sits on the donkey, a smile spread across his face. I watch the boy, wondering if he fears that Lake will open fire on him and his pet after the picture. Instead, after Bobby snaps the shot, Lake asks the boy if he has any Iraq currency—dinars. The boy exchanges currency with Lake, dollars for dinars, before turning his ride around and galloping away. I imagine he'll take that money to his parents, show them the crisp green picture of George Washington, and say, *He paid me for my photo.*

We climb back into the trucks and travel down a dirt road until we find a hardtop highway with signs pointing to Baghdad. This is the highway that takes troops to Baghdad, up through the sandy dunes, around tiny farms and begging children, into the heart of the capital city. Before leaving Kuwait, I overheard Grayson telling Newman that the route to Baghdad had been cleared of any war symbols—no charred bodies, no burning tanks. We all declared it a disappointment, Grayson even mentioning how discouraging it was going to be if he didn't get to see one dead Iraqi.

But we see very few people, dead or alive, along the highway. Occasionally we notice a man watching from a distance, hands clasped behind his back, silent. We come upon road signs, in Arabic and English, pointing us toward Baghdad, a faded white arrow pointing up.

It doesn't take us long before we see the remains of the war. Rogers, our lookout, yells, "A tank, a tank," and points off into the ditch; we all lean over to one side of the truck, our cameras ready, as we pass a wasted Iraqi tank. The tank is black, destroyed by flames, the broken tract laid out like a snake's skin. There is no man, burned beyond recognition, sprawled next to the tank, only the machine. A few minutes pass before Rogers yells out, "Here comes another one," and we again lean over to get a glimpse of another tank, this one in the same condition, each tank interesting and terrifying at the same time.

By the seventh tank we've lost interest, Rogers not even notifying us when we approach. We still look—another destroyed tank, no body, nothing special about this one. It won't be long before children will be climbing on the tanks as if they are jungle gyms, swinging from the barrel of the canon. Passing by the tank, I wonder how the children of this country feel about the machines, lying along the road as they pass. What do their mothers say to calm their questions and fears?

Bobby and I are sitting near the edge of the truck, settling back in after seeing the tanks. Ahead, I see another sign for Baghdad as the convoy takes the center lane of the three-lane highway. Bobby shifts over and I watch, as if in slow motion, as a magazine of ammunition slides out of his cargo pocket, falls onto the folded-down bench, and slides off the side of the vehicle, through the concertina wire rings. The magazine makes a sharp noise as it hits the pavement and bounces into the right lane of the highway. Our convoy continues up the road.

I look over at Bobby, who shrugs his shoulders, not worried that he just lost a magazine of ammunition, thirty rounds he is responsible for.

"You just lost a clip of ammo," I say to Bobby. "Don't you care?"

Bobby doesn't seem to understand responsibility. He doesn't understand the magnitude of his actions, as he looks down at his boots, avoiding my question. His actions and silences tell me that he has never learned these things, traits children learn from parents or older siblings: how to be responsible, how to admit your mistakes, how to speak up. I tap Rogers, explaining the incident. Rogers knocks on the cab and relays the message to Newman.

After Newman turns the truck around to retrieve the ammunition, Bobby is quiet. He watches the sand, the few people that dot the landscape. He doesn't speak, too embarrassed to make a sound. I watch the convoy snake up the road, vehicle after military vehicle, maneuvering up the highway. Then, as if out of nowhere, a blue van appears in the right lane of the highway, between our convoy of vehicles and the metal railing along the road. The rusty van pulls up next to our truck, four Iraqi men sitting in the back. The men notice me watching them. One man, with a young face and black eyebrows, pulls back the window and sticks his torso out of the van, a clear glass bottle filled with copper-colored liquid in his hand.

We immediately recognize the liquid. We've been sober for almost a month, ever since we set foot in a combat zone. The Iraqi man holds the bottle up, points at me with his dark index finger, before showing five fingers.

"Is that whiskey?" King asks.

"I think so," I say. "And it's five dollars."

We search our pockets for money. I look back at the Iraqi, nodding my head. The man motions for the driver to get closer. The driver pulls the van right up next to our truck. With the five-dollar bill in my hand, I reach through the side rail, through the concertina wire, and place the bill in the man's palm before slowly retracting my hand. Pulling my arm back into the truck, I nearly knick my arm on a razor blade, swearing as the blade grazes my uniform sleeve. The Iraqi hands the money to the other men inside the vehicle. He then gently lowers the bottle and tosses the container over the razor blades and into our truck. King catches the liquor with both hands.

King opens the bottle and smells the fumes coming from the container. "It smells like apple juice," he says before raising the bottle to his lips. He puckers a bit as he lowers the bottle, shaking his head. "Sure as hell doesn't taste like apple juice."

I look back at the van and notice that the Iraqi is now pointing at Bobby, trying to sell him a bottle of whiskey. I laugh as Bobby shakes his head. I look into the back of the van and notice an entire box of whiskey bottles; these guys are making a killing off of us. We pool the rest of our money and buy four more bottles, reaching four more times through the concertina wire, each bottle transferred from Iraqi hands to our hands, all while driving down the highway.

I want to pass a bottle around the truck, offer a swig to Bobby, make him feel the burn down his throat, but I don't. We quickly hide the bottles, knowing that we'd face serious consequences if we're caught.

Watching the van pull away, off to tempt other soldiers up the line, I realize the extent of our *own* neediness. We put up these bundles of wire to keep the Iraqis from grabbing our equipment and our gear. But when the roles are reversed, when we are the needy ones, we curse at the sharp barrier that prevents us from reaching beyond our truck. We grumble and yell at our inability to touch a world outside our own, a world full of people reaching out to grab our hands, and tanks that lie destroyed and broken in the ditches. We need these people—the people we've started comparing to wolves—just as much as they need us, and looking around the truck, at the smiles on our faces, people pleased with their new purchases, I realize that we are the wolves, every single, greedy soldier.

I've always been the big brother. Growing up with four younger brothers, I've gotten used to the role and even cherish the fact that I've gotten so good at it. But, when we were dating, I liked how you became the big brother I never had.

During Christmas, your protective nature was particularly evident. I remember being invited to ride around in a limousine and look at holiday decorations with two other couples. I didn't know the other couples very well (they were your friends), and I felt a little uncomfortable because one of the other guys was your ex-boyfriend. I remember feeling awkward sitting next to you, but then you put your arm around me, and I leaned into your body and felt the warmth of being held, and all that awkwardness disappeared. I hadn't really felt that before, so when you did it, I remembered.

Then there was the Christmas party we attended, the one with my friends. I took shots of tequila and drank beer after beer while I smoked cigarettes out on the apartment balcony. I think I ignored you for most of the night, and you were probably pissed about that. But at the end of the night, you took my keys and drove me home. You guided me into my apartment and onto the green, shag carpet in my bedroom. I had just moved in and didn't have a bed, so I passed out on the floor.

I like to think that you lingered in my room that night, watched me fall asleep on the carpet as the moonlight snuck in through the blinds and cast shadows onto the walls. I like to think of you covering me with a blanket, smoothing out my hair, maybe even lying down next to me and curling your arm around my shoulder. In my memory of this event, you stayed. In reality, I know you didn't. I know I'm romanticizing the event, but when you experience these feelings for the first time you have a hard time letting go. You remember what it feels like to be looked after, to be protected, to always have someone there, and no matter what happens after that, you remember how good it felt that first time.

I realize the magnitude of the world, the extent to which land is populated by millions of hungry mouths, all eager for something different. This world exceeds the half-dozen people I call friends, enjoying dinner and conversation without me; the hundreds of students copying notes from chalkboard to notepad, people I once identified with; or even the handful of soldiers, formerly poker players in Kuwait, now sharing a bumpy ride across the desert.

We stop the convoy just outside Baghdad. In the ditch, scattered among rubble, rock, and trash, someone has discarded a disposable camera. We dare each other to pick up the camera, each of us thinking that it could be a trap, a trigger to a roadside bomb planted for curious soldiers. Watching King walk up and toe the plastic camera, I imagine all the hands that touched it: the fingers that built the plastic shell, the meaty hands that placed the item on the shelf, the gentle hand of a mother buying the item to send to her son, a U.S. soldier sitting in Kuwait. I want to grab the camera, develop the film, and see the people important to someone else, the soldiers, family members, and landscapes that make other people press the black button.

We leave the camera in the ditch as we load the trucks. The towers of the mosques climb into the cloudy Baghdad sky as we approach the capital city. Our trucks drive around Baghdad, safely touching the outskirts of the city before connecting to a highway that takes us north, forty-five miles to Balad. Along the highway, reminders of a great empire still exist. On the wall of a compound just outside Baghdad, a billboard proudly displays Saddam, two silver swords crossed above his head. We stare at the billboard until it is out of sight, wondering if it will be there the next time we pass, and silently take in the ornate architecture of the faded buildings and the thick walls surrounding once-flourishing courtyards. Everything is so gray.

We reach Anaconda Army Airbase by early evening on May 3. The base is an old, run-down Iraqi military compound. I notice the stucco buildings dotting the field next to the runway, and the diamond-shaped concrete bunkers. We pull the trucks into a dusty parking lot near the middle of the base, again lining the vehicles up, and are greeted by Sergeant Major. He tells us that we'll again be sleeping under the stars, and in the morning we'll start building our new homes.

Bobby and I put together our cots on the ground between our truck and another. As the sun sets, the platoon sits around the trucks, staring off into the night sky. Bobby and I have a flashlight and are making shadow puppets against the wooden wall of the trailer box. I hold the flashlight as Bobby makes a dog with his hand, two knuckles forming ears and the tips of his fingers portraying the pointy teeth of beasts.

King watches the stars while lying on his cot. We're nostalgic tonight, and every now and then someone will mention family members or something they wished they were doing back home. Tuna is eating sardines, the tin lid peeled back to reveal a layer of stacked fish. He talks about being home, where he doesn't have to eat fish out of a can. He offers a sardine to King, who takes the fish between his fingers and slides the silver sliver down his throat.

"We all worry so much about our own lives," King says, "but looking at this night sky makes all our troubles fade away."

In the morning, we build the floors for the tents. In between building floors, Bobby and I have races flipping hammers. We take hammers and flip them into the air, catching them by the handle. We do this ten times, racing to see who can complete the cycle the fastest. I drop my hammer, dust scattering over my boots, and when I reach down to pick up the tool, I catch a smile on Bobby's face as he continues the race without me, easily finishing well before I do. His eyes are now a soft, warm brown, and I see comfort in his face that wasn't there before the trip into Iraq. He retells the Iraqi shoe salesman story every chance he gets, and I see him laugh for the first time in a couple of days.

The funny thing is that I used to be Bobby. I was just like him when I first joined the army. I didn't know what to do with myself, and I would often sit silently in the corner, waiting for someone to tell me where to go or what to do. But now, Bobby has become my little brother—a stand-in for Brandon. I like talking to him, helping him, or just goofing around with him while we wait to put up our tents. Helping Bobby makes me more connected with these men. I have a purpose—a role—and I'm not just a gay man out of place in Iraq.

And that in itself is an incredible relief. When I started this deployment, I thought the best thing for me to do was to keep quiet and continue to hide behind my mask. Five and a half years of hiding my sexuality from the military had taught me to do that. But now I realize that I can't do that anymore. I can't just fly under the radar and expect to survive this deployment. With Bobby, Jones, and a few others I've started to make genuine friendships, the kind that are needed among men at war because they are the kinds of friendships that keep you alive.

By the time evening sets in, we have the floors built and GP (general purpose) medium military tents constructed. The tents aren't the white canvas circus-style ones we used in Kuwait. These are standard-issue military tents, sixteen feet wide and thirty feet long, smaller than the white tents. We immediately roll up the side walls of the tents, tying each side up with green strings, leaving only a mesh screen between our cots and the Iraqi sand.

Bobby and I lie on our cots in the dark. I pat his shoulder, glad to be here, satisfied with our journey so far.

I feel the cool desert air rush in through the mesh screen, the same way it rushed through my tiny pup-tent window, and for a moment I don't feel like a nomad moving from place to place. I feel at home. Then I hear the swoosh of a canvas flap being pulled back, and as the curtain door opens, I hear the boots of another wandering soldier.

This Is Our Comfortable Hell

As the soldiers push the refrigerator toward the tent, the wind whips the sand into a fury. Particles rise up like flames around the appliance, devouring the box like termites. They walk the box forward, teetering the giant appliance back and forth like a mother escorting a child toward a grandparent. The men maneuver the large rectangle through the curtain doors and onto the wooden floor of the tent. They slide the appliance across the wood, the metal rubbing against grainy sand, and as they move it to the corner, the sound of grinding fills the tent. They don't mind the noise. They stand with their arms akimbo; white salt stains make circles on their T-shirts like patches of ringworm—blurry on the edge, damp in the middle. They brush away the sweat from their heads with their forearms and saunter out of the tent toward the next icebox.

From inside a Conex box (a large metal box for transferring equipment and supplies across land and sea) at the edge of our tents, I breathe a sigh of relief.

The temperature on Fredricks's thermometer reads 108 degrees. We've been sweating and swearing all morning. We sweat because of the sun, swear because we're forced to endure the heat all day inside a steel Conex box that bakes our bodies like Easter hams. We've stripped down to brown army T-shirts, the sun too hot for our long-sleeve camouflage uniforms, as we move boxes around the Conex, examining and inventorying the contents of each box. Trangsrud smokes Camel cigarettes near the edge of the box, his boot tapping against the steel floor. We all look at him in agitation. Newman is knee-deep in the mess, surrounded by ladders and wooden carpenter boxes. He opens one and looks over at me.

"Two hammers, four tape measures, two long-tooth saws, three auger bits, two levels, seven tool belts." He pauses to wipe away the sweat. I scratch the details down on the clipboard, lean against the side of the box, and wait for Newman to say the words: *Let's take a break.*

Because of the heat, we work only for about ten minutes before we are forced to surrender to the sun, forced to sit in the shade and drink lukewarm water from olive-colored canteens, and wonder what we are doing here.

I stare down the line of tents that have popped up almost overnight and think about the nomadic lifestyle we've been living. We're gypsies in the Middle East, nomads pushed forward by the beating sun. We pulled into Anaconda Army Airbase almost a week ago. It took us more than two months to get here—first taking a three-day bus ride from North Dakota to Colorado, then a fourteen-hour flight to Kuwait, and finally a 480-mile bumpy convoy into Iraq. Now we can finally unpack our gear, roll out our flags, push wooden stakes into the sand, and thank God we have a place to lay down our heads.

Our camp is centered around an old stucco Iraqi army building with a metal awning jutting off the back corner. We've built picnic tables and placed them under the awning—this has become our new chow hall. To the south of the building, Headquarters Company has raised a colony of tents. Alpha and Bravo's tents extend in three rows to the west of the building like insect legs protruding from the body. At the end of these rows is a single row of Conex boxes, where we've been sweating all day.

When we return to our tents at the end of the day, the refrigerator is waiting for us in the corner. It is the most beautiful thing we've ever seen.

"About damn time," King says. He throws his gear onto his cot and a puff of sand rises from his sleeping bag like a cloud of gas.

We walk up to the appliance mesmerized, running our hands down the white metal siding, over the handle on the door. It is a completely average-looking refrigerator. No stainless steel casing. No automatic ice maker. No side-by-side fridge/freezer doors. It is white and has a freezer on top, cooling coils in the back, and a temperature gauge inside. It is designed to cool water; that's the only thing that matters.

King opens the freezer door and places his hand inside, palm down.

"Nothing," he says as he turns back to us. He slams the door shut and walks over to his cot. "It's just teasing us."

Newman explains that the electricians are hooking the fridge up to the generators and should have the appliance up and running before nightfall. We wait. King and Rogers stack boxes of bottled water next to the fridge in preparation for being chilled. Cole peeks out the tent door every few minutes to gauge the electricians' progress. Lake opens and closes the freezer door, waiting for a wisp of cool air to come wafting out. We've all been waiting for a little bit of comfort, a little relief for the toll the sun has taken on our bodies and our minds.

When the fridge is connected and humming, we race to load it with bottles of water. Over the next couple of days, we anticipate cold water. We start to think of that fridge like a loved one—a wife perhaps—waiting at home for us with cold, cold water. Marching across the sand back to our tent, we picture her in our heads—her silver handle smiling at us as we pass through that door, sweat dripping from our brows as her fan sucks in air, and when we pull back that door, inside is the sweetest thing we've ever seen— water, stacked like cheerleaders in a pyramid, so cold it clouds the bottles.

When we were in Kuwait, Jones and I waited outside Camp New York's PX trailer for three hours, listening to a soldier discuss Dante's *Inferno*.

"If Dante were here," the soldier said, leaning against the yellow steel siding of the PX trailer, a cigarette dangling between his chapped lips, "he'd call Kuwait the fourth circle and Iraq the sixth."

Jones and I just stared at this man, amazed at his knowledge of Dante's poem. You don't see many soldiers waxing eloquent on the circles of hell. Yet soldiers can be a collection of contradictions, and as he went on about the climates of hell that differentiated Kuwait from Iraq, we listened in awe of his descriptions and his knowledge on a writer rarely referred to on military bases.

Kuwait didn't feel like Dante's fourth circle—a place for those obsessed with material possessions. But as I looked down the line of soldiers waiting to get into the PX at Camp New York and fill their pockets with Coke, Gatorade, *Playboy*, tobacco, and chocolate, it clicked. The sun was bearing down on us day after day. We'd been through at least two sandstorms, and the climate, combined with the war that was waging to the north, helped me realize how right this soldier was. Kuwait was hell, and our punishment was hours of waiting in lines.

Two weeks later, when I was convinced it couldn't get any worse, we arrived in Iraq.

During our first three days, late morning temperatures were never below 100 degrees. In the early morning we could see the heat coming. We'd rise from our cots, shake off the layer of sand that had accumulated over our sleeping bodies during the night, and walk to the tent door with toothbrushes and canteens in hand. Most mornings we practically ran from those tents right when the sun came up, for fear that we'd be roasted alive. We'd stand between our tent and the next, splashing water on our faces, trying to wake up from the nightmare that is Iraq.

Now, on May 5, I walk three paces from our back door and squeeze toothpaste onto my brush. I hold my canteen between my right elbow and ribs and unscrew the cap with my left hand before pouring water over the paste. I lift the brush to my mouth, my eyes to the horizon, where I see the heat rise up, light bouncing off the tents scattered near the runway beyond our camp. It starts here, in the morning, when the heat is still bearable and kind. It eventually builds to a sweltering triple-digit degree, showing no mercy to struggling soldiers just trying to make it through the day.

When I return to the tent, Newman is there, telling me to grab my gear because I'll be riding shotgun for Ivy on a post mission. Ivy motions for the tent door. We walk across the sand to a five-ton dump truck. From the passenger seat, I watch Ivy lift his heavy form into the truck. He is swearing because of the heat. He shifts the truck into gear and steers the vehicle out of the parking lot and onto one of the paved base roads. We pass a stucco building just outside the motor pool. The building is in dire need of a face-lift; it practically begs us to tear it down. I wonder if that will be part of our job in Iraq—to renovate this run-down base into a living, breathing, fully functioning military post. I look over at Ivy, who's concentrating on finding the right building. His forehead is wet from sweat, and he occasionally lifts his sleeve to wipe away the droplets.

"How hot do you think it'll get today?" I ask.

Ivy doesn't answer. He grunts and steers the truck into a crackling paved lot between two beige warehouses. The buildings are facing each other, each lined with six garage doors. As Ivy and I climb down from our truck, another soldier walks up to one of the garage doors and surveys the mess. The doors are open, and papers, pamphlets, and folders spill out the opening onto the pavement between the warehouses. The place has been looted, documents thrown about like confetti. I stand and watch for a minute. The two soldiers walk through the building, paging through a few documents and pulling open cabinet drawers. Slowly, I walk up to one of the doors and reach for a sheet of paper. The document is covered in Arabic letters, dark scratches across the pale paper. Instantly I feel guilty, like I'm looking at something I shouldn't. *These aren't my things.* These documents—laid out and discarded—are not mine. I have no place among this disaster. But I still want to look. I'm still curious what it was like to live on this post.

I carefully step over a pile of folders into the warehouse. The stalls are lined with silver filing cabinets. Some of the cabinets have fallen forward like tipped outhouses, sealed shut by their own weight. Other cabinets have hardly been touched, a few off-white sheets of paper peeking out the top drawer like stray chest hair climbing out of a T-shirt. Ivy walks over to me, explains that our job is to clean up the garbage, spare truck parts, and other metal outside the warehouses. We need to cart these things away to the dump. I watch as a Bobcat loader lifts the metal into the bed of our truck. Load after load, the Bobcat clears the debris from outside these buildings, and every time the loader dumps the trash into our truck, I think about the letters and documents I am standing on. What do the documents say? Why do we have to destroy these documents?

And most importantly, to whom do these things belong?

The more I think about the discarded warehouses the more I am reminded of my childhood home in central North Dakota. I grew up in a two-story farmhouse on a small hill overlooking a branch of the Sheyenne River. When farming became rough, my father took a job managing an ice-cream warehouse in town, and we eventually abandoned the farm in favor of a red ranch house in town, complete with a finished basement and attached garage. But we kept the house and farmland it stood on for the four years I was in high school. We kept the animals there—several head of sheep, two dogs, and a few horses—and every day someone from the family drove five miles from town to the farm to feed the animals and play with the dogs.

Shortly after we moved, my father asked me to drive out to the farm. While I can't say that I lived a nomadic childhood (unlike some children, particularly military brats who move from post to post, my family only moved once—from a farm into town), I've always had an Odysseus-like obsession with returning home. As I drove the gravel roads to the farm, I was reminded of my childhood memories in that house, the only place that felt like home.

I pulled my Ford Escort into the driveway, the bumper pushed up against the steel gate that spread across the road like double doors. I stepped from the vehicle and looked up at the house. The house held no joy. It looked cold and dark. No light shown through the windows. No smoke billowed from the chimney. No laughter came from the house. I knew, before even seeing the house again, that it would look like this, abandoned and left to die on the North Dakota prairie.

The gate's lock felt cold in my hand as I pushed the key into the slot and snapped the lock open. Pushing the gates forward, I felt a great wind at my back, like I was pushing open a door to my past. Instead of getting back in the car, I walked the long driveway.

As I walked, I glanced over at the piece of land on the other side of the dry creek. When I was ten, my father told Brandon and me that he had put the land in our names, our own piece of acreage. We never fully understood why our father did this, but did it matter? What ten-year-old can brag about owning his own land? We used to dream about building houses on the land—on the hill across the creek from our parents—where we'd help out with the farm, raise our own families, watch our parents grow old, and live happily on the North Dakota prairie. We would stand on the hill and take in the view—our view, our land, our futures—before jumping onto our sleds and racing down the snowy hill, our red plastic sleds stopping just before the frozen creek. But as I neared the house and saw the peeling paint, I realized how impossible that dream had become.

My father had boarded up the picture window that faced the barn and creek—two large sheets of plywood nailed haphazardly across the front of the building, a mouth wired shut. I passed the boarded-up window and shivered as I stepped up the two stone stairs and pushed open the heavy wooden door at the back of the house.

The house was small. Each room led into the next—the kitchen bled into the dining room, the dining room into the living room, the living room to the enclosed stairwell. The bathroom was just off the back door, added onto the square house as an afterthought. I gazed into the bathroom and saw a broken toilet bowl, cracked in half. Half of the ceramic bowl had fallen off and leaned against what was left of the toilet. I stepped beyond the bathroom and through the kitchen. Since moving, my father decided to store the horse tackle in the abandoned house. Sitting where our table used to be were a couple of saddles, the tackle box we took to the county fair every summer, and an assortment of bridles and ropes.

The living room was dark from the boarded-up picture window, but a rogue beam of light shown through the tiny window above the front door, which we rarely ever used, even when we lived there. The door to the stairs was open, and as I stepped onto the bottom landing of the staircase a rush of childhood memories came at me. These stairs held so many memories. Here I raced my brothers up and down, sent toy cars crashing over the steps, and pouted on the top step whenever I didn't get my way. I looked up and saw those memories laid out—almost literally—as I gazed upon an avalanche of children's clothes spread down the wooden steps.

This is what was left behind—my childhood in the form of Sesame Street T-shirts and cotton pajamas. I stepped on the clothes as I climbed the stairs, my feet slipping on the items as they slid below my shoes. I was afraid to look down, afraid that rats would rise up from the abandoned clothing and scurry across my shoes. At the middle of the staircase, I thought about stopping, turning back now that I'd seen the discarded items. I rested against the outside wall, part of me wishing that the wall behind my back would disappear, sending me out of this house and onto the grass where I could hold on to the rosy picture of this place.

I stopped on the top landing and collapsed onto the step, much like I did when I was a child. That house would always hold the memories of my childhood: how my brother and I rummaged through the high school yearbooks my mother stored under the bed he and I shared; how my siblings and I took newborn baby lambs into the house and sat with them next to the floorboard heating vents, warming our extremities from the cold midwestern winters; or the summers when we sat below the dining room window and played with our Tonka trucks as the music from *Days of Our Lives* drifted out into the warm, sticky air. Those memories remained. But after seeing the house I had this new memory—an old wooden box, white paint peeling on the outside, and relics of the past weighing down the inside, until the structure finally becomes too hard on the eyes and is ripped from the landscape by a wrecking ball, tornado, fire, or general decay. Then it is gone.

When Ivy calls my name, I am standing squarely on a pile of Arabic documents, misty-eyed and lonely. I'm still holding the sheet of paper, my fist clenching it like it was my favorite childhood T-shirt.

"Lemer, let's go," Ivy bellows.

We take the first truckload of trash to the dump down the road. As Ivy and I dump the papers into a pile with other trash from around the base, I am reminded of items that must hold some importance to somebody. *They are only documents*, I try to tell myself with each load. Old utility bills or instruction manuals. They are not love letters or childhood scribblings. *Nobody would ever want these things. They have all run off.*

At the end of the day, we return to our tents. We are welcomed by the news that the shower tents are finally operational, and the lieutenant is taking a truckload of soldiers to the facility. We haven't showered in almost a week, since we left Kuwait. Our sweat has caked our bodies in salt, so much so that white rings form around the necklines of our uniforms. At least we hardly notice how bad we smell because nobody around here smells clean.

On the ride to the shower tent, I notice mini-camps of tents along the route. The base looks like a concentration camp. Each battalion has staked out a plot of land, and as we drive I notice a team of soldiers stirring gasoline fires from the latrines, people wandering from one tent to the next, watching their boots kick around the sand. Nobody looks happy. When we arrive at the shower tents, we quickly get in line. The soldiers stand around, all dressed in PTs, waiting to get into the tent. We don't talk. We just wait. Darkness is setting in around us. Instead of looking inviting—a luxury after so many hot days—the tents look dark and gloomy. At the front of the line, just before the attendant pulls back the curtain to reveal the dark showers inside, Fredricks looks back at me and says, "It feels like I'm going into a gas chamber."

One day Lake returns from one of the bunkers near our camp with an Iraqi soldier's helmet and an old, tattered uniform. I watch as he rolls the helmet around in his hands and shakes the dirt from the uniform. I can't help but wonder why someone left these things behind.

I have become obsessed with this notion of things left behind. There is a sort of mystery in examining these things—documents, old uniforms, even writing on walls. They all say something of people who've been here before us. I almost majored in sociology in college, and now I'm obsessed with figuring our how societies form, how they function, why they exist, and why they sometimes disappear.

It all started with outhouse graffiti. There is something exciting about deciphering outhouse graffiti. It says so much about the kind of soldier who passed through a place. Most of the messages are typical notes from bored soldiers: SO AND SO WAS HERE or SO AND SO IS GAY or something about SO AND SO's mother. There are battle cries—ALPHA COMPANY LEADS THE WAY—and simple statements from homesick soldiers—THREE DAYS AND A WAKE UP AND I'LL BE GOING HOME. In Kuwait I saw a limerick etched into the plastic siding of an outhouse. The limerick said:

I've fucked in London.
I've fucked in Spain.

I've even fucked on the coast of Maine.
But I'll never be happy,
I'll never be free,
Until I've fucked the army
the way it fucked me.

I repeated the limerick to Jones and Lake because it seemed entirely fitting to our situation.

But there is also something disturbing about outhouse graffiti. When I was in Kosovo, I first started to notice graffiti invitations for sex, from one male soldier to another, and I began to wonder about the seedy underbelly created by the "don't ask, don't tell" policy. Straight soldiers could simply be themselves; there were all kinds of rumors about male soldiers having sex with female soldiers while deployed. Gay soldiers, however, had to resort to graffiti invitation for sex. There were physical descriptions etched into the outhouse walls, and next to the descriptions were times and dates for meeting up. I was both creeped out and intrigued by these invitations. While I had no intention of answering these invitations, I was glad that there were other soldiers like me—gay men hiding behind the military uniform. The outhouse graffiti was my only proof that I wasn't alone.

We are all damned.

It's called karma—plain and simple karma. What goes around comes around. Iraq is our hell, our personal punishment for some wrong we've committed, and we're doomed to spend the rest of eternity wandering the desert under the sweltering sun.

I can't understand what it is I've done wrong. What have I done to deserve this? I rack my brain for why I belong in this hell. Could this be my punishment for punching a classmate in the junior high locker room and gloating about it? Could this be the result of my unholy life, laughing at Father Vern's accent after his sermons, or disbelieving the existence of God? Or, as I've been told by the "religious Right," is it because of the homosexual lifestyle I've been leading?

The refrigerator has been connected for three days, but it has yet to cool any water. The bottles are stuffed into the main compartment so tightly that when we grab the cap of a bottle and pull, we have to hold the rest of the bottles back to prevent the entire puzzle from tumbling out.

Ivy stands near the fridge yelling himself hoarse.

"Who the *fuck* tried to put Coke in the freezer?" he yells at Tuna and King, who are lying on their dusty cots. "Why isn't there any damn cold water? The fucking Cokes are taking up all the room."

We ignore Ivy because that is usually the best option. He then blames us for not restocking the fridge, pointing fingers at whomever's near.

"You cocksuckers aren't stocking the fridge," he yelps. "I am the only one doing it!"

The temperature climbs to 102 today. When the sun sets and the desert finally cools down, the chiggers come out to eat our tan flesh. Newman sits outside the tent scratching himself; red dime-sized bumps dot both his arms and legs. Rogers and Elijah are comparing bites while discussing how hot it got today. Viv shoots across the tent in his underwear, screaming about losing his PTs and smiling ear to ear.

We have no cold water, the sand fleas are eating us alive, and, as if that weren't enough, the gods are mocking us, as somewhere off in the distance someone's boom box is playing The Cure's "Just Like Heaven." Add in the stress of being away from our families and stuck in the middle of a war, and we have our own private hell.

The motor pool is covered in ash. It's actually sand, so finely ground that when you set foot into the lot the particles rise up and surround your boots like morning fog. The sand is the color of Pacific beaches, light tan particles found in childhood sandboxes and Kuwait landscapes. But the texture of this sand is different. It is a fine powder spread evenly across the lot. As troops trounce across the motor pool, to and from trucks and Hummers, wispy brown puffs climb into the sky and explode like bombs over tiny sand cities.

"It's like walking through dry ash," Bobby says.

Bobby has taken to collecting the sand/ash in miniature bottles of Tabasco sauce found in MREs. He shows me four bottles cradled in his palm. The tiny vessels rest inside his hand, red caps keeping the sand sealed inside the glass. I pick up one of the bottles between my forefinger and thumb, gently tipping the bottle back and forth. The bottles of sand are just one piece in the collection of artifacts we are taking from this country. I imagine Bobby keeping the bottles for years after the deployment next to an Iraqi Republican Guard helmet, a scorpion pressed under glass, and an Islamic prayer blanket inside a chest. I see him picking up the bottles with his wrinkled fingers and showing the sand to his children and grandchildren. His grandchildren will shake the bottles, wonder whose ashes their grandfather is keeping, but never understand.

Six boots kick a wild cloud of sand across the motor-pool lot. It is May 7, and I have motor-pool guard with two other members of Bravo Company. We walk toward one of Horizontal Platoon's dozers parked along the concertina wire fence that surrounds the lot. We climb up the dozer, coming to a rest atop the steel square that shades the driver from the sun. McGoff and Adams lay their weapons on top of the cab and pull a cribbage board from their bags. I sit in one corner and look out over the motor pool.

Under a million tiny stars, I stare at the sand and think of Babylon—where civilization began. I think about this ancient place, only miles from where I am now. I read about Babylon in an issue of the *Stars and Stripes*, how shortly after the invasion U.S. troops took control of the ruins. Archaeologists criticized the troops for causing harm to the ruins, making even more of a mess than when Saddam tried to rebuild Babylon in the mid-1980s.

These ruins—the three vast mounds on the east bank of the Euphrates, the Ishtar Gate—are what remain of Babylon, but they are not what the troops will remember. Soldiers wouldn't remember the mounds, the names of which they can hardly pronounce. What they will remember is the sand. The sand is what ancient civilizations left behind—to cover us while we sleep, to become lodged in the nooks and crannies of our bodies, to stick to our sweaty limbs, to keep us entertained, to give us souvenirs. I think about the number of people who've lived and died on this sand, fine like ash, each tiny particle representing a life lived here. Between the stars and the sand—both in the millions—we trounce around this country, kicking the ash of people as we go.

This sand—like the cabinets of Arabic papers, the avalanche of children's clothes, and the outhouse graffiti—is what remains of people who've long since moved on.

I sit up and look across our patch of tents, thinking about where we'll move to next. I don't think Dante had a place for the gypsies, the nomads, the wanderers. But then again nobody did. They didn't belong anywhere, which is why I feel so completely and absolutely powerless here, as we're shoved from country to country, pushed into another land in conflict, forced to wear a uniform that makes us all look the same—nameless soldiers blending into the sand. I could die here, be buried in the sand—my limbs tangled with another soldier's under this grainy ash—and nobody would ever know. I'd blend right in.

A Hummer leaves the lot, kicking up another cloud of dust that floats into our tents and coats the sleeping soldiers. This ash is burying us alive, and all we can do is play cribbage and endure.

At the end of our shift, we pack up the game and climb down. From the top of the dozer, I watch Adams climb onto the hood of the vehicle before jumping down into the sand; his boots make a cloud of dust so thick he disappears.

It takes us almost a week to figure out why the fridge isn't cooling water properly: we've stuffed the compartment so full that the appliance is having a hard time cooling all the bottles. We take a few out, leave a little wiggle room, and watch as the icebox finally does its job, delivering cold water to hot, tired soldiers.

I grab a bottle from the fridge and my rifle from my cot, and walk out the tent door.

"Ready?" Roach says.

"Let's go," I say as the curtain closes behind me.

Bobby, Roach, and I have the keys to one of the Hummers and have decided to drive around to the other side of the base. As we walk down the line of tents, I notice a group of soldiers around a bonfire. The group is playing cards on a makeshift table as a boom box plays rock music nearby. Men are lounging in canvas folding chairs and drinking water like it's beer on poker night. The mood is jovial, and as I pass, I think about camping back home, living in a tent, and not worrying about work or war.

As I pass the first bonfire, I notice another, a few tents down this time. I see yet another fire at the back of our little colony of tents. For the first time since we've been here, the camp is filled with a sense of excitement, people happy with their surroundings. *We've finally settled in*, I think as we step into the motor pool and over to the Hummer. *This is our comfortable hell.*

Roach steers the Hummer out of the lot, a wild cloud of dust flies into the air, and Bobby laughs like a lunatic in the back seat. I smile as I look back at him and the fog of the gray dust we've kicked up.

We take the perimeter road, keeping an eye out for the runway in the middle of the post. We pass the north entrance to the camp, where soldiers stand near the gate looking out onto a dark, desert road. The sun is setting, and in the guard towers, troops lean against the front railing, gazing out over a field. As we drive along the north side of the base, the setting sun creates long shadows of the guards in the towers, pushing their dark forms over the perimeter fence and out onto the grass beyond base. *The sun isn't on our side*, I think as the shadows are pushed beyond the post, into the dangers beyond.

As we near the runway, we notice whole chunks of destroyed Iraqi plane parts littering the airfield. We drive past what looks like part of a cockpit pushed up against the perimeter fence in between two of the guard towers. It's like a piece of trash, a wind-whipped plastic bag pinned against the fence. We find the rest of the plane farther up the road, scattered around the runway as if it has crashed here and nobody bothered to clear the debris. That is when it occurs to me—we're survivors of some plane crash, abandoned and shipwrecked on some shitty island called Iraq.

I want to tell Roach and Bobby my theory, but just then Bobby points at a small block building near the far end of the runway. Roach steers the Hummer into a paved driveway next to the building.

Leaning against the building is a wooden billboard painted with the face of a man. The face has been mostly punched out; scraps of wood lie on the sand behind the billboard. The poster looks out of place, as if someone placed it there for a purpose, perhaps to display a message. We get out of the vehicle and stand with our hands over our eyes to shield them from the damn sun. Roach snaps a couple of pictures. We are all standing there in silence, looking at the plane parts on the runway behind the building and the punched-out portrait, when Roach says, "Look at the eye."

One of the eyes is still intact, hanging alone as if in a Picasso painting. It doesn't take us long to recognize that eye; it has been plastered all over the media back home and on billboards throughout this country. It is Saddam's eye, the only recognizable thing left.

When we get back to camp, Charlie Company has arrived and is camped out in the motor pool. They lie around on cots like we used to, dirty and tired from the trip into Iraq. As I walk from the Hummer back to our tent, I step on a tan sheet of notebook paper, folded in quarters and half covered in sandy ash. I reach down, shake the sand from the paper, and as I unfold the document I watch the Arabic letters appear, still bright and crisp, as if they still mean something to someone.

Icarus in Iraq

On May 14, we move to Baghdad, where, once we're settled, we'll begin work on repair missions in the violent city. As we pull out of the south gate of Anaconda, I notice a lone child standing in a field of weeds. From the back of a truck, I squint to see him. He stands near the road, knee-deep in twisted weeds, wearing a gray burlap sack. His eyes are wide as our vehicles pass. I catch his eye and hold his gaze, feeling his loneliness right down to my boots. There is sadness in the way he watches our trucks pass. He doesn't smile or wave. He doesn't chase after our truck or yell "Mee-sta, Mee-sta!" like the other kids do, demanding food or water. He stands still, silently wounding us with his stare.

I don't see anyone around and wonder if the child is lost or, even worse, homeless. There are no other people in the field, and his silhouette looks out of place, like a sunflower in a field of dandelions. He holds a clump of weeds in one hand and grips the side of his thigh with the other. There is something about his demeanor that sticks with me long after we've passed the child and followed the gravel road to the highway. It is the way he watches us, how he appears so helpless in that field and looks like no other child I've seen—in this country or back home—that makes me want to help the Iraqi people.

I shake away the image of the boy as we near the highway. Jones and I set up our positions in the back of the truck. We're standing near the cab, aiming our weapons out ahead of the vehicle. It is early evening, and we've managed to catch the citizens of Iraq as they settle in for the night. The streets of the tiny villages along the highway are clogged with men in white cloaks and women in black burkas. Young men in dirty T-shirts and jeans gather outside a greasy garage, smoking and laughing, as a multicolored car—orange trunk lid, white side doors—pokes out from a dark stall. They motion to us as we pass, whisper quiet remarks to each other, and tap ash off their cigarettes before taking in long drags. A group of young women crouch in a doorway, thighs touching calves, hands picking at the pebbles around their feet. They wave as we pass, and we wave back. Jones and I take turns yelling at the children playing soccer in the gray fields as if we were their mothers. "Hey," Jones yells. "You there," I scream to the goalie. We demand their attention. Then, when they look up at us as if they're in trouble, Jones and I wave back and laugh to ourselves because we have so much control over these kids. The kids shake their heads and yell *Hey* right back.

On the highway, an old man honks his horn at us and does a little dance in the cab of his truck, a crooked, half-toothed smile across his face. Another man holds his daughter in his lap as he drives down the highway; the toddler's small hands grip the metal steering wheel. The father points at me. He whispers something to his daughter as his dark, bushy eyebrows tickle the skin above her ear. She looks at me and waves. I take my finger off the trigger, wave back, and adjust the M16 rifle I had tucked into my shoulder.

It is all very surreal and paradelike; it almost feels like a homecoming. We are the heroes driving down the center of this country, swooping in to save the day. We wave and smile and rest in the back of our trucks as we zip across a country of people who are pretending they want us here. The odd thing is that seeing these people wave and the children laugh, I actually feel good about being here. I am getting excited about doing some good, about the role we're about to play in these people's lives. *This is why we are here*, I think.

Yet part of me knows better. I know there are people who don't want us here. I see them along the road as we near Baghdad. They are the people who don't wave, don't even look up. They ignore us. Some stand around in groups, pointing and growling at us or relaxing in plastic chairs outside their houses, stone-cold looks on their faces. They don't have to say anything; I see the disgust in their faces.

When we turn off the highway and onto the boulevard leading to the airport, we are met with scrawling words of hate and disdain. On a concrete wall along the road, a graffiti message says, "YES SADDAM YES SADDAM" in red block letters. Farther down the road, on the other side of the street, we come upon a blunt message on the wall near the airport: "LEAVE OUR COUNTRY." We aren't leaving. Instead, we're moving to another base, spreading out across this land.

The early evening sun makes a shadow of the winged man, casting dark lines across the road. In the back of the truck I chew my lower lip and wait for the guards to let us into Saddam International Airport. I squint into the sun to see the man, a stone statue poised on a two-story, star-shaped platform. He is stepping forward, one leg bent, his torso slanted away from the sun as if at any minute the figure will burst forth from the pedestal and lift into the Baghdad sky. I imagine the man laughing as his wings stretch and flap, wind carrying the creature higher and higher, until he circles the sky above our truck and darts off toward the sun.

We've traveled forty-five miles south to the capital city, eventually connecting to the boulevard that takes travelers away from the heart of Baghdad and into the maze of concrete barriers and concertina wire that is the city's main airport. I watch two soldiers step aside as we steer our trucks through the gate and onto the airport grounds. I turn back to look at the statue and notice a tall billboard on the opposite side of the road. There is Saddam's broad face, his slick black hair, and his large hand held palm-out to wave goodbye to people leaving the airport. The billboard attempts to make Saddam seem kind of like a proud parent waving at his children—the father of Iraq. But I'm not buying it. The billboard is eerie, the image of a stalker watching people come and go. I turn away, but I can't help but feel his eyes on me, like he's watching us enter this airport named after him.

The trucks speed past the tall grass and weeds in the dry ditches. I look out over the field, past the grass, and see the main terminal at the far end of a long road, beige wings shooting out from the main body of the building. Deep blue letters are printed across the building in both English and Arabic: Saddam International Airport. The airport was built in 1982 at a cost of more than 900 million dollars. It has three terminals, each named after an ancient empire: Babylon, Samara, and Nineveh. Originally the airport was designed to accommodate 7.5 million passengers a year. Now, I imagine, few people enter or leave this place by air.

As we get deeper into the heart of the airport, I see other signs of the airport's former life. A ten-story building creeps into the sky as if it's not sure whether it should be there. The building is gray and peeling paint. On the front of the building, about five stories up, is a billboard showing Saddam saluting passersby. I cringe at seeing Saddam again—it's as if we can't get away from him. Stop signs in Arabic and English dangle from posts like broken limbs. A piece of a plane lies in the grassy ditch. Abandoned trucks line the fence near a former fueling station. I don't see any complete planes, but as we move up the road I see signs of military life. Vehicles are lined up in the sand lots; whole lines of tanks and Hummers make aisles in the former airport parking lots. A crop of tents is scattered about the pavement around the post.

I watch the dusty dual-language signs pass by, arrows pointing off in all directions. Just then we see another image of Saddam as he beams from a stone monument near the road. The monument is on a strip of sand between the two roads leading to the main terminal. In the picture he sits on a gold throne and watches the passing trucks, an Iraqi flag waving in the background. He smiles at us—a proud Saddam greeting airport visitors— and as we zip by him, I notice his hand, held out as if gesturing for peace. We've been at the airport for fifteen minutes, and we've already seen three Saddams. There is something unsettling about this, especially now that we've run him off by invading his country. This place has an air of mystery, a ghostlike feel of something deserted and reclaimed; only now, an odd lurking presence remains. It is a drastic change from the streets of Baghdad that bustled with activity as we passed on our way here.

In a narrow lot, we pull the trucks into a line, park, and settle in for the night. Captain Roar tells us that we'll be sleeping in the motor pool this evening, and in the morning we'll move into our new home. I jump down from the truck, shake the sand off my uniform, and remove my goggles. We're all exhausted from the trip. I glance over at the airport terminal, where the sun is setting behind its beige walls, and watch as troops stand around smoking and joking, hands on hips as we take in the new environment.

When the sun sets, we set up camp for the night. I grab my cot and climb onto the headache rack of our truck. I unfold the cot, roll out my sleeping bag, and settle in. I am tired, hot, and stupefied at what I've seen. I stare at the nearby airport terminal and think about the people again— the children with their frantic waves that cut right through me; the women in shabby dresses smiling at us like we're suitors or saints; the old men who hardly look at us, hardly acknowledge our presence. They are all there along the road to Baghdad—spread out as if on display for the passing troops. Then the image of the boy in the field returns. He isn't like other children in this country. He doesn't wave or laugh or do what children should be doing, and I wonder why. I conclude that the child is missing something—a parent, a mentor, a teacher, anyone to guide him. He is homeless in a country that is essentially fatherless. We've run off this country's leader, and now, instead of looking to Saddam for help, they look to us.

I realize that what we've gone through today is not a parade. It is more akin to an adoption meeting where we meet, for the first time, our new responsibility.

I first learned of the myth of Deadalus and Icarus through music.

I played alto saxophone in junior high school concert band. We attempted a portion of Igor Markevitch's *L'Envol d'Icare* one year. The music portrays the entire rise and fall of Icarus—from the labyrinth where he and Deadalus were trapped to the crystal-clear water the boy's body splashed into. I remember the way the music builds up, the warbling flutes and beating bass signifying the flapping of Icarus's wings; the way the horns and saxophones wail on the ascent; how my classmate's wrists snap the mallet against the timpani as Icarus nears the sun. The whole score promises a train-wreck ending, climaxing at the point where the wax of Icarus's wings melts and he plummets into the ocean, swallowed whole by the great, angry sea.

It was a disaster for any junior high band to attempt, but we tried it anyway. Every time we got to the climax, I blasted my saxophone as loud as it would go, squawking out note after dramatic note in order to get the full effect of the tragedy. I imagined an audience listening to the tragedy unfold with our music. The women would weep; the men would get lumps in their throats; and everyone—man, woman, and child—would stand and applaud as we brought the story to a close.

What I took away from the song was the profound love Deadalus had for Icarus. Deadalus constructed wings from feathers and wax for his son, warned the boy about the dangers of the sun and the ocean, before pushing him off into the sky. He was the first of the Brady Bunch fathers—always looking to protect their sons with profound spoonfuls of knowledge and tidbits of common thought. It was a relationship that broke my heart because I felt that I'd never had a genuine moment like that with my own father.

While my brothers found common bonds with him—hunting, fishing, wrestling—I struggled to find anything to connect myself with my dad. During holidays, when my brothers put each other in headlocks, and my sister and mother argued over dirty dishes and leftovers, I was left with my silent father. He twiddled his thumbs, rubbed his hands together, and stared at the ceiling. I cracked my knuckles, cleared my throat, and wondered what it was that made us so different. We were different to the point of discomfort. We both twitched around in our seats, not looking at each other, until he rose from his chair, walked to his favorite cabinet, and returned with a Western novel.

I always thought at least we could bond over literature and words, but I know nothing about Louis l'Amour. Maybe I should.

I remember how rough his hands got in the summer from pounding fence posts, pulling at horse bridles, and carrying buckets of water to the sheep. He sat in the living room and lathered his hands in Cornhusker's lotion. The thick syrupy smell mixed with the humid air, and at night I smelled the lotion on my pajamas as we played in front of the television.

It was later—when I'd grown old enough to lend a hand—that he enlisted my help with farm chores: feeding the animals, gathering the square bales, helping a ewe through labor. *After all*, he'd say, *what are kids good for if not manual labor?* That is why he had six children.

He taught us how to ride bikes, tractors, and horses. Once, while teaching me how to drive a stick shift with his Ford pickup, I stalled the vehicle at a stop sign in town and couldn't figure out how to correctly let my foot off the clutch. We sat at that intersection for fifteen minutes as I tried to get it right. Each time I lifted my foot, the truck died. We then sat in silence, father and son, as one of the city cops watched from the armory across the street.

I never mastered that clutch.

But I learned more from my father than he'll ever know. He taught me determination—that if there is something I want, I should work hard to get it. He did everything he could to prepare me for the world. Yet there is only so much fathers can do before they let go and trust that their advice will stick. They must give their children the right tools to survive— man-made wings or common sense—before patting them on the back and sending them out into the wide world. It is then up to the children to decide how to use their newly acquired knowledge.

Icarus, however, was a stupid, stupid boy.

Is that piss?" King asks, pointing at a plastic water bottle sitting half full in the corner.

"I think so," Roach says as we all look on from the doorway.

We're standing in our new home—one of the second-rate side terminals down the runway from the main airport terminal—staring at a bottle of urine. I look out over the upper level of the two-story building. The place is a mess. A line of floor-to-ceiling windows peers out at a runway full of military helicopters, poised like grasshoppers on the hot concrete. Beyond the helicopters, an old plane lies on its side at the edge of the runway, its wing snapped off like a limbless dragonfly.

I step from the doorway up to the windows and make a handprint on the pane, white fingers surrounded by dust—a stamp of disapproval. About half of the windows are busted out, and a pile of garbage and broken glass lies beneath each empty hole. The windows that remain are caked in a layer of dirt—both inside and out. The sand has been whipped up against the glass by the helicopters and never wiped clean.

There is a hole in the wall at the end of the windows. Three soldiers stand near the hole, looking down at the rubble that lies on the concrete below. Pieces hang from the opening like stuffing from a coat. It's almost as if a missile has pierced the terminal and left a fleshy scar. There are no plastic seats for waiting passengers to watch the planes taxi. No check-in airline counter. No snippy airline employees. No coffee stands pushing caffeine on weary travelers. The bay is open, filled with dirt and garbage. We find the urine bottle in one of the two rooms at the end of the bay and speculate that the soldiers downstairs on the first floor used these rooms to relieve themselves and get rid of their trash.

"No way, man," someone yells. "You do it."

A handful of soldiers argue over who has to remove the bottle of urine. I walk from the window to the half-balcony wall and look out at the soldiers below. The first floor is about three times the size of the second and lined with cots and sleeping soldiers. They're packed in like stranded tourists. At the far left is a makeshift gym. Several second-hand weight plates are scattered about; a homemade wooden bench press sits in the center of the area as if it's an elegant couch. The area is devoid of any weight-lifting troops. Morning light shines through the green siding along the front of the building, casting a lime-colored beam over several sleeping soldiers. An oscillating fan does overtime as it sweeps across a group of men sleeping near one of the two giant staircases leading to the second floor. The fan clicks as it reaches the limits of its span, as if to express its disgust at constantly being used.

Above it all—the cots, the fans, the water, the weight-lifting equipment— a flight-information display system hangs from the ceiling like a watchful eye. The board is black with rusty edges and displays no arrivals and no departures. When we first entered the building, I half hoped the device would announce our arrival: Bravo Company, 142nd Engineers, arriving at gate 4. I could almost see the ancient letters flip forward as they spelled out our arrival. But they didn't. The board remained silent, no clickity-click of letters breezing past as it tried to spell out another destination.

The empty display board adds to the mystery of this place. I imagine a time when letters appeared on that board and travelers hurried through this terminal, not having to worry about waking sleeping soldiers or being trapped in a dead-end corridor blocked off by a line of military cots. I try to think of this place as it was before we got here, when helicopters didn't dot the runway, and planes still lifted people into the sky.

I turn back to see six soldiers standing in a circle playing rock-paper-scissors. Paper covers rock followed by a collective groan as one of the soldiers in first platoon loses the game. I watch the soldier slip on a pair of gloves and approach the bottle.

"Lemer," Newman says as he walks up to me. "The LT says the PX is open. Why don't you go try and see if they have any cleaning supplies?"

I can't say how I found the PX—I have no idea where anything is on this base—but I attribute it to animal instinct—how animals just *know* where the food is. The whole base is a strange, new world, different yet familiar. I see the familiar—the bottled water shipped in, the Hummers and helicopters scattered about the base—but this is nothing like airports back home. There are no car rental companies where you can rent a Ford Taurus and zip off into the city. There are no duty-free shops, souvenir boutiques, or magazine racks. We're living like primitive survivors, building whatever we don't have.

The PX is housed in a large warehouse with white siding and a huge, green garage door that is spilling out a line of soldiers in camouflage. I walk to the end of the line and wait. The wait doesn't even faze me: after five years in the military, where you stand in line for everything, waiting two hours to get inside a general supply store doesn't seem the least bit unusual. I could wait here all afternoon and still feel it was worth it for a taste of Coca-Cola and junk food. After two hours, I set foot inside the building, grab a plastic basket, and get back in line. The line heads north down one wall, turns right at the corner, and runs along the back wall before turning south again and running along the opposite wall until it reaches the checkout lines near the door. It is a giant U made entirely out of moving, sweating soldiers.

I rip a flap off one of the large cargo boxes lining the inside of the building and fan myself. The box is full of sunflower seeds—bags and bags of Spitz. The line follows the boxes around the building. Soldiers get in line, place their basket on the sandy cement floor in front of their feet, and wait to inch forward to the next box. Each box offers a different luxury. I come to a box filled with Oreos and another with Pop Tarts. As we move, we push our baskets forward with our feet, the plastic rubbing against the sand. The noise dominoes down the line each time one of the three cashiers yells *Next*, making it impossible to even talk with your neighbor.

At the back of the warehouse, I find a box full of towels and another with greeting cards. Soldiers reach into the boxes and fill their baskets with junk food and toiletries. I find very few cleaning supplies. As I near the checkout lane, after waiting for nearly four hours, I come upon three boxes full of underwear in plastic packages. I then realize how ridiculous the whole situation seems. Who back home would stand in line for four hours just to buy cookies and underwear?

I really don't know what we're doing here. Some members of our platoon are the only people to have gone into Baghdad. But for the most part it seems like we're spending more time on post than doing missions in the city. Mostly we just sit around, building picnic tables, and helping ourselves.

I watch Roach kick a pile of two-by-fours. We've been tasked with building two wooden picnic tables from the pile. I laugh as Roach—a plumber—scratches his head and steps back from the stacked wood. He's in charge of our group—a ragged band of misfits made up of two carpenters, two electricians, a plumber, and four rock crushers. The thing I like best about being engineers is that if we don't have something, we build it. We're engineers and we're resourceful, so building a couple of picnic tables seems simple.

But I'm a terrible carpenter, and I'm comfortable with this realization. As Roach tries to draw the plans for the picnic tables in his tiny pocket notebook, I think back to Camp Bondsteel, the 955-acre military post near Ferizaj, Kosovo, where I spent seven months in 2000. The base was truly man-made. It was built on the rolling hills and farmland at the foot of a mountain and was made up of nearly 250 wooden SEA huts. From the scraps, I built a wobbly nightstand with two slanted shelves. I took a picture of it, like a proud mother would a child, and sent the photo to my friends. They commented on the nails sticking out the side (I told them I used them to hang my dog tags) and how everything on the second shelf slanted slightly to the left. But I felt no shame.

Now Roach turns to me for advice. We talk about the plans, instructing the four rock crushers to start laying out the wood and handing tape measurers to the two electricians. I watch the electricians extend their tape measures and make their lines as Roach and I figure out each measurement. The other carpenter is at the saw we've set up nearby. Once the boards are measured, the rock crushers feed the boards into the saw, the other carpenter chopping the pile of wood into pieces.

Then comes the tricky part. We have a hard time putting the tables together. The angles are all wrong; the legs refuse to extend from the table top the way we wanted them to. The spaces between the boards are uneven. Both tables wobble. When we have the tables assembled, I sit down on one bench, my weight making the opposite bench lift into the air. I remove my boonie hat and wipe the sweat from my forehead. The wind carries a handful of sawdust off the sand and over the tables, making the tiny particles stick to my forehead. I take a drink from my canteen and splash some water on my forehead. The sawdust scent triggers memories of childhood woodworking projects—birdhouses, tool boxes, footstools. I used to take such pride in these projects, knowing that this birdhouse was the fruit of my labor, that the hard work I put into this stepstool or tool box would result in something concrete and permanent. The projects were examples of a job well done. But as Roach sits on the opposite side of the table and the bench rises beneath me, I feel my father's shame deep down in my gut. If he could see me—sitting on these shitty, crooked tables—he would look at me with shame and shake his head. He wouldn't say it, but I know he'd be disappointed.

I am mostly disappointed in my own abilities and lack of interest in carpentry. I take no pride in it, and these picnic tables show that. But it doesn't really sink in until I'm sitting on these rickety tables, wobbling back and forth, that I may be no good to the people of Iraq; I may have nothing to offer. After all, how can I help others when I can't even help myself and my platoon by completing simple carpentry projects?

Roach looks over at me and points up toward the road running by the motor pool. "Want to go check out Saddam?"

I follow his finger and see the Saddam monument we noticed on our arrival here. We all walk toward the monument, climbing up the steep ditch and across the road to reach it.

As we near, I notice that the picture of Saddam is made of tiles— five-by-five-inch squares depicting the proud former leader. The picture has been defaced—graffiti sprawled across Saddam's face, his hand, and the throne he sits on. The poster has become a sort of guest book for U.S. troops visiting the airport. Most troops have written their names, units, and hometowns. I notice that someone has already placed 142nd ENG—NORTH DAKOTA on the running tally of units here.

We read the messages and run our hands over the tiles. On Saddam's hand someone has written in block letters: "I Pissed Here. Love, Your Friend Smith." Nearby, another soldier has signed the monument "Sgt. King, Spring Break 2003." A few of the notes are phrased as letters, like a note I found near Saddam's knee: "Dear Sara, Well We're Here. We've Taken Care Of Saddam So Our Children Will Never Have To Come Over Here. Love, Dan." Roach laughs. He points at a message near Saddam's head that reads "I Jerked Off On This Poster You Shithead."

I walk back to get a picture of the entire poster. I stand, framing the shot, and imagine the other soldiers who have already taken their pictures in front of it. I imagine them standing in front of Saddam, unaware that their proud smiles match that of the leader depicted behind them. It has been so easy taking over this airport—defacing what we don't like, building what we don't have—that I wonder if we even realize what we're doing here. The messages proudly sprawled across the poster depict people almost too comfortable with their situation, soldiers too cocky and foolish to realize the importance of their presence here.

I take the picture. Before leaving, I notice a message written near the bottom of the monument, from a soldier staying at one of Saddam's former mansions near the airport. The message, again in block letters, is a letter written to Saddam himself: "Dear Saddam, We're Staying In Your Palace. Thanks For Your Hospitality. Love, Sgt. Rick And 2nd Platoon. P.S. We Took A Shit In The Living Room. Bill Us Later."

Walking back to our terminal, I notice a rectangular, stone monument just outside the door of the building. For some reason, I haven't noticed the plaque before. Beige blocks surround a white marble plaque with letters, both English and Arabic, etched into the stone. The English is written on the right side of the block, the Arabic on the left. I squat down to read the message:

Constructed in the era of the
Leader president
SADDAM HUSSEIN
Secretary General of the regional
leadership of the Arab Baath Socialist Party
President of the republic.

Below the message, in black, even letters, a soldier has written in marker: TERMINATED 08APR03 BY GEORGE W. BUSH!!!

Over the next few weeks we see further demonstrations of this termination. We change all the names of things: Saddam International Airport is renamed Baghdad International Airport, or BIAP (pronounced *Buy-op* by the soldiers). Someone spray-paints HOTEL CALIFORNIA on the sign along the road. Even the terminals, which once held history in their names, are simplified and stripped down to terminals A, B, and C.

The tiled monument of Saddam disappears; the image is painted over by coalition troops. The billboard showing a waving Saddam as visitors exit the airport also vanishes. Saddam is being erased from this country. Wiped clean. He no longer smiles or waves. He ceases to exist here.

On May 16 I volunteer to travel back to Anaconda for a day, to get supplies and mail. When we leave BIAP's east gate, the winged man is still there, unchanged. He looks the same, still threatening to lift off from his cement platform and dart toward the sun. He has the same stern look of determination—a look that shows both hope and sadness. He reminds me that there are people beyond this post and that thus far in Iraq, we've only managed to help ourselves. He reminds me that more must be done in this country. We act like children in an amusement park: fighting over cleaning up piss, getting giddy over American cookies, and defacing posters of Saddam. But we are not the children here.

We need to show Icarus how to fly.

Abbas Ibn Firnas always knew he wanted to fly.

The Spanish-Arab humanitarian, technologist, chemist, and poet watched a daredevil named Armen Firman fly off a tower in Córdoba in 852 CE. I believe he was instantly impressed at how the man glided through the air using a huge winglike cloak, how the wind lifted the daredevil's hair, and how all the people pointed and stared in amazement. The feat was one of the first of its kind, a challenge to astronomers and engineers working on ways to make humans fly like birds.

Ironically, it was a man called Blackbird who first recognized the talents of Ibn Firnas. Blackbird was a patron of the sciences and saw potential in Ibn Firnas. He noticed the way the young man was fascinated by chemistry, physics, and astronomy. He watched Ibn Firnas design a water clock and devise means of manufacturing glass from the millions of particles of sand in the Middle East.

Then, in 875, Abbas Ibn Firnas attempted to fly. He built his own glider, invited his friends and neighbors, and launched himself from a tower. Ibn Firnas was finally in flight, soaring over a crowd of spectators—now a spectacle himself. He laughed and flapped his wings, noticed the crowded streets below, and felt like a bird. In the faces of the people, he instantly recognized his fame as one of the first people to fly.

Ibn Firnas is the Islamic equivalent of the Wright Brothers. Westerners teach their children about the Wright Brothers, a pair of American pilots credited with making the first, controlled, powered flight in 1903. But the Islamic people tell their children about Ibn Firnas, who flew under his own steam a thousand years before the Wrights. They remember him in Libya through a postage stamp honoring his flight. A crater on the moon is also named in his honor. And in Baghdad, Iraqis honor him with a statue of a winged man, who stands proudly outside the recently captured international airport.

We've traveled back to Anaconda to retrieve our mail and to get supplies for upcoming missions in Baghdad. As Newman and Grayson gather supplies, the rest of us sit in the shade. While sorting through our company's mail, I come across an envelope full of letters from my aunt's fourth grade class.

Most of the notes are stereotypical letters to the troops. The children talk about themselves mostly, explain how old they are, what their parents do, or if they have any pets. A majority of them offer up interesting theories about where Saddam is hiding. I flip to a letter written in pink, cursive handwriting and read through the half-page paragraph: "Dear Bronson, I might know ware the leader of Iraq hide out is at. It is under the sand someware. I think there is a door under the sand. But be careful, he has a bomb with him. Good luck. Be careful! Your friend, Carly Jo." Another student, Logan, holds a similar theory. He's even drawn a picture to give me a visual image of Saddam's hiding place.

I come across one letter that makes my day—my entire year actually—with just this first line: "Dear Bronson, You are the coolest man ever." In the middle of the letter, as if to make it stand out as the most important question ever, he has written: "WHO IS YOUR GIRLFRIEND" followed by five exclamation marks. I laugh and flip to the next letter.

Reading through them makes me smile and wish I could go back to grade school, where I could practice my cursive handwriting and do math problems all day. Most of the boys have drawn some kind of tank or gun. Some are even witty. One kid has written on the back of his card: "CDs: $14. Sunglasses: $3. Dog: $50. Keeping the nation safe: priceless."

But I most identify with a letter I find at the bottom of the pile. The child's name is Seth. He has written in gray, cursive pencil: "I hate it when

we have wars. Lots of people die from it. I like to draw stars." He then draws a giant red, blue, and orange five-point star, and signs his name. Even with the constant war coverage and newspaper headlines tallying the dead soldiers in Iraq, Seth has managed to look beyond the destruction. As he draws stars in North Dakota, I envy his naïveté and his youth. Being on this deployment, having to do a job I don't entirely enjoy, makes me envy Seth. I wish I could forget about this place sometimes, this odd thing called war. I wish I could be back home, doing what I love, instead of driving back and forth across the desert, pretending to be a carpenter and acting like I'm doing some good over here.

Newman and Grayson pull up into the shade with the Hummer. I stuff the letters in my pocket and climb into the back seat. On the ride back to BIAP, I watch the children play soccer in the fields and the young girls wave and giggle at us. On the road, I see a man riding a scooter. The man looks like an old friend I used to work with back home. He has the same facial features, same thinning hair, and same slender figure. I stare at the man until he zips past our Hummer. As we are entering Baghdad, the Hummer gets a flat tire. The entire convoy of five vehicles pulls to the shoulder of the road, and we get out and look at the shredded tire. We're stopped at the top of a huge bypass on the edge of the city.

As three of the soldiers from Maintenance Platoon look at the tire, the rest of us walk to the guard rail and look out over an open field below. Soon, a group of about twenty kids comes running over and stands at the bottom of the ditch, looking up at us as we line the rail. They range in age from three to twelve and are wearing multicolored cloaks. They are asking for food, patting their stomachs, and sticking their fingers inside their mouths. Lake walks back to the Hummer and retrieves a handful of items— MREs, bottles of water, granola bars—and throws the food to the children like he's feeding dogs. I watch the children fight and claw at each other. The boys push aside a little girl with sad eyes as they dart forward to grab the MRE packages. Nearby, I notice three adults watching the kids push and shove for food: two men are smoking, and a woman sits bowlegged on a stool while washing clothes in a steel bucket.

When all items have been claimed, an older boy with dark red hair raises his index and middle fingers to his lips. He sucks in and moves his fingers away from his mouth and repeats the gesture.

"Is he imitating smoking?" Lake asks.

"I think so," I say.

"I'm not giving him cigarettes," Lake says, laughing.

Lake gets out his Arabic Command and Control Card. The card has English to Arabic translations of various commands like "lower your hands" and "drop your weapons." The card also translates numbers—so you can explain that there are ten thousand of us coming into this country— and helpful words and phrases to use such as "Nah-nuu Am-ree-kee-uun," which means: "We are Americans." Lake turns the card over in his hands. He finds the right question and looks over the crowd of children at the bottom of the ditch.

"Man hu-wa al-mas-'uul?" Lake asks.

The children laugh. They look at one another and talk quietly in Arabic. Slowly, the redhead raises his right hand into the sky and steps forward.

"Are you in charge?" Lake asks, pointing at the redhead.

The boy nods his head timidly. Lake reaches into his pocket and tosses a dozen loose cigarettes down to the redhead. The children race to grab the cigarettes, some of which snap in half as they're tugged between tiny hands. They fight for them like they did for food. I notice Lake smile, and I shake my head. I can't tell if he enjoys seeing them fight or if he finds some pleasure in corrupting Iraqi youth. As we walk back to our trucks, Lake jokes with a couple of the other soldiers about being a bad influence.

As we drive away, I shake my head at the picture we've just painted of ourselves. We should be role models here. We should give this country everything it doesn't already have: leadership, guidance, hope. Instead, we make fun of the hajjis along the roads, share disgust at the lack of beautiful women in Iraq, and toss cigarettes to three-year-old children in highway ditches. We aren't the leaders we should be over here. Instead we're just like the children that gawk and beg and act foolish. We're no different.

If American children saw us over here—building picnic tables or complaining over the price of PX cigarettes—I wonder how their image of a hero would change.

In Jack Kerouac's novel *Dharma Bums*, Japhy and Ray are hiking outside San Francisco when Ray turns to Japhy and states that there is nothing in the world he wants more than a Hershey bar. Sitting on our rickety picnic bench behind the terminal, I couldn't agree more. We've become so accustomed to getting what we want that I have a hard time coping with not having a chocolate bar now. However, the sun doesn't allow chocolate bars to last long in Iraq.

The picnic table groans under my weight. I watch a half-dozen birds coast over the terminal and out toward the gate, and I think about Abbas Ibn Firnas. His flight was mostly successful, yet what parents fail to tell their children is that doctors attributed his death—twelve years after his flight—to what happened when he tried to land.

The landing was, by all accounts, rough. Ibn Firnas felt comfortable being in the air. If he could have stayed up in the air, circling round and round until his body tired of the activity, he could have survived. But then again, everything that goes up must come down. So when Ibn Firnas tried to land, he injured his back. Critics say he hadn't taken proper account of the way birds pull up into a stall and land on their tails. Ibn Firnas had no tail to land on.

I look out over the line of helicopters dotting the pavement. The helicopters sit on the runway like they've always belonged there. Nearby, soldiers walk to and from the PX with plastic bags as if it's a shopping mall. We've managed to build a labyrinth we have no desire of ever leaving. While we've managed to travel into the city on a few missions, we've spent a great deal more time here at BIAP, making this place feel like home when it is anything but.

I watch nine black guys try to steal a ball from the one white soldier on the basketball court near the picnic tables. The backboard behind the hoop reads in spray-painted letters: BRAVO COMPANY LEADS THE WAY! Nearby, six Bravo Company soldiers sit inside a wooden man-made tub filled with cold water. A handful of the truck drivers in the company built the tub the same day we built the picnic tables. They lined the tub with a plastic tarp and filled it with water. Now, I watch the group soak in the cold water, their bare shoulders poking out of the water as their heads tilt back in comfort.

We'll move on and leave this terminal for good. Our names will appear on the empty flight display screen: Bravo Company, 142nd Engineers, departing for HOME at gate 1. But before we do, I want to know I'm doing some good over here. I want us to act like leaders, role models or parents; we should be Deadalus and the Iraqi people our Icarus. I want to feel as if my time isn't being wasted. It sounds a little selfish, but I need this to help me get by. I'm here to help people like the boy in the field, and I need something—anything—to be proud of. The more I think about it, the more I realize I have very little to be proud of in my life. I no longer play the saxophone. I rarely run anymore (except in my mind). I don't have a significant other or children or even a college degree. I'm a horrible carpenter who can't even build a couple of picnic tables. Sometimes I even think I'm a horrible soldier because I don't get excited and giddy every time another monument of Saddam is knocked down or we capture another former Iraqi leader. And because I can't speak out about being gay while in the military, I can't take pride in my sexuality, like so many other people do. I have nothing to be proud of, so I need to make a difference over here.

We complain about the price of cigarettes, bitch about the heat, and pamper ourselves because nobody is there to stop us. Looking at the men playing basketball and soaking in their homemade tub, I know we're already too comfortable here.

We're already too close to the sun.

Baghdad in My Boots

We call them hajjis. Most of us don't even know what the word means. We heard it one day outside the wire, and now we can't stop calling them that. There are hajji men—dressed in dirty slacks and T-shirts, standing on the street corners or peering from behind steering wheels. There are hajji women—covered in black as they walk down back alleys and slink down in back seats. There are hundreds of hajji children; we see them the most as they throw out their hands every time we pass by. Hajji dogs. Hajji buildings. Hajji behavior and, even, when we're particularly pissed, hajji weather. *I'm so sick of seeing hajjis everywhere* becomes a common refrain on days like that.

For a while Roach tried calling the Iraqi people LBMs—Little Brown Men—but that didn't catch on, so he dropped it. Now, to us, every Iraqi person is a hajji.

On May 18, I wake at 5 a.m. and make my way to the motor pool for my first mission into the city. A few days earlier other members of the platoon came back from a mission into Baghdad, and while I listened to their stories, I wondered when I'd get my chance to go "out there." I'd heard the news reports about how violent Baghdad can be. Soldiers killed along the streets. Trucks ambushed. Roadside bombs found by Hummer tires and American feet. Even though I've felt that thus far we've only made ourselves comfortable in Iraq, part of me doesn't want to go into Baghdad. Part of me wants to stay at BIAP, a stone's throw away from the heart of the city. If this war was a beast, I was comfortable with the occasional brush against it, but I had no desire to slice open the chest of the animal and gaze at its still-beating heart.

The commander stands in the motor pool, spewing forth details about our mission. We are engineers, so we'll be helping the Iraqi people by repairing the city and making life a little easier for them. We line up our vehicles—three five-ton dump trucks, a couple of Hummers for the officers, a covered two-and-a-half-ton truck to haul the troops, and a flatbed trailer with a couple of tractor loaders. Inside the back of the two-and-a-half-ton truck, I glance around and wonder if anyone else feels nervous energy jolting through their body.

The truck is quiet as we leave BIAP's north gate. Once we get out past the airport boulevard and onto a city street, I am overcome with anxiety. Already, I feel the pull of the city, its people grabbing hold of me with their eyes as we ride down the road. At the intersections, I expect the children to rush our vehicles and latch onto our boots, their thin fingers clinging to our bootlaces. Beyond the people, I hear the city rise up and welcome us— jarring car horns blaring out as we cross the city streets, quick Arabic slurs, a baby's muffled wail. It isn't even 8 a.m. and I am already mesmerized by this city, and its sights and sounds.

We pull into a gravel lot. I climb out of the truck and look around. I rub my eyes, stretch, grab my weapon with both hands, and feel the magazine of ammunition I have slapped into the chamber. I half expect people to rush our vehicles, for there to be bullets whizzing past our heads. It may be that I have this Hollywood war movie image in my head, where the troops rush out of their vehicles and are picked off by enemy snipers. Instead, I listen to the silent morning and cough at the smell of gasoline and garbage that wafts over this neighborhood.

We've made a horseshoe with our trucks around the lot, and at the edge of the horseshoe, just beyond our trucks, is a giant pile of trash. I look around and notice smaller piles—fruit peels, plastic bottles, empty cartons. We have pulled into the middle of a neighborhood dump.

Slowly, I start to feel the city come back to life around me. Members of a military police unit rope off the horseshoe to create a sort of safe haven, a place where we aren't exposed to people and garbage. As Newman explains the mission, I look past our trucks and notice the tan stucco houses that surround the lot. From doorways, I see dark eyes peer out at us. Slowly, people appear, popping out from their houses to watch us work. Most of the platoon are headed to a nearby school where they'll be helping to repair classrooms, while some of the troops from Horizontal Platoon cart away the garbage in the lot. I want to take it all in, to see the people and experience this place. Therefore, I volunteer to escort a specialist with Headquarters

Company, two military intelligence officers, and an interpreter into the streets surrounding the lot.

Bouret is a communications specialist with HSC. She has come along to take pictures of the mission, to show the people back in North Dakota what good work we're doing over here. As we near the edge of our trucks, ready to step out into the streets of Baghdad, she looks over at me and asks, "Ready?"

The streets of Baghdad, particularly this neighborhood, aren't any different from those of other run-down countries. There are crumbling walls lining the streets, each a barrier between the dark houses and the road. Women stand in the gateways, one foot in their front-yard gardens and one foot out into the street. Men have gathered on the corner, some smoking cigarettes while they quietly talk. Nobody seems to notice the sewage that has backed up and is spilling out into the road. We step over a puddle as we cross the street, careful not to let our feet sink down into the slush and grime. Children rush to our side, sliding right through the sewage to shake our hands.

I expected the children to be grabbing at my uniform, reaching inside my pockets, and running away with whatever they found. I expected rocks to be thrown, slurs to be used. I expected to see needy faces and big eyes of wonder. Instead, I look over a dozen smiling faces.

"Mee-sta, Mee-sta," a little boy says as he runs up in front of us. I shake his tiny hand, nod to the other neighborhood children around him. They are all dark hair and smiles, giving us the thumbs up as if they approve of us being here. From afar they seem joyful and full of energy. Bouret takes out her camera and takes a few pictures. They smile back, give peace signs. But then they start asking for food. One child points down his open mouth with one hand and holds his other hand out to us, palm up. Another boy holds out his hand and imitates cutting off his wrist. We look over at the interpreter, who tells us that that gesture means money. They have suddenly turned into little men.

They look like children back home, but when I look into their eyes, expecting to see a happy glow, instead I see a hardness that children shouldn't have. They shouldn't have to worry about begging for food and money. I shake a few hands like I'm a senator on the campaign trail, and make my way through the crowd and across the street. A Hummer from the military intelligence unit slowly trundles its way down the street, a speaker atop the vehicle broadcasting an Arabic message.

"To tell the people what you're doing today," the interpreter explains.

Walking into someone else's neighborhood with everyone watching, I feel on display. I feel their eyes watching me, their dark fingers pointing as I walk down the street. I feel uneasy walking between Bouret and the interpreter, so unnatural being the center of so many people's attention.

At the corner, where a dozen men are watching us approach, the two military intelligence officers and the interpreter are talking to a young man. I look around at their faces, worn and creased by the conflict in this city. I nod at the women, shake hands with the children. I laugh at a boy juggling rocks along the side of the road. A teenage boy steps in front of me and points his long, thin finger at my chest.

"You," he says and then points at Bouret.

He places his two index fingers side by side, like bony bride and groom figures you'd see on a wedding cake. He looks into my eyes. I look down at his fingers and realize that he's asking if Bouret is my girlfriend or wife.

"No," I say, shaking my head and looking back at Bouret.

She is standing near the military intelligence officers and listening as the interpreter translates what a group of Iraqi men are saying. She notices me looking at her and steps over to where I'm standing.

"He just asked me if we were a couple," I tell her. We laugh and both shake our heads again.

I look at the boy and realize that even in Iraq, stereotypes exist. I'm sure they see us all the same—straight American soldiers, eager for power, money, and women. They see us all dressed alike and think we all must have the same desires, the same needs, the same wants. In a way, they are right. Most of us want similar things—an end to the conflict over here, a cool breeze, a chance to see our loved ones, the day when we can go home. But I also want to tell the boy how wrong he is. I want to point at one of the male American police officers across the street, then point at myself, and then place my two index fingers together. But I don't. I'm not sure he'll understand.

The boy says something in Arabic, and when Bouret and I stare back at him speechless, he shakes his head and walks away. It is hard to understand what the Iraqi people want. Sometimes—like when the children point down their mouths or use their fingers to make universal gestures—I pick up on what they're saying, but most of the time I shake my head, shrug my shoulders, and throw up my hands, or just ignore their comments altogether. In doing this I realize that we view them the same way they view us. To us, every Iraqi child we meet on the street—with his mouth open and palms outstretched—is the same kid, recycled over and over again. And to them, I look just like the other soldiers they've seen marching around the city.

As we watch the boy walk down the street, an older man grabs my arm and pulls me over to an open gateway near the road. A short woman, shrouded in black, stands in the entrance to a house, looking meek. She is hesitant to talk, but when the man gestures at her, prods her with his Arabic words, she talks angrily. Her eyebrows form into sharp arches, and she gestures with her arms, first up at the sky, then over at the soldiers in the lot.

"I don't understand," I say to her, shaking my head.

Bouret has stepped over next to me. I ask her if she understands, and we both look back at the woman and shake our heads. I see beyond the gate into the small garden lined with vegetables. I notice the man walk down the path, through the garden, and into the house. He returns to the doorway holding a propane tank.

"Oh, propane," Bouret says. "To cook food."

Minutes later the interpreter comes over and explains that since we've entered the country and run off Saddam, the people haven't been able to get propane. The woman stands quietly behind the interpreter, her hands folded in front of her. She doesn't look angry anymore, just disappointed and upset at the Americans' inability to provide for her family.

We leave the woman and the people gathering on the corner, and walk to the school a block away. The afternoon continues in much the same fashion. Children swarm around us, begging for food and money. At the school, a half-dozen older children are helping soldiers clean up trash. Bouret and I are sitting on the front steps of the school, watching the kids push the trash into piles with the shovels we've given them. Rainman stands on the playground, children swarming around him like flies. He is handing out candy. He places a few pieces in dirty hands, then turns to leave, but is met with more hands. He has fed the wolves but now can't get away.

"Mee-sta," one of the boys with shovels says loudly.

I turn to look at the boy.

"Disco?" the boy says as his hips gyrate back and forth, his two index fingers pointing at the sky as he twirls around. He has a huge smile on his face.

Bouret and I laugh and clap our hands. Another boy notices the attention we're giving out, so he drops his shovel and steps up next to the first boy.

"Michael Jackson?" the second boy asks. He joins the other boy in disco dancing. How is it that children in Iraq know about Michael Jackson? From American music videos? From siblings? From relatives in the States? I look at the boys and laugh at the universal appeal the pop singer has gained.

"Yes, I know Michael Jackson," I say. "But you're a couple of decades behind. Michael Jackson went out in the eighties."

The boys don't care; they still dance to the song running through their heads. I imagine the song is "Thriller."

"You," the first boy says, pointing at me. "You."

They want me to dance. I walk over near the boys, my weapon now moved from out in front of me to being slung behind my back, and I dance with the children. The boys laugh and giggle. We've made a connection, and we all smile.

As Bouret and I walk back to the trucks, young women pour out of a courtyard across the alley. It is an all-women's school getting out for the day. They see Bouret and instantly surround her, asking questions. I imagine that they don't see too many female American soldiers. Other children, begging and wanting to shake our hands, flood the alley. I move through the crowd quickly, gently pushing the children as I step down the road. I manage to make it back to the parking lot, but when I look back down the alley, I notice Bouret surrounded by eager hands and open mouths. They have engulfed her on all sides like wolves ready for the kill. These children prey on the slow, and they've caught Bouret right in their trap. She tries to push forward, but she's met by dozens of hands reaching up to touch her, several mouths asking her Arabic questions.

The alley has filled with children, and Bouret pushes her way forward. I don't think to panic, to call for help. They're just children. But watching Bouret inch forward, I realize how these people have managed to swallow us whole. They've managed to stick in our minds in ways we'll have a hard time shaking.

Back at BIAP, I sit down on my cot and pull off my right boot. I tip the boot upside down and watch the sand and dirt fall to the floor at the end of my cot. I look around and notice other soldiers doing the same—dumping Baghdad from their boots. We've taken the city with us, and brought it back here, along with the old woman begging for propane and the boys asking me to dance like Michael Jackson. I don't quite know why yet, but I know that days—maybe even years—from now I'll have a hard time forgetting these things.

By the time we arrived in Iraq, we were used to having a shower only every third day. But after starting Task Force Neighborhood missions, we *needed* a shower to wash away the city. We needed to get the smell of gasoline and garbage out of our hair, to feel clean again after all those dirty hands grabbing our limbs and the harsh sun making us sweat.

The airport terminal doesn't come with fully functional toilets, let alone showers. But being the resourceful carpenters and plumbers we are, we build our own showers out in front of our terminal—six phone booth–sized wooden stalls complete with soap holders and towel racks. On top of each stall is a barrel that we fill from our company's water tanker. Inside each booth, a hose hangs down from the barrel with a half-liter bottle punctured with holes serving as a shower head. It isn't the Marriott, but it will have to do.

There is one stall that isn't like the others, one stall a little bit closer to Marriott standards than the rest. We call this stall The Golden Shower.

"It has an actual shower head with a valve instead of a water bottle," Roach says. He is one of the plumbers who helped build the showers. "Trust me, you can feel the difference."

I am standing in line for the showers, half-listening to Roach describe The Golden Shower. People are settling in for another night in Iraq. The sun is casting an orange haze behind the main airport terminal. I hear helicopters flying overhead and the gentle hum of oscillating fans from inside the terminal. A line of ants moves perpendicular to the shower line as they march back to their hill. It has been a week since our first mission into Baghdad, and the people are still on my mind. Yesterday, while sitting on the picnic tables behind our terminal, I imagined I saw the old woman carrying her propane tank across the strip of runway outside our terminal. She drifted between the helicopters, waving one hand and dragging the tank with the other. She was trying to get someone to notice her, trying to get us to do something about her situation, but we ignored her, turned our heads away. I knew it was the heat that made my mind run wild, but I also knew that the Iraqi people still had a hold on me days after that mission.

A couple of days ago, Newman sent Jones and me to the finance office to get $450 in one-dollar bills. We needed the money to pay the two hundred hajjis we are hiring on our next mission. As Jones was talking to the teller behind the window, I could see the confused look on the man's face, as if to say, *What do you need that many ones for?* Jones cradled five bundles of ones in his hands all the way back to our terminal.

"I just want to hold it and love it all the way back," he said. "I wanted to say to the teller, 'I want to take my entire platoon out to the strip club.'"

Jones isn't the kind of guy you'd expect to see in the strip club. He's quiet and withdrawn, but as we walked down the street carrying all that money, we felt like kings, men with power. It was the power of all those one-dollar bills. It was also the power we'd recently gained from going into the city. After that first mission, I felt important and powerful, like I was invincible.

Roach is still talking about The Golden Shower as the line inches forward. People come and go. Roach says something about getting The Golden Shower, but only one in six people get to use it, so his chances aren't very good.

"I just thought someone had peed in the shower and then written 'Golden Shower' on the wall," Tuna says, laughing.

"No way," Roach says. "It's real."

I'm not very disappointed when I don't get The Golden Shower. I'm too tired to care. After my shower, I return to my cot to find the terminal dark and nearly quiet. I notice the rise and fall of chests in the dark, hear Rainman and Elijah softly snoring. I take off my shirt and lie down on my cot, sweat already forming on my chest. I stare at the ceiling and wonder how I ended up here. In high school, when I signed those papers to join the National Guard, I never imagined I'd be seeing Iraq. But here I am, sweating through May in a country I had no interest in ever setting foot in, surrounded by men, women, and children I had no interest in ever helping. I turn onto my side, look out the terminal window. I don't really know what I'm doing in Iraq, but if I start to understand the Iraqi people's lives, I may start to understand why I'm here. It seems simple. I mean, how hard can it be to put yourself in someone else's shoes?

They call us fags. On college campuses and in neighborhood bars, they call us fags for not being like them. They call us fags in restaurants and truck stops and car garages, parking lots, grocery aisles, and Wal-Mart. They call us fags when we have our parades and drag shows and talks about tolerance and acceptance because it is written someplace in a great book that being a fag is wrong and sinful. They call us fags when they don't think we are listening, in the privacy of their own homes, where they hope and pray their children don't turn out like us. Most of the time they do nothing more than throw around a few hurtful words—words they don't want to understand. They write it in colored chalk all over campus sidewalks. *FAGS!* in thin, childish letters, curled right around the sign for Coming Out Week, which we'd drawn onto the cement footpaths.

And they call us fags on the weekend, when they dress up in uniforms and meet other part-time soldiers to talk about their nagging wives and girlfriends and complain about "fags taking over their neighborhood." They call us fags because they think they are so radically different from us. They don't think about the men sitting next to them. They assume everyone wearing the army green is just like them.

Watch out for the fetus," King says as I step across the loose gravel.

King is convinced there's a fetus among the rubble on the road. He jokes about stepping on one, telling each person who walks the path between the hospital and the empty lot to watch out for dead babies. I find a dirty syringe lying in the sand behind the hospital. I look farther up the path and notice that the ground is littered with used hospital items— bloody bandages, dark tongue depressors, used needles. I shiver as I try to think about what else lies out in this field.

It is May 28 and we're on another mission in Baghdad. We're repairing the walls of a hospital. The building is a huge block structure at the corner of two city streets. Across the street is a line of shops, and behind the building, where we've lined up our trucks, is a dirty alleyway that separates the hospital from a sandy lot filled with craters and trash.

I help my platoon unload bags of concrete and lime from our truck and lay them against the hospital wall. We unload our wheelbarrow, grab a handful of masonry trowels, and form a line to relay the cinder blocks from the back of the truck to the area where we'll be building our wall. Yesterday I rode along on a FOO (Field Ordering Operation) into Baghdad to buy these blocks. We went from shop to shop until we found a merchant who would sell to us. Then, as our truck was backed into the driveway of the merchant's shop, I noticed a middle-aged woman rushing across the street carrying a young boy. The boy was awake and even smiling, but we noticed his deformed arm right away. The interpreter told us that the woman wanted us to take the boy with us, back to our base, where we could fix his arm. The woman looked defeated when the interpreter told her that we couldn't take the child, that we had no way of helping her.

As I hand each block down the line, I am reminded how determined that woman was, how hopeful she seemed that we could help her son, only to find out that we couldn't do what she asked us to. After failing to procure propane for the Iraqi woman during our first mission, this was strike two for us. We haven't done anything the Iraqi people have asked us to do. We can't take children with us, even if it was our guns that did the damage. I feel that we might not be able to do *any* of the things the Iraqi people would like us to.

King fills two buckets with water. He puffs on a cigarette as the water fills. I watch as he tiptoes around a mound of rubble, the cigarette stuck to one side of his mouth. His boots barely miss a stack of bloody bandages. "This is just sick," King says through his teeth. "I had to cover up some bloody bandages earlier because I was so grossed out."

We awoke at 3 a.m. this morning. As we loaded our trucks with equipment, water, and MREs, I looked east and saw the moonlight illuminating the city, making it look calm and romantic. It's hard to imagine the city that way, silent and still asleep, but I like to think that there was once a time when Baghdad was a desirable place.

On the trip into the city, I noticed that someone had spray painted the words DIRTY BUSH on a wall. The letters were large and dark red, blood-stained. We've come across a mix of supportive and hateful messages throughout Baghdad, and I've gotten used to them. It isn't the supportive messages that worry me; they are everywhere. It is the threats that give me concern. They stick with you like a failing report card or bad news.

I look off into the field behind the hospital. There are mounds of dirt scattered over the field and garbage littering the short grass and weeds. I'm afraid to walk out into the field for fear of stumbling upon empty glass medicine bottles and blood-soaked gauze or, worse yet, a body. The city and children seem calmer today, less eager to grab hold of our wrists and beg for our attention. It could be that for once we aren't near a school and children are few and far between. But around lunchtime, while pulling security near the road, I see a few children walk by. I follow them with my eyes, hoping that they've grown tired of begging. But every now and then, I am surprised by one or two children who come running up from behind.

"Mee-sta," one boy says as he waves at me. He has a toothless grin and strappy sandals.

"Bad Saddam. Good Bush," the boy says, giving me the peace sign.

I can tell that the boy wants me to acknowledge his attempt at English, to give him a thumbs up or nod my head in agreement. But I just look at the child, wondering why he'd say that. For the rest of the day, children run up to me and make similar statements. It doesn't seem like the kind of thing children learn in school, and from what I understand about the average Iraqi citizen, most adults don't know much English, so the children aren't hearing it at home. I wonder if it's a phrase someone told them to tell the U.S. soldiers, a reaffirming line of comfort for the troops.

They are eager to defy their runaway former ruler and eager to give praise to the man who sent me to this country. I wonder how I could ever trust the Iraqis, a people who turn on someone so quickly. I want to believe what they are saying. I want to know that this country is about to change and that I am a part of that change. But I have a hard time believing these children. Some simply say, "Good Bush," possibly too scared to defame Saddam. Others put emphasis on the Saddam part. Either way, I know the children don't fully understand what they're saying. I know they don't fully believe the words that spill out of their mouths. They are just phrases picked up on school playgrounds, dirty street corners, or behind thin doors. Our interpreter tells us that there are people who want us here, people who are glad to see our sand-colored camouflage in their streets, but I don't believe him. He, just like the children, is filling our minds with compliments while we hear reports that insurgents in Baghdad are killing more American soldiers.

When we get back to BIAP, we again go through what has become a ritual—tipping the sand from our boots. I empty my boots and think about the last couple of missions, how I've started to resent the very people I thought I'd be helping. I started these missions hopeful that I could do some good. But the heat, combined with the stress of being in the violent city, has made me cynical. I've started to question why I'm even here. We're taking so much sand from this city, but what are we giving back?

I like to imagine what the pile of sand at the end of my cot would look like if I didn't clean it up. I imagine a whole city rising from the sand I've collected—my own private Baghdad. In this Baghdad, the people don't seem so innocent. There are no wide-eyed children, no begging mothers holding children. There are no men silently smoking cigarettes on street corners, or children dancing like Michael Jackson. Instead, I imagine a city that is loud and dusty and full of whispers. I imagine people clawing at the soldiers who've taken over their city, running their nails against their uniforms, ripping into their pant-legs, scratching a line into their cheeks. I imagine the soldiers turning around to see not children and women begging for help but wolves, red-eyed and vicious, waiting and ready to pounce.

This is what I believe Baghdad to be—a place where knowledge is illusive, the situation is complex, and the people are never how they appear.

I spend most of the days in between missions napping in a pool of my own sweat. I am awakened by the sound of another helicopter setting down on the landing strip outside our terminal. I open my eyes and see the spaghetti-strap ceiling we've created with electrical wire. We've run the wire through the ceiling tiles in an effort to provide the entire bay with the electricity needed to power a dozen blowing fans. The wires look like jungle vines. I hear the whipping sound of chopper blades nearby, and as I sit up I watch a cloud of dust lift into the air and float down the runway, pebbles shooting out from below the chopper as it lands.

We sometimes have three or four days off between missions, where we sit around the terminal playing cards, watching movies, or lifting weights. I hear Lake and Cole in the homemade gym at the bottom of the stairs. The metal plates clank against each other as they're put on and taken off the bars. Grayson and Newman are sitting on their cots and talking, while down at the end of the bay a group of soldiers crowds around a television playing a pirated copy of *Matrix: Reloaded*. After a month of missions I cherish days like this, days away from the city. I don't have to worry about swarms of children and watchful stares.

I walk to the two Deepfreezes along the back wall. We picked these up on a FOO and instantly packed them full of bottled water. I lift the lid, feel the cool puff of air hit my face, and grab a cold bottle of water. As I walk back to my cot I catch the temperature on the thermometer: 116 degrees.

Elijah is sitting alone on his cot, his head in his hands. His wife is expecting their first child soon, and he's been waiting three days for the orders sending him home for the birth. As I pass by his cot, I see the anticipation in his face, the way his eyes have a hard time focusing on anything without his mind drifting back to his wife and his absence from the birth.

"How's it going?" I ask, stopping next to his cot.

He looks up at me with his sweaty face. His glasses lie in his lap. At his feet are his bags, packed and ready to go—he just needs the word and he's gone. But looking at his face, I can tell that his mind is already somewhere else. He looks away from me and out the window at the helicopters.

"You know your priorities are messed up when all you want is a cold bottle of water and you're happy," he says.

I can tell that the anticipation and heat have gotten to him. When he turns back to look at me, I hand him my bottle of water, pat him on the shoulder, and, with a smile, walk away.

Jones is quietly reading on his cot as I approach and sit down across from him.

"Listen to this," he says without looking up. "Iraq holds the world's second largest oil reserves, many of which have been undeveloped and are waiting to be tapped."

Jones is normally very withdrawn and quiet. He is quiet to the point of almost seeming meek. But lately his wife has been sending him conspiracy theory articles on why we're really in Iraq. He gets animated and excited when reading them and goes off for ten minutes about the latest theory or how much he hates the war.

"It's all about the fucking oil," he says. "It's about money and power and oil. We are here because Bush wants to take control of all this untapped oil. It has nothing to do with the people."

I let him go on about the conspiracy theories circulating in the media. We've been told that we're in this country to help the people. When the war began we were led to believe that we were doing some good over here. And I've believed that we were indeed helping the people. I wanted to believe that I was in this country for more than just the oil. While I have yet to fully understand what I am doing in this country, I think about what Jones is saying. I have yet to see the direct result of our missions. I have yet to get any kind of reaffirming gesture that what I am doing is appreciated or welcomed. My heart tells me that I am doing something important, but my brain reminds me of the woman with the propane tank and the one with the deformed child, and the looks on their faces when we told them we couldn't help.

That night, as I watch the jungle wires gently sway in the fan's breeze, I realize that I've been fooling myself thinking that my job in this country is important. I've been holding onto a lie, a statement I chose to accept because I needed some reason to justify why I had to leave my life in America to help other lives in Iraq. We've all had our lives interrupted in order to secure more oil. Lives will be changed by this war. Wives will leave husbands. Children will grow up. Elijah won't get to see his first child born. We've all had to put our lives on hold for money and power, and it makes me cringe as I feel the lie I've been led to believe slipping away.

It's *not* about the oil, I try to tell myself. I have a hard time believing what Jones is selling, but deep down I feel like there is some small kernel of truth in what he is saying.

> There is a photograph of us that I can't seem to forget. The picture was taken on the day you left. We are standing in front of my apartment building like new homeowners. My arm is around your shoulder, your hand cupped around my waist. We look happy, and if I could choose only one photo to represent our

relationship, I would choose this one, because in that photo I look happier than I've ever been. I'd just been through my first relationship with another man, and even though we were breaking up and going our separate ways, I felt like I'd achieved something, like I was finally living the life I wanted to live.

But people move on and sometimes there is nothing we can do to stop them from leaving. You made up your mind all by yourself, and I was fine with that. If you would have stayed for another two years, the roles would have been reversed, and you would have been the one watching me go—shipped off to a war I have a possibility of not returning from.

I don't think I ever told you what our friend Kelly said after she and I helped move you to Minnesota. We were driving back to Fargo, and as my car climbed the hill outside New Ulm, she turned to me and said that she wasn't sad to see you go. She was happy, actually, because she knew—absolutely, deep-down-in-the-bottom-of-her-gut knew—you and I would get back together. She knew you and I would find each other again. There was a long silence in the car after that. I didn't agree or disagree with her. There was a possible truth in what she said, a small sliver of possibility. I remember that conversation and that photograph now, and on the nights when I'm lying awake listening to the helicopters land and lift off, when the voices of the Iraqi children echo through my head and images of Iraqi women holding propane tanks replay over and over in my mind, I can't help but wonder if she was right.

The thermometer reads 120 degrees Fahrenheit. It is June 2 and I am sweating salt rings around my collar as I drive through the streets of Baghdad. My shirt is soaked in sweat, double rings forming around my arm pits because I don't like driving big trucks through crowded cities. But I don't show that fear; instead, as I turn these city corners, I feel the power of this vehicle under me, the strength I have at my fingertips as I plow my way into this city. I feel the eyes of a million hajjis upon me, and I feel uneasy because everyone is watching.

A motorcycle zips past our truck and darts across the street.

"Get the hell outta the way," I yell.

Rainman laughs. I've gotten cocky and cynical lately; we all have. These missions have helped us perfect ignoring the citizens of Baghdad. We like the attention the people are giving us. It feels good to be celebrities, where people praise our every move and run up to us asking for us to look at them, to recognize their existence. But like Hollywood celebrities, the fame has gone to our heads. We don't even look down at the children anymore. We complain when we see them coming, trying to duck behind a truck or building and hoping they won't notice us. Sitting in our vehicles, we know that after we're done with this mission we'll return to our base, where Burger King is about to open and hot showers are waiting to cool our sweaty bodies. We'll return to mail from loved ones and the security of knowing we will eventually be able to leave Iraq.

An old man on a bicycle takes his time crossing the street. To our left is an open market where Iraqi farmers are selling vegetables from wooden street carts. The market is alive and buzzing with people, and I detect the spicy scent of cooked lamb wafting into our open windows. I look over and see a pile of purple eggplants, long rows of dark cucumbers, baskets full of nuts, and ripe cherry tomatoes spilling out of a cart. As we slowly roll past the market, the people turn and look our way, eying us suspiciously. I look back, and we all acknowledge the nervous tension that hangs in the air.

I feel that at any moment a kid will dart out in front of the truck and I'll catch his head with the truck's bumper, sending his small body under the vehicle. With every sudden move, I slam on the brakes and hear a half-dozen yelps from the rest of the squad in the back of the truck.

We're looking for a school where we'll repair classrooms, build desks, and rewire light fixtures, but we're lost. We drive down a narrow alleyway, and from the truck's cab I look over the ornate gates and into the backyards of the houses. It feels so much like spying, as if I am privy to what people prefer to keep behind locked gates. Tidy gardens with neat rows of vegetables are fenced off from a small patio area. In the doorway of one house, three little girls watch us pass. They lift their tiny arms and wave; I lift my hand from the steering wheel and wave back.

We eventually find the school, just in time to see the students let out for the day. I sit in the truck while Newman and Grayson do recon on the site.

It is a girl's school, and I watch as dozens of female students fill the street, darting off in all directions. They all wear matching blue uniforms, some carrying backpacks, some simply holding their books. They walk in twos and threes down the street and away from the school. I wait to see if they'll come running our way; I expect the littlest girls to start begging, to at least wave at us. But they don't. The girls walk away from the school, ignoring the three, huge, steel truck bodies parked in front of the building.

We are so used to being praised that we almost expect it. But for some reason the girls don't even flinch or look twice at our weapons, our sunglasses, our helmets. This could be a scene from any high school, even back in America. But then I notice a few of the girls stop and watch us as we wait alongside the road. Finally, some recognition, I think. Jones and Roach, standing by the road, are waving at the girls. The girls don't wave back. Some point at us, some stop to watch us before whispering to their friends. Most ignore us, and for the first time I feel shunned by the Iraqi people, the way they point at us and giggle. How they talk among themselves and ignore us doesn't sit right with me.

I can't help but feel a little guilty about our position in this country as I watch the girls point and whisper. It seems wrong to get this much pleasure from driving through these city streets. We used to be taken aback by the enormity of this city, swallowed whole by its ancient streets, its angry eyes, and its swollen defiance. We used to sit in our trucks, our weapons aimed out the windows, and stare at the children standing on the side of the highways, wide-eyed boys holding gas cans and rubber hoses, looking both lost and mischievous. We used to smack our lips over street-vendor food—shaved lamb, roasted vegetables, and pancake-thin flat bread—and ask for more. But now we stare at the silent women, yell at the hardened men, and ignore the needy children. We wander from neighborhood to neighborhood like we own this city, our eyes never staying too long on dirty children playing in street sewage or the misfits that walk the streets begging for handouts. We think we know what these people want and how to help them, but we also know that if we stay too long they'll tear us apart.

Back at BIAP at the end of the day, I find myself thinking about my own private Baghdad, the one I've imagined at the end of my cot. I want nothing more than to stomp out this city. I want to step on the schoolgirls who laughed at us, to squash the children who play in the street. I want them all to disappear—the needy children, the propane woman, all Iraqi women with wounded children. I want nothing to do with them.

Do they have Burger Kings in France, French Kid?" Bobby says to me.

Bobby has taken to calling me French Kid, or, when he's feeling rather brave, French Slut. After eating MREs for lunch for three weeks straight, he turned to me and asked, "Do they have MREs in the French army, French Slut?" I actually enjoy the nicknames; they lighten up the mood and make the fact that we're walking around an Iraqi airport less absurd. *He could be calling me something a whole lot worse.*

On June 10 I find myself standing in line at the first Burger King Restaurant in Iraq. The restaurant, however, is at BIAP and only for the troops. We've managed to build up a "home away from home" here in Iraq. We now have a PX with daily shipments of Gatorade, cookies, cigarettes, and Coca-Cola; a gift shop with Arabic items such as prayer rugs and hookahs; and a barber shop where we get "high-and-tights." It almost feels like home.

Bobby and I are sick of eating MREs, so we've decided to stand in line for as long as it takes on the opening day of the restaurant. The restaurant is a restaurant only in name; it is actually more like a county fair concession stand—a steel shed across from the PX. Flaps are opened at the front of the tiny steel building to reveal a line of cash registers and several employees dressed in blue and yellow polo shirts and matching baseball caps. The lines form behind the cash registers, two beige boots stepping forward each time an order is completed.

Bobby looks impatient. I give him the *Do you want to go back to eating MREs?* and *What else do we have to do today?* looks as he hops around in line. I smell the charbroiled burgers covered in melted cheese and topped with lettuce, tomato, and onion. I look around and can tell that other soldiers are thinking the same thing. We stand in line, salivating over greasy burgers and golden "freedom fries," and for a moment it seems like we aren't even in Iraq. *This isn't war,* I tell myself. *How bad can it be when we have burgers and fries?*

At the front of the line, I fumble over my order and the six other orders I've told my platoon I'd bring back for them. I look down at the list and read off a dozen Whoppers and six cartons of fries before looking the Asian employee in the eyes. He doesn't even blink. He's probably been getting this all day.

I hold the greasy sacks in my hand and realize that I can get almost anything I want here. Bobby and I step over to the Iraqi gift shop nearby, where we find a pack of the fifty-five Iraq's Most Wanted List playing cards. I take the cards out of the box and flip through the stack.

"They should have made Saddam the joker," I say to Bobby, showing him the ace of spades card with Saddam's face on it. I flip through the other cards, laughing at the mustaches on the faces of the men. Of the pictured men, only four are mustache free. The only woman pictured is Huda Salih Mahdi Ammash, a "weapons of mass destruction" scientist and Baath Party regional command member. As I flip past her card—the five of hearts—she salutes me with the tips of her fragile fingers.

Bobby finds a stash of Iraqi dollar bills in plastic sleeves along the back wall. On one side of the bill, it reads "Central Bank of Iraq—Twenty Five Dinars" in English and shows pictures of Babylon. On the opposite side, Saddam appears, surrounded by Arabic letters. In the center is a group of hajjis riding horses into some unseen battle. They hold spears above their heads and wave flags as they move across the paper money.

As we walk back to the terminal with burgers for the platoon, Bobby and I feel like kings. We have food, the greasy patties we're used to back home. We have treasures from a country we never thought we'd ever see. Our walk is a kind of pompous swagger. It feels great to get what you want. We enter the terminal, and soldiers rush to our sides for their orders. Seeing their smiling faces and watching everyone feast on the burgers and fries we've delivered, we couldn't feel more praised.

They call us all kinds of things, mostly behind our backs. They call us scum, American devils, murderers. They sneer and laugh and point at us. In newspapers, we read about troops being killed by roadside bombs and army captains who hold the charred helmets of dead American soldiers and proclaim, *This is what they think of us.* In a video being passed around, an Arabic-speaking journalist asks Iraqis in Baghdad what they think of the American soldiers. One child holds up a snake, shakes it at the journalist, and replies, *They're vipers.*

I watch a bearded man cradle a large bundle of bananas—bananas that look so ripe and fresh he could have only recently ripped them from a tree. He zips across the street, weaving and darting in and out of traffic. I am standing between two five-ton trucks on a thin strip of median that separates the two lanes of this boulevard, pulling security as Newman and Grayson use an interpreter to barter for steel plumbing fixtures. We're on a FOO in Baghdad. There have been a half-dozen days like this where I stand watching the people of Iraq. With each one I've gotten more and more irritated at this city, at its people, and at the reason I'm over here.

After wandering this city for a month, I can't seem to shake the place. I feel Baghdad on my entire body. I smell the scent of this city on my uniform—a mixture of garbage, grease, and cooked lamb. At night, I hear the way the children say *mee-sta* like the rat-tat-tat of a machine gun looping through my dreams. I feel the salt and sand that has risen up and settled into the deep crevices of my body. I find the city behind my ears, at the nape of my neck, and inside the bend of my arm, tucked neatly between two folds of skin. Plus there is the sand I've poured from my boots, a whole dune being hauled out of this city every day by soldiers. I used to admire how much of the city stuck with me, but now I shiver at the thought of this city never leaving me.

I shift my weight to my right foot, push away a pebble in my boot with my toe. The man with the bananas is waving at traffic. He lifts the bananas out in front of him and waves his tan arm above his head. He yelps at the passing vehicles, his dark fingers catching nobody's attention, his soft yell finding no open ears. It is still warm, and I see the sweat form on the man's forehead. He is slightly hunched over, and I watch as the sweat falls onto the hot concrete street. He isn't forceful with his yelling, and people pass him by, nobody stopping to purchase his fruit. The women won't even look at the man. They cast their eyes forward, watch the litter blow across the sidewalk, and move on.

I feel bad for the man. I want to call him over, buy one of his bananas— maybe ten—and talk with him about the difficulty of selling fruit in Baghdad, maybe even give him tips on how to sell more. But I'm hesitant to talk to any Iraqis. I'm too tired and sweaty to play any role but that of a tourist, silently watching from the sidelines and occasionally oohing and aahing at the broken scenery. Plus, I know better than to get involved.

The streets are full of cars and trucks; it is bumper-to-bumper traffic today. Lake, wearing a pair of sunglasses, sits atop the truck. I glance up and notice the traffic reflected through the lenses as he stares down the street. Most of the cars are patched together from other vehicles—dark brown doors on a white Mustang. The vehicles move slowly down the street, past our vehicles. I gaze inside the windows and see white-knuckled men gripping steering wheels with both hands while women in head scarves hold small children in the backseats, their eyes peering out the windows at our uniforms, our trucks, and our guns. A couple of motorcyclists glide by—young men with no helmets. They slide between parked and moving cars. I watch as a dump truck lumbers by, coughing up smog into the city street, where it mixes in with the scent of gasoline and sweat.

I take it all in like I'm watching a live theater performance, occasionally wincing when a motorcycle nearly gets creamed. A street vendor has set up shop across from our vehicles. Roach stands behind one of the trucks, a small gathering of children begging at his feet. He gives one of the children a dollar and points at the cart. The child runs across the street to the vendor. He doesn't hesitate or race off with Roach's money. Instead, he returns with four cold cans of Coke. Roach thanks the boy and passes the dripping wet cans around—one for Lake, one for Roach, one for me, and one for the boy.

In between sips, I look around for the banana man. I don't see the man and think that maybe he has given up, headed home to his wife and six hungry children. Instead, I notice another walking merchant—a one-armed man with two dozen hand-sewn purses looped around his good arm. The purses dangle from his arm like raindrops. They are straw-colored and shaped liked diamonds, each with an odd loop of fabric at the bottom. The man walks stiffly, shaking his arm at the men and women who pass. He is much louder than the banana man; his sales approach is more forceful, more direct. He sticks his arm out as if he's ready to knock someone down with the purses, demanding that people look at him, his deformity, and his merchandise. A young man stops to admire a purse, touches it, fingers the loop at the bottom, and releases the bag back to the man's arm, the purse gently swinging like a pendulum. I watch the man drift down the street. I try not to stare, but I want to know where this man is headed and if he sells any purses.

Walking merchants are a common occurrence on FOOs, and every time we're out in Baghdad I'm tempted to purchase genuine Iraqi items from these merchants. I *want* to help them out, thinking that maybe the one thing I can give back to these people is a few American dollars that they can use to feed either their families or addictions—nicotine and alcohol. But I'm hesitant to approach the one-armed man, the banana man, or anyone else. Instead, I think, *I'll buy my Iraqi souvenirs from the base PX.*

I look over at Roach to see if he's noticed the one-armed merchant, but he's too busy entertaining a group of children. Roach is a father, and I'm not surprised at how easy it is for him to interact with the children. When I turn back, the man is gone. I look up and down the street, but he is nowhere to be seen. *He must have found an interested customer or a busier street*, I think, knowing that it is more likely he has given up and collapsed next to a street vendor or in someone's garden.

Two minutes later, I'm watching people come and go from the shop across the street when I hear someone say, "Mee-sta!" behind me. The word is loud and sharp, and I jump. I turn around to see the one-armed man dangling his line of purses out in front of his body like a cape.

"Jesus," I say, holding my right hand over my Kevlar-protected heart. "You scared me."

The man looks back at me with wide eyes, as if he doesn't know what it's like to be scared. But I know that for someone living in Iraq, lack of such an emotion is nearly impossible.

He waves the purses in front of me and repeats his phrase.

"No," I say, shooing the man along. "Now go. Go!"

I point down the street. The man doesn't seem shaken by my comments; he probably gets this all the time. He turns and slowly shuffles down the street, his body sticking to our trucks like a man on the edge of a cliff as he slides down the median. I watch the man slowly step out into the street and dart out between traffic. He ducks into a shop and is gone.

Roach is making origami swans out of scrap pieces of paper the children are bringing him. Lake has taken off his sunglasses and is leaning hard into his weapon as he stares down the street. I turn back to find that the banana man has returned. He is zipping across the street again, trying to make another go at selling his fruit. I admire his determination, his will-power to continue on here. Looking around, I feel like I've been in Iraq for years, like these are everyday situations that no longer seem all that unusual to me. Roach has always been this playful with Iraqi children; Lake always looks this angry.

I watch four Iraqi boys dart by with origami swans. Roach is watching the children run down the street. Roach is happy here, content among the children, and I admire his ability to find them amusing, even after a month of grabby hands and sharp *mee-sta, mee-sta*s.

The street is still busy when Grayson and Newman come back from the shop. As Roach helps them load up the supplies, a family standing across the street watches us. The man is tall and angular, a dark beard around his chin. His wife stands next to him, a young girl in her arms, and a shy young boy—maybe two or three years old—peeks out from between her legs. The man notices me. He grabs the boy from behind the woman, wraps his strong forearm around the child, and carries his son across the street. He stops right in front of me and holds up his son so the child is dangling in front of my face.

"Osami," the man says, smiling. I assume that is the child's name.

I don't know what to say; I'm not used to people just walking up to me. I want to tell the man what I already know, what I have come to realize about why I'm in this country. I want to explain to him the full circle of emotions I've gone through since entering this city: questioning why I am here, starting to believe the conspiracy theories, hearing the schoolgirls' giggling, which made me realize that these missions are not *only* about the oil. In the Baghdad I want to build, we are helping children like Osami. I hate to think in such clichéd terms, but the truth is that we're here to help these people learn how to help themselves, to teach them how to create their own futures, for their children and for their people. It seems to me, in a roundabout way, that the man dangling his son in front of me is trying to say, *Look—this is our future.*

The man holds the boy out stiff, the child's feet swinging in the wind. The child is inches from my face. I notice the boy smiling, his tiny teeth shining against his tan face, dark forehead, and black hair. His smile instantly brightens his face. His legs swing back and forth, and he reaches forward to touch my helmet.

"Hi," I say.

The child giggles. Without another word, the father hoists the boy up on his shoulders, turns, and crosses the street again, back to where his wife and daughter are waiting.

Roach and I finish loading our supplies. I climb in the back of the truck, and as we pull out into the street I notice an old man in a long, dirty robe walking down the sidewalk as children dart in all directions around him. The man is waving a stick, blindly stepping across the pavement straight toward a stone wall. I try not to stare, but as the blind man nears the wall I briefly think about asking Newman to stop the truck. I want to hop down and steer the old man away from the building. I want to show him that there doesn't need to be this separation between us and them. But then I see a younger Iraqi come up from behind the blind man, place money in the old man's hand, and turn him in the right direction.

As we drive away, I realize I've been waiting for a sign that what I am doing in this country is paying off, and I've just received two. Watching the young man guide the blind Iraqi down the sidewalk, I am finally content with being in Iraq. It is a step in the right direction, a future that doesn't include us. Our presence in Iraq is about oil *and* helping these people. While I don't deny that we didn't enter this country thinking about oil, I am determined to leave this place thinking about the people, knowing we've helped them survive.

Don't Tell

The magazines come in the care packages, tucked between logs of chewing tobacco, our favorite candies, and letters from schoolchildren back home. Most of them are weeklies— *Time* and *Newsweek* are the most popular. On our days off, we sit or lie on our cots, flip through them, and read up on the latest news.

I've started reading any and every magazine I can get my hands on, just to quench my desire for information. It seems like we live inside a bubble in Iraq, and any information—whether it's the latest political scandal, health fads, or celebrity gossip—is welcomed and helps me feel more at home. I grab magazines from the TV room and other soldiers' cots, sneak off to my little area, and spend the afternoon catching up on what is going on in the world.

I read most of the articles quickly and without slowing down to think about the information. But one article makes me stop and think. "Forever a Prisoner" by Bobby Ghosh appeared in the May 2003 issue of *Time* magazine. In the article, Lahib Nouman, a former Iraqi criminal lawyer, defends a man who insulted the girlfriend of Uday Hussein—Saddam's eldest son. Nouman then finds herself in prisons and mental institutions, enduring rape, beatings, and torture. After being released, she returns to Baghdad and tries to tell her story to her neighbors, but nobody will listen. Instead, she fills the walls of her shack with Arabic and French writing, some words in bright red lipstick, others in orange paint or gray charcoal. In the picture that accompanies the article, a copper-haired woman stares at the ceiling, her hand clutching her chest and her mouth slightly open in a half-scream.

While the story is outstanding, it is the picture that sticks in my head for days. Mostly I see flashes of Nouman's face in my mind—her sad eyes looking heavenward, her wrinkled brow, and especially her twisted mouth. I feel for Nouman as if she were a friend or relative because she told her story, stood up for what she believed; in return, she was punished.

We are waiting in line outside the administrative office when the guys start talking about visiting a gay bar back home.

"I just want to find out which of my neighbors is gay," Grayson says. "Wouldn't you want to know?"

A few of the other soldiers laugh and play along. Some talk about knowing friends or old roommates who've been to a gay bar, often dragged there by their girlfriends or forced to go on a dare. From down the line I listen, smile as if I agree, but say nothing. Their conversation reminds me why I hate the "don't ask, don't tell" policy. It's not the "don't ask" part. I actually don't mind that people cannot ask me if I'm gay because I prefer to keep my personal life separate from my life as a soldier. It's the "don't tell" part that really makes me angry. The policy creates an environment where it is OK to ridicule someone because of their sexuality since gay men and women cannot stick up for themselves or others without fear of being ostracized and outcast, and that is the last thing a soldier wants during a deployment. The policy reinforces ignorance and stupidity by forcing people to keep their mouths shut. It also stifles a community that cannot grow, trust, or support each other because some of the members aren't allowed to speak up or express who they are.

The conversation doesn't go on for long, and for the most part, it is harmless curiosity that fuels conversations like these. Luckily, it doesn't turn into a discussion about witch-hunting and "rounding up all the fags," which it easily could. But I still want to say something, to tell the other men my own experiences as a gay man. I think by silencing gay men and women the military is really missing an opportunity to educate the troops about acceptance and tolerance. I want to tell—the way Nouman told her story and inspired me to think more about the Iraqi people and their culture, and how we are ridding Iraq of a ruthless leader who doesn't allow his people to speak and tell their stories—but I can't.

The other soldiers don't ask, and I don't tell.

If Charles Bronson Were Here

The longer we're in Iraq the more I think about luck and superstition. I had read stories about GI superstitions and seen them depicted in movies, but I never really realized how widespread superstitions were until I found myself in the middle of a war. When you're at war you have a hard time not thinking about luck. During every mission you think about how lucky you are to be alive, how any minute you could be taken out by a sniper or blown to bits by a roadside bomb if it weren't for some lucky rabbit's foot or horseshoe you've been dragging along.

Superstition exists in all of us in the platoon. Rogers has a lucky pendant. He pulls it out during missions and kisses it, crosses himself, and places it back against his chest. In his helmet, Rainman has a picture of his wife, much like Lieutenant Cross carrying photographs of Martha in *The Things They Carried*. Trangsrud is full of superstition. He doesn't like the numbers 1, 4, and 2, or any combination of the three. He also does a number of odd chants and gestures for good luck. Most of the time we think he's making them up.

I carry a broken copper ring in my rucksack. I used to wear the ring, a good luck charm I'd worn since high school, on my left middle finger. The ring showed a snake wrapping itself around my finger and curling halfway up my first knuckle toward my nail. It was given to me by an ex-girlfriend in high school, before I realized I was gay. In the middle of January 2003 the ring snapped in half, partly because of old age, partly because of the cold winter. Two weeks later, I received the call deploying me to Iraq, and I can't help but think that the ring breaking caused the deployment.

I am superstitious because of my father. When I was in high school he nonchalantly told me about a curse on Lemer children who are named after their fathers. Any Lemer father who names his son after himself damns the child to die a painful death. Every time he tells the story he uses the same examples: a great-uncle who fell from a hay loft, and another Lemer son who was dragged by a horse. But the best example is my father's own brother.

My uncle J.R. isn't dead. When he was in his early twenties, he was involved in a car accident that left him paralyzed. My father never went into details. All he said was that J.R. was lucky the curse didn't kill him and then he would point to the place on Highway 52 south of Minot, North Dakota, where my uncle's car went off the road. When it came time to name me, my mother argued for naming me Nick Junior, but my father wildly protested. He brought up the curse and said he couldn't do that to his son. Instead, he named me after his favorite movie star, Charles Bronson. That is why, in the Lemer family, there are only daughters named after fathers—Toni Marie named after my uncle Tony, and my sister Nikki, named after my father.

Now, in Iraq, I carry Charles Bronson inside of me. He's my guardian angel, my watchdog, my memory of home. He's my good-luck charm, and he's never going to break.

On June 19, Lake leads a line of soldiers to the motor pool for our first fight. A boxing ring is marked off with green tape—a square laid out across the rocks. Four fuel cans serve as corner posts, and behind the cans are two chairs for the competitors. One of the sergeants in the company is already at the ring when we arrive. He has volunteered to referee and is noisily pacing inside the ring, rocks clinking together under his shoes.

Thursday Night Fights began as a necessity. We needed some way to burn off steam, to help relieve stress, and to take our minds off being away from home. During a FOO, Lake purchased boxing gloves and pads from a sporting goods store in Baghdad. He came back to BIAP with a bag full of gear—two sets of red and white boxing gloves, two slightly beat-up headgear, and mouth guards that we were afraid to use for fear of catching some desert disease. He came up with a plan for Thursday nights—boxing—and he started signing up names.

Lake has paired off everyone according to height and weight. It starts with the little guys—Fredricks and Rogers—and moves all the way up to the heavyweights—Lake and a soldier from Headquarters Company. Somehow I've gotten roped into boxing Tuna. I'm not much of a fighter. Unlike my brother Brandon, who, my father claims, received his temper from my mother's side of the family, I don't have the temperament for fighting. I am far too laid back for swinging and punching. I let everything just roll right off my back. But when provoked, when poked and prodded, I'll fight.

In junior high, my classmates egged me for weeks until I finally agreed to fight Nick Shear in the boys' locker room. I don't really remember why they wanted me to fight him, just that everybody else was telling me to do it, so I did. I put up my fists and punched him square in the nose. One punch and it was over. I remember lots of yelling and blood.

Lake steps into the middle of the ring and calls out the first pair. Around the ring, most of Bravo Company is camped out to see the fight. Some people stand near the ring. Others sit on the hoods of five-ton trucks, hooting and hollering. A couple of the women have cameras to document the experience. Fredricks and Rogers go off to their corners, escorted by a couple of soldiers. They lace up their gloves and squeeze their heads into the padded helmets.

The fights consist of three one-minute rounds, with a one-minute break in between rounds. Three judges decide a winner if there hasn't been a knockout or forfeit. Into the evening, we cheer on our fellow soldiers as they jump around the rocks, throwing punches and grunting. We get into watching each other fight. Smith, the tallest man in the company, takes a couple of punches to knock out one of the truck drivers. He uses his long arms to keep his opponent away, clocking him over and over until the truck driver falls to the rocks during the first round. Fly defeats King with a few good punches and general scrappiness, something that surprises most of the platoon.

When I get into the ring my heart is racing from the adrenaline of watching others box. They made it look so easy, but as Lake laces up my gloves and places the helmet over my head, I realize that I have no idea what I am doing. Others in the platoon had told me what to do—*Keep your arms up. Protect your face. Jab with your strong arm.*

The thing I like about Tuna is how laid back *he* is. In a lot of respects we are similar. We're both easygoing. We both like to act goofy, but we know when to shut our mouths. We're approximately the same height and weight. It makes for the perfect matchup. Yet watching him hop around the ring as he warms up for our fight, I see a different man. He's transformed into something else—something more fierce and angry than I've ever seen him. He has this really intense look on his face, and when the referee blows his whistle, he comes out swinging.

Part of me didn't want to fight back, but when someone is swinging for your head you swing back. You keep your left arm over your face and swing with your right. You dart around the ring, jumping and moving so your opponent can't pin you down to one place. You think about his next move, how you'll counter it with your own. You imagine everything you've ever been angry about and let it build up inside you until it must be released, until the power surges through your chest and down your arms. You curl your fingers forward, digging into your gloves, and let that anger come out through a left jab to the face, a good sucker punch in the throat. You fight.

I don't mean to fight dirty, but I do. In the last ten seconds of the match, I start swinging randomly. In the end, I throw one too many punches to the back of Tuna's head, costing me a point and the match. When you have that much adrenaline pulsing through your veins, you just fight and worry about the consequences later. That seems to be my motto for the entire deployment: fight now, worry later.

Before the match, I told Tuna that I was going to give him a nice uppercut that would send him on his ass. After the match, while we are talking about how exhausting it was, how hard it was to fight on rocks, Tuna says, "I was waiting for your uppercut, but it never happened."

"Yeah," I say. "I was saving it for the third round, but I got too tired."

Walking back to the terminal to take a shower, I am still buzzing from the fight. I'm not an athletic guy. In my family, I leave the athletics to my three brothers. They're the ones who are always rolling around the floor wrestling or trying to start a game of touch football at family gatherings. But something about that fight got me going. Something has been awakened inside of me—an animal I never knew existed. It stands furiously growling, drenched in sweat but ready for a fight.

There is something extremely sexy about women in dresses," Rogers says.

He has a pair of binoculars and is looking out at the women who pass by the military checkpoint. We are on another Task Force Neighborhood mission, this time to a school next to one of the army's checkpoints through-out Baghdad. Rogers and I have been watching people all morning.

"I don't know what it is, but man, they look good walking around in those black dresses," Rogers says. "Don't you think?"

No. They look like the ghosts from Ms. Pacman, I want to say. I used to be pretty good at talking about women with straight men. I often returned volley during drill weekends, when the guys commented about one of the female soldiers or talked about sex with their girlfriends. But I no longer feel the need to discuss women with them. I'm tired of lying. Instead, I simply nod at Rogers and look away.

Rogers shifts his weight to his right foot, adjusts his weapon. He's one of the smaller guys in the platoon—five feet four and stocky. This is the first time I've been on a mission with him, so I'm quickly learning his proclivity for watching women.

"You know why they wear black, don't you?" he asks.

"I think so."

I had no idea. I'd seen these women walking around the streets of Baghdad, shrouded from head to toe in black cloth. The cloth covers everything except their hands and faces. The garments go all the way to the dusty ground, making them appear to have no feet, like wandering souls. On windy days the black shroud billows behind them in the wind.

"They are called *abayas*," Rogers says. "I asked an interpreter why they wore them, and he said that married women will wear them to show their devotion to their husbands."

Rogers lowers the binoculars and wipes a bead of sweat from his forehead. It's the end of June, the temperature easily in the triple digits.

"Some kid tried to tell me it was because they were mourning Saddam," he continues. "That kid was full of shit."

I watch Rogers follow three younger women with his binoculars. We are standing before a field full of garbage and debris, between the school, where the rest of the platoon is working, and an army checkpoint. The women are walking on a trail about fifty yards away. They don't even notice Rogers watching them. When the women disappear behind a house, Rogers takes to watching cars.

"It's funny. Once they see me watching they speed up and get out of the area."

He laughs and turns slightly to catch another car off at the edge of the field.

"Yeah, that's right. I'm watching you."

Many of the Task Force Neighborhood missions begin this way. I watch the people around me, taking in my environment and the people who populate it. I spend hours soaking up the locale. I make note of what everything looks like, who is peering in at the edges of the scene, where I can take cover, and the quickest way out of the neighborhood in case we need to make a rapid exit. I do this partly out of training; this is my job and the military has trained me to be this observant. But I also do this because I don't want to be caught off guard. I'm still waiting for that third strike—the curse—to take me out, so I'm always on guard, always on my toes.

In the afternoon, after eating MREs in the courtyard of the school, Rogers and I move over to the other edge of the perimeter, near a neighborhood street. The street is relatively quiet, but slowly people appear. We get the usual kids running and shaking our hands, asking for food and money. Across the street, a couple of women stand in their doorways and watch Rogers and me, much in the same way we watched them this morning. An hour into the afternoon shift, an Iraqi man in his early twenties—the same age as we are—walks over to where we are standing. He starts to speak to Rogers in English. Rogers looks over at me in amazement. We've been doing Task Force Neighborhood missions for several months now, and this man has the best English of anyone we've met. He introduces himself and tells us that he is a student at Baghdad University.

"What are you studying?" I ask.

"Poetry, drama, novel, composition," he says, listing the subjects off on his fingers.

I smile and realize that I've just found my Iraqi counterpart.

I tell him that I study English back home, and we get into a conversation about literature and writing. I start to talk to him like I would a classmate back in college. We discuss Shakespeare (he tells me about his fondness for Shakespeare, but that he really likes Christopher Marlow). I tell him about the British and American authors I'd read during survey classes in college. He mentions Jane Austen. He takes a few minutes as he tries to remember the title of one of her books. I ask if it's *Sense and Sensibility*, and he gets excited at hearing the title, knowing that he's made a connection with an American soldier about something other than war, Iraq, or Saddam.

And for once, I actually forget I'm talking to someone from Iraq. I relish the fact that I can finally talk with someone about literature. The more I talk with him the more I start to believe that we are the same person—he and I. We both enjoy literature and writing. We both talk passionately about poetry and drama. But as we talk, I wonder what else this man thinks about. He's a young man stuck in a struggling country torn apart by warfare. Does he think about fighting for his country, about protecting his family and his way of life? He has to think about more than just Christopher Marlow and Jane Austen. I wonder if he ever thinks about fighting, like I do. I wonder if he fears being killed walking home from college and if that fear motivates him to take up arms. I wonder if, like me, he thinks about luck and fate and destiny, and how he will survive another day in Iraq.

Eventually, the man says goodbye and walks off down the street. I am standing along the edge of the school, watching the children wander away toward home and wondering what it would be like to grow up in this country. That's when I hear the gunfire. It is close; I hear it echoing off the buildings. I stand frozen beside the school. Rogers and a few other soldiers are also still, waiting to hear more, wondering if it is enemy or friendly fire. We stand like that for a moment, until a Hummer with three military police goes barreling off across the field, in the direction of the gunfire. We watch the Hummer vanish between two houses, and we wait in anticipation of more gunfire, but nothing follows.

Hearing that gunfire, there was something inside of me that wanted to run toward the sound. I wanted to take off in the direction I'd heard the shots, my rifle in both hands, yelling at the top of my lungs, until I found the finger that pulled that trigger, until I found the person who fired those shots. It is the same warrior who'd been awakened by the boxing. He wants out. He wants to fight, but I won't let him.

Instead, I ask Rogers for his binoculars, raise them to my eyes, and look off in the direction from which I'd heard the gunfire, hoping that maybe seeing a few Iraqi gunmen will quench my desire to fight.

When we were in Kuwait we tried to catch scorpions.

The plan we came up with was nothing more than a half-dozen soldiers running across the desert chasing after what looked like moving sand. King, Cole, and Lake spent whole afternoons out scouting for scorpions and other sand creatures. In the mornings, Cole would tip his boot upside down and say, "Come out scorpions that have crawled up into my boot during the night. Come out." During the hot afternoons, while the rest of the platoon watched from the shade, the three guys sneaked around the motor pool like spies, peering around Conex boxes and under trailers, anywhere cool and dry, hoping scorpions would come scurrying out.

In the end all they caught were two desert lizards.

They built a cage from scrap pieces of wood and played with the lizards for days. The lizards had huge stomachs that stuck out like disks from their abdomens. They both had razor-edged tails that they'd swing at us when we peered into their cage. We'd stand around and watch King and Lake provoke the lizards, poking at them, moving them to opposite corners in an attempt to get them to fight. The lizards looked back angrily at the men, as if they were confused at why they were being encouraged to fight.

We wanted a good fight. It was ironic really, given that we were a week away from heading into our own fight with the Iraqi people. But it was all the anxiety we'd been building up, waiting in the desert. After a couple of weeks we couldn't wait any longer, and when Lake saw that the lizards weren't going to fight, he released the creatures back into the desert and began to think of another plan.

One of Charlie Company's soldiers had caught a tiny scorpion, and, after some persuading, Lake convinced the soldier to stage a death match between the scorpion and a mouse. We placed the two animals inside the empty lizard cage and stood around waiting for a fight. At first the animals did nothing; they were too petrified by a few dozen soldiers peering down at them. But eventually, as if it realized that we needed a fight, the scorpion made the first move.

The scorpion swung its tail up over its body, piercing the mouse in the neck. The mouse hardly seemed fazed by the move. The scorpion backed away and waited for the mouse to approach. When the mouse came near, the scorpion attacked again, but this time the mouse bit into the scorpion's tail, snapping it clean off the body. We all gasped in amazement.

In the end, the mouse left the scorpion tailless and legless. It had managed to outdo the scorpion on its home turf. It was something we admired as we waited in the Kuwaiti desert, ready to advance north, into an unknown country full of scorpions. There was something about that mouse exceeding our expectations that stuck with us as we made our way into Iraq.

Soldiers are stuffing a building full of explosives. The building, the only one left inside the southern corner of Abu Ghraib prison, is scheduled to be demolished. It needs to be removed to make way for a tent city for Iraqi prisons. It is hot, the middle of July, and I am trying not to think about Iraq. But my mind keeps drifting back to the prison we're currently working at. The prison itself is huge—the size of a small city. Before we invaded Iraq, the facility was Saddam Hussein's most notorious jail. I had read about it in the magazines sent from home, how it was dreaded for its torture chambers and mass executions. But after we invaded Iraq, the prison was abandoned by the Iraqi government. We arrived to a deserted facility, full of trash and garbage, and were asked to turn it back into a jail.

We're on the outermost ring of Abu Ghraib, right inside the wall that runs around the entire prison. Captain Roar is standing against his

Hummer, talking with Paul Bremer, director of reconstruction and humanitarian assistance for postwar Iraq. Captain Roar is explaining the plans for the site, how Bravo Company will first clear the site of all debris, then demolish buildings, and finally build containment sites for the new Iraqi prisoners. From the way Captain Roar explains the project and the way Bremer leans toward Captain Roar to hear, I can tell the U.S. military has big plans for this place.

After Bremer leaves, I walk back to the Hummer where the LT, Lake, and Rogers have been waiting. They are talking about death.

"Do you guys know what Saddam's favorite method of torture was?" the LT asks, looking around the Hummer.

I slide into the empty seat and unhook the chin strap of my Kevlar helmet.

"He liked to bury someone in the sand up to their head and leave them there to die," the LT says as he stares out the front windshield of the Hummer.

A few days earlier, on my first trip out to Abu Ghraib, I followed Newman and Elijah to one of Saddam's torture chambers. We took our cameras and shot pictures of the insides of a cement room that looked like a locker room shower. I stood along the wall and imagined all the people who could have been tortured in the room, and I actually felt something standing in that torture cell. I felt bad for all the people who suffered at the hands of Saddam: the ones who were tortured and killed, the family members who never saw brothers or uncles again, the children who grew up fatherless. I felt something because I was actually a part of this event; I wasn't at home watching the whole thing unfold on television. I felt proud being a part of the military force that ended Saddam's reign of terror.

"That would be a horrible way to die," Lake says. "Slow and painful. Almost like getting burned at the stake. I think if I had the choice I'd want to drown to death. Quick and painless."

"I want to die peacefully in my sleep," the LT says.

"I think we all hope for that," I say, laughing.

We all chuckle and laugh at how naïve the LT can be. The man has no edges; he's like a grown Ken doll in GI camouflage.

"Not I," Rogers says. "I want to be eighty-five and I want to go skydiving without a parachute. As I'm floating to my death, I'm going to have this huge smile on my face as I see the earth for the last time."

Something about Rogers's death scenario sounds comforting. Maybe it's the image of an old man floating to his death. Maybe it's the idea of going out of this world with a bang. I like the thought of leaving this world knowing I've accomplished something.

Around five o'clock, Lake, Rogers, and I take the Hummer and drive around Abu Ghraib. We don't get very far. Next to the area we've been working in is a large grassy field full of debris and trash. As we're driving across the field we notice a pack of five rough-looking dogs running around the debris. Lake stops the vehicle. We stand before the Hummer, watching the dogs. The dogs are scrounging around for scraps, digging their noses into the car parts and tires littering the field. A black dog looks up in our direction. I see its dark eyes look right at me before it darts off between the shell of a vehicle and a pile of rubbish, leading the other dogs across the field.

I turn away. Lake is standing off to the left with his weapon raised. He is aiming at the dogs.

"Let's take them out," he says softly, a quiet intensity in his voice as he follows the animals with his rifle.

You give a young man a rifle, and he's going to want to fire it. You spend months teaching the young man how to disassemble and reassemble the rifle. You teach him how to fire at pop-up targets, how to aim through the weapon's sights, how to clean the dirt away from the firing piston. You give him ammunition, tell him to always carry the weapon, but demand that he fire that weapon only when instructed or threatened. You send that man into Baghdad, make him watch people swarm his convoy, and force him to hear the gunfire ricocheting around the city. The young man *always* wants to fire his weapon. His desire is the power the weapon brings, how one shot from the instrument can instantly justify his presence in war.

I look over at Lake and can tell he's eager to kill the dogs. I see it in his eyes every time we leave post; I see it in all our eyes. It's the Charles Bronson inside us all. We all want to shoot at something in Iraq, just to get the satisfaction of killing another living thing. I've been waiting for that moment to release my inner Charles Bronson; watching Lake aim at the dogs, I think that maybe this will be as good as it gets. But Lake lowers his weapon and walks back toward the Hummer.

"It's just not worth it," he says.

An hour later, as we're getting ready to leave the prison, I hear gunshots coming from that field. I turn around to see three soldiers running after the dogs, their weapons aimed, firing shots. The dogs blend right into the sand and grass as they zip across the field. I imagine the soldiers are bored with waiting around the base. Maybe they're tired of waiting for the animals to kill themselves by running in front of our vehicles or slowly starving to death. Maybe, like Charles Bronson's character in *Death Wish*, they're simply tired of nobody doing anything about the dirty animals, so they decide to take matters into their own hands.

I watch the dogs scatter and feel a little sympathy for the animals. They have nowhere else to go. They were born, and will die, in this shitty country. They can't help the circumstances they are in. But another part of me knows what it's like to be stuck in the middle of a war with nothing to do. I know what's it's like to want to fight.

It is this part of me that scares me the most.

The men are in a jovial mood. They are standing on the runway outside our barracks at BIAP, sweating in the heat, the temperature threatening to rise to 130 degrees Fahrenheit. They've stripped off their camouflaged tops and are walking around in mud-brown T-shirts, their biceps stretching against the fabric as they hammer nails into wooden walls. They are building guard towers for the prison, and they are singing.

It starts with REM's "Losing My Religion." They struggle with the first verse, but when the chorus hits, every man is singing along. They fumble over a few lines and laugh when they forget the words, but when they return to the chorus, everyone chimes in. There is no talking—only the sound of hammering accompanied by the off-key bellowing of an REM song on an airport runway in Iraq.

Later, the men move on to Starship's "We Built This City," except instead of *city* they insert the word *prison*. I step back and watch the men hammer and sing. They don't know any of the words besides the ones in the title; therefore they're stuck repeating the same line over and over. They sound like a broken record looping the same tired line.

We've spent the better part of July working on the prison. In the corner of Abu Ghraib, we managed to set up eight containment pads, each with a five-stall shower unit. We've spent weeks building the shower units at BIAP, and another week installing the structures at the prison. Now we've moved on to the guard towers. At the end of the month, the days slow to a crawl. Each day seems stretched out by the heat. When the heat is bearable we continue to build projects for the prison. When the heat is just too much for us to work in, we sit around the terminal making ourselves miserable by thinking about home and annoying one another. We watch pirated movies we picked up in Baghdad. We read the books that have been floating around the company. Leaf, Cole, and King take their frustration out in the homemade gym at the bottom of the stairs. On Thursday nights we head to the motor pool for another night of boxing, and this helps with the stress, but we slowly grow tired of beating up on one another. Eventually, our favorite pastime becomes gossiping. We like sitting around spreading rumors about when we think we'll go home. The military has yet to issue us re-deployment papers or tell us we're in Iraq for the long haul. Once a week Captain Roar gathers the company together and squelches any rumors and dispenses new information on when we'll be going home. One week it's: *Worst case scenario—we'll be home for Thanksgiving.* The next week: *I'll have you home for Christmas.*

On July 23, when the first North Dakotan is killed in Iraq, nobody seems surprised. Newman tells us during a squad meeting. A member of 957 Multi-Role Bridge Company, another North Dakota National Guard unit in Iraq, was killed by a rocket-propelled grenade near Ar Ramadi. We don't mean any disrespect, but we've gotten used to hearing about soldiers being killed across the country.

"The other soldier in the truck was a twenty-year-old from Bismarck," Newman says. "He lost his arm below the elbow."

I hold my right forearm with my left hand and look down at my boots. I don't like hearing about anyone losing any part of himself. While waiting in Kuwait, I read John Irving's "The Fourth Hand," a story about a television reporter who loses his left hand to a lion in India. The actual scene of the lion taking the hand made me cringe. But more than anything, I was struck by the emotional impact of losing a part of yourself in a country where you didn't belong. It makes me uneasy stepping across Iraq. I'm always afraid I'll step on something—a buried bomb, some homemade device—and lose my leg to the sand. I'd hate to leave anything behind here.

Inside me, I feel Charles Bronson coming to a boil. If he were in Iraq, he'd take revenge for the North Dakota soldier's death. He'd be a Marine and storm Baghdad homes and knock down doors. He'd question civilians, take down names, ransack back rooms. He wouldn't take shit from anybody, especially not in Iraq. And every time another soldier is killed in Iraq, he wouldn't think that he might be next, like I do.

"The kid will probably return to North Dakota a war hero," Newman continues.

War hero. It's a difficult title to swallow. Does being in the wrong place at the wrong time make you a war hero? I feel for the injured soldier, but as I look around at the other men in my squad, I wonder if any of us could be called heroes.

A month earlier, on our last Task Force Neighborhood mission, the curse almost got me.

Fly, Jones, Newman, and I got lost in Baghdad. We needed to go back to the school where the rest of the company was waiting. Instead of driving a couple of blocks and finding the school, we found ourselves alone in Baghdad, lost, in the worst possible scenario. In my head, I could see insurgents rushing our vehicle. I could see them using women and children to lure us into a false sense of comfort before they'd launch a round of missiles our way. Fly would become agitated and afraid and steer the vehicle off the road. They'd rush our truck and drag us from the Hummer, much like we'd seen the Somalis do to helicopter pilots in *Black Hawk Down*. It was the kind of thing we'd read about in magazine articles about the war; it was the kind of thing that happened to Jessica Lynch.

As we drove down the road, every Iraqi standing in the street seemed to be watching us. They saw every worry line on Newman's face. They saw every single one of our heads darting around the truck, trying to figure out where we were going. They knew we were lost. We were sitting ducks inside an army Hummer. Our luck had finally run out.

Jones had his M16 pointed out the window, his face a blank slate of stone. Fly was full of nervous energy. He kept asking Newman which direction to turn, where to go. I closed my eyes and listened to Newman trying to contact our company over the radio, and I waited for it all to be over, for everything to fade to white. But nothing happened, and that was when it hit me.

I knew I had failed my platoon as a carpenter. I was no good at that profession, and I'd long ago become bitter with my decision to join the military. But I *was* good at something, and back home my friends had always been amazed by my sense of direction. Whenever we left BIAP and traveled into the city, I peered outside the truck and tried to make note of my surroundings. There was a mosque. Over there—a picture of Saddam. Across that field—a school, a ministry building, an open market, a group of children playing with a furry dog. I was good at directions, and when we got lost I knew I had to step in.

"Turn left here," I said. "I remember this block when we were coming in. The school is the other way."

The Charles Bronson inside of me wanted to do more than just give directions. He wanted the bad guys to attack our truck. He wished for the opportunity to fend them off with his machine gun and anger. He wanted to be the hero and save the other men. He wanted to wander the streets of

Baghdad and gun down anyone who threatened our presence in this country. He wanted to wear the long trench coat, carry the pistol, shoot men in their guts, and shrug it off as his God-given right. He wanted to shoot all the stray dogs in the city. He wanted action, blood-spewing, high-adrenaline, bullet-pumping situations where he could get mean and dirty, times when he could feel justified for having to carry, but never being able to fire, a rifle in Iraq. And he wanted to roar and howl about the injustices *within* the American forces, things like incompetent lieutenants, sexual harassment, and policies like "don't ask, don't tell" that weaken the armed forces. He wanted to cause a lot of trouble, but I wouldn't let him because there were other things to worry about now—keeping cool, doing our jobs, staying alive.

Instead, I gave directions to Fly, instructing him to turn at the corner by the mosque, to follow the highway to the statue, and turn left down the road to the school. I'd been waiting for my true war experience, the time when I'd have to prove myself in Iraq, and getting lost in Baghdad was the closest I came. I knew the curse was waiting out there, and I wasn't going to let it take me down.

The prison mission is complete and prisoners have finally arrived. On August 1, we pull into Abu Ghraib and notice a handful of men wandering around one of the containment pads near the road. Each pad is surrounded by concertina wire. Inside, men in dirty robes crouch in the sand. There's a tent and a shower unit, and above them a guard tower. A few soldiers stand in each guard tower, watching the dirty prisoners.

Rogers parks the Hummer at the edge of the compound. I get out of the vehicle and walk over to one of the pads. I'd never really seen prisoners before. Even though the men before me are the least dangerous criminals in Iraq, I want to see what we are up against in this country.

The prison guards have let an Iraqi child onto the compound to sell Coke. He stands near the edge of the compound, watching us watching the prisoners. I walk up to the boy and buy a Coke. I look out over the compound. There are three guards near the front gate. In each tower are more guards. Across the field, the LT is talking with Captain Roar. They boastfully peer out at the completed compound. They look so proud standing before the prisoners; watching them, I realize how much power we hold in this country. We've been stepping across this country for three months now, forcing our way into homes, rounding up Iraqis who are up to no good. We're doing what Charles Bronson's character did in *Death*

Wish except we're not killing these people. Instead, we're keeping them alive so they can watch us turn this country around.

I stand before the prisoners, almost teasing them by sipping from my Coke. Some of the men are looking at me. The gentle breeze makes their robes billow out a bit. All summer I'd wanted a fight—we all did. We wanted a real part of this war, where each and every one of us let our inner Charles Bronsons out to roam. I think every man who goes to war wants to feel justified that his time there isn't wasted. Most of the time that justification came in the form of fighting, of firing your weapon, and fending off the enemy. What I've realized is that I don't need to see that kind of fighting in Iraq. I don't need to fire my weapon to feel like I've done some good over here. I know I've made a difference—completing projects during Task Force Neighborhood missions, seeing the people who waved and shook our hands, watching these prisoners wander around the containment pads I helped create, and giving direction to my lost squad members. And even though I wouldn't let the Charles Bronson inside of me speak out about the unfair and unjust "don't ask, don't tell" policy, I tell myself that when I return I will let him out to roam and howl, and I'll do my part to eliminate that policy. That will be my contribution to improving the military, and being part of this war makes me realize that I must do something.

I don't need to kill something to feel like a real soldier.

On September 1, I'm standing in battalion headquarters at Anaconda Army Airbase, watching CNN, when I hear that Charles Bronson has died. I see his name scroll across the banner at the bottom of the screen and gasp. I'd spent a long, hot summer in Baghdad, repairing schools, adding onto hospitals, and improving the neighborhoods of the city. Now we had traveled back to Anaconda Army Airbase, where most of us expected that we'd remain for the rest of our deployment, away from the suicide bombers and Iraqi snipers who roamed Iraq. We'd probably see the Iraqi people only when we did guard duty in the perimeter towers or wave at them on our way home. But still I didn't feel safe at Anaconda, and now I no longer had my lucky charm, my personal Charles Bronson, to protect me in Iraq.

How to Build Your Own Coffin

We know very little about the dead mechanic. He didn't sleep in our tent or share in our nightly bouts of laughter when Cole and King reverted back to teenagers. We don't know his name, his hometown, if he had a wife, kids, or pets. We don't know why he joined the army, if he liked being a mechanic, or if he woke every morning hopeful and excited (like we are) about being another day closer to going home.

We know very little about *any* of the men and women being killed in Iraq. Yet we all share an understanding for what it feels like to walk around this country with targets on our backs. We've all perfected the act of tiptoeing lightly around death.

We receive the *Stars and Stripes* in the late afternoons, with the mail, and each evening we page through to find the news about Iraq: how many soldiers were killed in the latest attack, how the hunt for Saddam is progressing, and what Bush is saying about the war. We read about other dead soldiers, people killed while patrolling Baghdad or charred beyond recognition when their helicopter is shot down over the country. But the dead mechanic wasn't killed in battle like the men and women in the newspaper. He didn't step on a roadside bomb or catch a wild bullet in the streets of Baghdad. He was killed when a tire rim struck him unconscious while working on a five-ton truck at Anaconda Army Airbase. It was all just an accident.

"Shit," someone says after Newman explains the incident. We are in Newman's tent, all eight men in our squad, listening to Newman list off news and information passed down from the battalion.

Newman looks up from his notes. "A couple of carpenters in Alpha Company had to build a temporary coffin for the guy," he says.

I sit on a canvas cot between Jones and Roach, staring at my boots. I am afraid to look up at the other guys in my squad, eight men each silently thinking about death. We had all thought about death during the deployment: upon seeing charred tanks while riding into Iraq, during Task Force Neighborhood missions when we could have been picked off by insurgents, or when we got lost in Baghdad and felt alone in the violent city. But somehow we felt safe here at Anaconda Army Airbase, separated from the Iraqis and roadside bombs, and it was devastating to hear that Death was no longer just in the streets of Baghdad, patrolling the Sunni Triangle, or waiting along the roads. He had taken a break to come here, to the motorpool lot of our section of this base, where he stood squarely in the sand.

Newman continues with the squad meeting but I can't hear what he is saying. Instead, I think about what it would be like to build a coffin for a man I don't know. The army doesn't exactly teach coffin-building when training carpenters, and I'm thankful for that. I am also thankful that I'm not one of the carpenters who had to build the dead mechanic's box. I don't want the responsibility of making sure the side walls are long enough and the base wide enough to hold the body. I'm such a horrible carpenter, I'm afraid I'd screw it up. The haunting thought of someone lying in a wooden box—built not of pine or oak or cedar but of plywood, by third-rate, part-time carpenters, as it travels across the Atlantic to a crying mother back home—makes me uneasy. It's a military carpenter's worst nightmare.

Roach slaps my leg as he rises from the cot and exits the tent. I get up and follow my squad out the door.

A fucking tire rim, I think as I exit Newman's tent. *I'd hate to go like that.*

I try to imagine how it happened and what was running through the mechanic's mind before he was killed. Maybe he was thinking about summer back in Missouri or Louisiana or Minnesota, any place where it doesn't climb into the triple digits and stay there all summer long. Maybe he was thinking about coolers full of beer, the sound a baseball bat makes when connecting with a ball, or the smell of his mother's pot roast or red-apple pie. Maybe he was thinking about what his wife looked like naked or the way his baby boy crawled across the carpet. He may have been simply thinking about doing his job—changing a tire—and the next thing he knew he was dead. I try to speculate about what went wrong, but the more I think about the dead mechanic, the more difficult it becomes to face the fact that I could die over here.

It is early evening and the sun is getting ready to set behind the basketball court we built on the western edge of camp. One of the squad leaders is asleep in a lawn chair between the tents. He looks old. His entire face sags with his bushy mustache. Cole and Lake are dressed in their PTs, leading a team of soldiers to the empty field beyond the basketball court for a game of soccer. I listen to the rocks shift and slide under their tennis shoes as the teams pass. I walk slowly to my tent and barely miss Rogers, who comes running out the door.

"We don't allow fags inside our tent," King says as he chases Rogers away. He shakes his fist, laughs, and ducks back inside the tent.

I want to say, *Well, you already have one living in the tent*, but I can't. I don't want to ruin what I have going with these men.

I am surprised how jovial the mood is around camp. The rest of the platoon is playing soccer and making jokes, but I can't seem to shake the dead mechanic. It may be because I don't like Death in our backyard. I don't like the way he plays with our fears or how he makes me always think twice about trusting Iraqis or tire rims. Or, it may be that I've finally realized the importance of my job and fear the day I have to build a coffin for one of the men in my squad.

I hear Cole, Lake, and their teams playing soccer. They sound like children, happy as they kick a ball around the sand. I stop, just for a minute, to listen to the joyful sound of people having fun, and I try to remember what that was like.

I am living with a bunch of teenagers.

I don't know if it is the stress of being away from home or the fact that we are eight men living in a tent no bigger than a meat locker, but the men in tent 17 have quickly reverted back to being adolescents. Add a case of beer and this could be high school all over again.

We've moved from BIAP to Anaconda Army Airbase. It is the last week in August, before the mechanic is killed by a tire rim, and the heat is still unbearable. Inside our new air-conditioned tent, we unpack and settle in. Rogers, Lake, and Cole are talking about the size of their dicks. It all started when Rogers returned from an Alpha Company tent where three men were living with four women in the same tent.

"The women would just come walking in and undress right in front of us," Rogers says. He is giddy like a little boy. "I just stood there and stared."

Rogers looks around the tent to see who is listening. Cole and King are laughing. Jones looks up from his magazine and smiles. Bobby is silent in the corner. Lake stands near the door, unfolding a rug he bought from an

Iraqi salesman in Baghdad. He lays the rug in front of the door as a welcome mat to our tent.

"They would all do it, the men too. I guess this one guy has a huge cock," Rogers continues. "He didn't show it to me, but I guess it's a big joke with everyone there."

Cole is unpacking his gear. He laughs and looks over at Rogers. "Was he good-looking too?"

"Well yeah," Roger says without hesitation. "He wasn't ugly."

"Damn," Cole says. "It's unfair. You shouldn't get to be good-looking *and* have a huge cock."

I watch it all unfold from the sidelines, laughing right along with Cole and Rogers. Mostly, I laugh because I don't hear conversations like this at bars back home—where men don't jockey for position among other men by discussing the size of their dicks. Back home, I don't spend much time around men. Most of my close friends are women, and the few male friends I have (usually through school or work) rarely talk about things like that. But in Iraq, after months away from home, I laugh because I miss this kind of companionship, the kind I had with my oldest brother when we were growing up. I like being around these men because they remind me of a time when I was young and could simply *pretend* to play war.

We've been living together for almost seven months, and the barriers of unacceptable conversation have crumbled to the ground. Now we talk about anything—women, sex, how many times we've masturbated in the wooden outhouses. When you live and work this close with men, everything is fair game. At night you can reach out and touch the man sleeping next to you. You can slap your neighbor's arm in order to stop his snoring or wake him for his shift on guard duty—it all depends on how hard you hit that arm.

As evening approaches, the tent settles into silence. Jones is wearing his headphones and lying on his cot, staring at the ceiling. Lake is meticulously placing his gear under his cot. King hasn't unpacked. His bags lie open on the dusty plywood floor while he spreads out on his cot reading a magazine.

Then, without warning, Cole starts lighting his farts on fire. He lies on his cot, his legs curled up like a dead beetle, his thick thumb clicking away at a lighter. King puts down his magazine and bursts into laughter. He reaches across the aisle to Cole's cot.

"Here," he says. "Let me try."

They take turns with the lighter. We all stop what we're doing and watch the spectacle before us. They pass the lighter between the cots each time they feel another one coming. After five minutes, the tent smells so bad we have to prop open both doors, letting the cool evening air clear the stench. The smell, and our laughter, drifts out into the silent desert night.

"Damn, you guys," Fly says, walking into the tent. "It's like a fucking gas chamber in here."

We all laugh. It *is* a gas chamber. We joke about being killed by the smell. If Cole and King continue, I will die in this tent, gassed out by my own platoon, and it will give a whole new meaning to the term "friendly fire."

Fly likes the name so much that he creates a sign out of a piece of cardboard and hangs it outside above our door. It reads in bold, block letters: THE GAS CHAMBER. For once during this deployment, I feel part of something special, some small, shared experience, even if it is as insignificant as a tent full of gassy men. I am a resident of the Gas Chamber and it feels good.

The Gas Chamber is alive with the sound of funk music.

Rogers is playing a funk CD from his boom box and dancing down the middle aisle of the tent. He shakes his hips to the music, jives down low to the dusty, wood floor, and springs back up, rising with the beat of the song. He swings around the two poles that prop up our tent and for a minute we all mistake him for a stripper as he curls his legs around the pole and slides up and down, his small body easily moving around the poles. The entire time he has this intense look on his face, a look that tells us that he's into every note and every dance move.

"She's a brick . . . houuuuuuuuuuse!" King sings as he stands on his cot, his lips puckered in a howl as the lyrics escape his mouth. He's jiving and dancing as well. The dancing is contagious and soon the entire tent is into the music. Even Bobby, who's been silent most of the week, smiles as he watches the rest of us. I even think I see his foot tap a couple of times.

I don't hold back. I sway and jive and laugh with the men like this is natural, like dancing to funk music in Iraq is something we do every Friday night. Hearing the music, seeing everyone lose their inhibitions in the song, I almost forget we're in Iraq. This could be any group of men letting loose after a long week. But then I remember that men in America don't do this. They talk about sports and trucks and women's bodies. They chew tobacco and spit out the side of their mouths. But men I know don't do this. They don't dance around poles like strippers and lose themselves in music. There is something about our situation—bored in Iraq—that creates a whole new breed of men, and I laugh at how absurd and free it feels to dance, how good it feels to let go.

Later, I sit on the porch outside the Gas Chamber, smoking a cigar with Roach and Fly. We are talking about Lake, who recently punched another member of Bravo Company, knocking the soldier to the ground with his heavy fist. Captain Roar heard about the incident, and now Lake is getting demoted from specialist down to private first class.

"You know," Roach says, taking a puff of his cigar, "Headquarters Company is planning boxing matches for Labor Day this weekend. Do you think they'll let him fight?"

I hate the taste of stale cigars. I normally turn down an invitation to smoke, but something about being among these men, being part of this group living in the Gas Chamber, is enticing. There is something about their worry-free attitudes that makes me want to be one of the boys. Plus, I look cool when I'm smoking, so I take a puff of my cigar and look over at Roach.

"No way," I say. "Not after that stunt."

He nods, puffs at his cigar, and sits back. Smoke floats around the porch. We're sitting on canvas lawn chairs, relaxing after the funk music routine.

"Maybe they should match up Lake and Washington," Fly says. "You know, round two."

We laugh. I don't like the Lake who knocks people to the ground. He walks around camp with an attitude, a sort of cocky swagger about his gait, but inside our tent, on nights when we're acting like children, I see a different side of Lake, a side he doesn't show everyone. He has this big smile spread across his face as he laughs along with us and makes comments about us setting ourselves on fire. When he's one of the gang, Lake is jovial, light-hearted, fun; alone, when he lets the army get him down, he's angry and mean. He's our own Jekyll and Hyde.

A few nights later, for instance, I am watching a movie in the MWR (Morale, Welfare and Recreation) room (one of the rooms inside the sole building we've built our camp around) with a dozen other soldiers when I hear my first mortar attack. *THUWNK, THUWNK.* The low thuds send a dull vibration through the room. I listen to the rounds being released, the second right after the first, and am reminded of junior high, of the low and hollow noise of spitballs being shot out of a straw. I am taken back to study hall, where I hear the sound and am instantly alert, waiting for the wad of wet paper to hit the back of my head.

But now, in Iraq, the sound isn't as innocent, and this isn't junior high anymore.

"Was that a mortar attack?" someone asks. We sit listening for a moment. Earlier in the week, we'd been told to take cover during mortar attacks, and if we had to go outside we were supposed to take along our flak jacket and Kevlar helmet, just in case a round fell on us. The attacks came once a week, and Headquarters Company believed the rounds were being shot from somewhere just beyond the perimeter, possibly from the small village just outside the base.

But now we sit and listen, waiting for more rounds—more spitballs—or the horrifying screaming of wounded soldiers. This is the part I hate—the anticipation. I hate waiting for the next attack, knowing that I can't do anything but sit, listen, and wait. *THUWNK*. We hear a third round. I perk up my ears and try to hear if the rounds have landed anywhere, if there are casualties or screaming troops. I hear nothing. After a couple of minutes, someone in the back of the room asks another soldier to rewind the film, and the room returns to normal.

I sneak out the door, down the hallway, and push open the outside door. Most of the people in the battalion, the ones who've been at Anaconda the entire deployment, are used to these mortar attacks, but I am not. I want to witness their destruction myself.

I stand at the entrance of the building and look out over the collection of tents. From here, everything seems OK. There are no flaming soldiers frantically racing about, no tents with a mortar round sticking out the top. Everything seems fine, just how I left it before the movie. As I'm walking back to the Gas Chamber, I notice a few Charlie Company soldiers walking around wearing flak jackets and Kevlar helmets. Seeing them, I think about picking up the pace, running back to my tent because I am caught out in the open, fully vulnerable to another mortar attack, like a child in the middle of a rainstorm. I hear the dull *THUWNK* of another round being released, and I start to jog.

Outside the Gas Chamber, Lake is standing in his PT uniform—no flak jacket, no helmet—videotaping other members of the company who've come outside to listen to the attack. As people walk by he points the camera at them and asks, "How was your first mortar attack? Were you scared? What's going through your mind?" A huge, toothy smile spreads across his face as he stares into the tiny video camera screen and comments on the hilarity of his documentation. There isn't a worry on his face, and I watch as he moves the camera over to another soldier, chuckling to himself while he conducts another round of interviews. I like Lake this way— mocking and sarcastic—when not even the possibility of a mortar round slicing our tent in two could take away the humor of men at war.

It is still hot in the middle of September, so we stay inside on the afternoons we don't have to work. Cole and Lake are tossing a football back and forth, occasionally commenting about how tight their spirals are and laughing when the ball goes askew and hits Cole's fan or bounces off the hanging lightbulb. King sits in the crossfire of their game, reading a magazine and laughing whenever the ball grazes his head. The mood in the tent is jovial. I am reminded of the feeling I used to get when I was child trapped inside during a North Dakota snowstorm, all cozy and content as my siblings and I scrambled around the house.

Every now and then Cole will giggle to himself, and soon after a rank smell will waft around the tent.

"Man, that smells like baby shit," Lake says, pinching his nose.

"I love it when he says they smell like baby shit," Cole says to the rest of us, a big smile on his face. Cole laughs, looks over at Lake, and says nothing. He doesn't have to. I watch Lake shake his head, smile, and light some incense. Soon the pungent smell of baby shit is replaced with the smell of cloves and frankincense.

It is times like these that I admire these men. They may act like children—crass and rude—but I admire their openness, their civility, and their respect for one another, even when it doesn't seem that way. They have no hesitation to tell each other how they feel, and even now there's closeness between them that I don't see between men back home. The war has created this bond between us. What I like most are nights like tonight, when they can give each other a look and, after living together for seven months, understand each other's joys and fears, all in that one look.

Fly comes to the door and tells us to meet in Newman's tent for a squad meeting. We follow Fly across the sand and rock, to our squad leader's tent, where Newman tells us about the dead mechanic.

If there is ever a humbling experience, a moment of pure reality and squalor, it is burning your own shit.

I get stuck with first sergeant detail, which means I have to do anything the first sergeant says, including burning the outhouse waste. I pull the elastic straps of the respirator over my ears and fit the gloves to my hands. Then, with a determination I feel in my eyes, I march toward the wooden outhouses. The outhouses are lined up near the basketball court—six booths strapped together in one large unit of filth. Each booth has a door in the front, for entering and exiting, and a door in the rear that lifts up to reveal a sawed-off barrel drum filled with diesel fuel and shit.

I lift up the rear flap of the first outhouse and grab hold of the handle welded to the barrel drum. I am surprised by the smell—more diesel fuel than shit. I drag the barrel off to the side of the outhouses and go back for the next barrel. Once all six barrels are pulled from the outhouses and placed strategically apart, I take a match, strike it against the box, and toss it into the first barrel. The barrel erupts in an orange and green flame. A dark, orange flame with an olive green base leaps from the barrel, reaches around, and licks the side of the drum, occasionally lashing out at the barrel next to it as if it wants contact with another flame. Black smoke lifts into the sky and floats across the camp. You can always tell when someone is burning shit—the smell always gives it away.

I grab the metal rod, dip it into the first barrel, and walk to the other barrels, setting each one on fire. I step back and admire my work, watching six orange-green flames rise and fall as they burn. It has been six days since Newman told us about the dead mechanic and the coffin. I stand watching the flames and thinking about the man. If I die over here, I don't want to be shipped back in some makeshift coffin, and I don't want my squad members to have to build my box. I don't want to return home like that. Instead, set me on fire, let my body burn into ash and bone like the shit and waste in these barrels. Let my remains blend into the sand and leave me here. It would save everyone a whole lot of trouble. But as the flames settle and go out I wonder if that is really what I want. How does someone decide something like that?

When the flames are out, I look into each barrel and notice a fine layer of ash at the bottom. I lift each barrel by the handles and dump the ash into a larger barrel behind the outhouses, the remains blending in with the remains of yesterday, last week, last month. I clap my hands together, brushing off the last of the ash, and compliment myself on a job well done.

By October the mood in the Gas Chamber has soured. As the days get cooler, the people get colder, more withdrawn, and increasingly grumpy. Everyone seems on edge. Cole lashes out at Lake for always leaving his television on. Lake complains about King's mess, his uniforms and gear spread out haphazardly across the tent. I get angry at Cole and his fan, which constantly blows during the night.

It seems obvious that the honeymoon is over.

I walk into the Gas Chamber and notice Cole building a miniature hut out of plywood over his cot. He has the half-walls constructed and is working on the pointed roof. He has built himself a roofed cubicle in order to seal himself off from the rest of the tent—a coffin of sorts. King and Lake are sitting nearby, pretending not to care. There is no funk music tonight, no lighting of farts, no jokes about the size of other people's dicks. There is only awkward silence in between the sound of Cole hammering nails.

The deployment has taken its toll on everyone; we are all agitated and angry at one another. I don't like the mood in the tent; I don't like the men this war has created. They used to talk excitedly about everything, but now morale has bottomed out and nobody seems happy. When Newman walks into the Gas Chamber and asks me if I want to move across the aisle to another tent, I immediately accept his offer. I fear that the mood in the Gas Chamber is only going to get worse. I pack up my gear, my uniforms, whatever else I've acquired, and make a couple of trips to my new tent. On my last trip back, I stop at the doorway and look around, just for a second, partially to make sure I haven't left anything behind but also to acknowledge that I am no longer a member of the Gas Chamber.

It has been easy for me to think of myself as part of this group of men, one of the boys. It is the concept of forced proximity—we're forced to live with one another like families do. I wouldn't live this close to these men back home. But over here, it has helped me swallow the idea of being in a place where I could be killed simply for wearing the camouflaged uniform. It has helped to know that I am not alone; there are other targets walking right beside me. It has also made me forget that someday I may have to build a coffin for the man sleeping next to me, a man who snores and farts and likes to be loud, but also a man I respect and admire because we're both sharing something as odd and frightening and surreal as war.

But families also separate. Parents break up. Children leave home. People move on.

The pigeon shit is unbearable. Green and white splotches cover what is left of the floor in one of the airplane hangars near the runway. We're standing in the middle of the hangar, admiring the large hole in the roof and the even larger hole in the cement floor. One of the officers who works in the hangar explains that a missile destroyed the roof during the war, landed "right the fuck" on the hangar. Now birds fly in and out through the hole, bouncing from rafter to rafter, swooping down low, landing on the two small airplanes inside the building, and shitting wherever they please.

Newman tells us to start unpacking the truck. I walk over to the five-ton and unload the wood and equipment. Our job is to cover the hole in the floor. I start setting up the circular saw and laying out the wood we'll need for the job. The rest of the platoon quickly gets to work constructing other small wood projects as Newman surveys the hole.

A few hours later we notice a group of soldiers, including the officer who told us about the roof, gathering in the hangar, near the hole. They set up a podium and two wooden steps covered in sand-colored camo netting. On the top step, a rifle stands on end, the tip of the attached bayonet stuck into the step.

I stop to watch the group set up. Soon the entire squad stops working to watch the soldiers lay out a series of chairs and a sign with the unit's insignia.

"Is this another enlistment ceremony or did someone die?" Fly whispers.

"I think that's obvious," Elijah says without even looking at Fly. "It's a memorial."

We watch the soldiers make the final touches to their setting: a Kevlar helmet and a pair of dog tags. I turn away when I see the dog tags. Our battalion has yet to hold a memorial for a fallen soldier—we've made it seven months without losing someone. But the memorial reminds me that someone could die at any moment. I look around at the group of men watching the memorial. I love these men like little boys love trouble. It's taken me years to understand this kind of love for another man. I have this love for the men in my platoon, but not my brothers, because these men and I share an understanding for the frailty of life, how easily a tire rim can kill a man or a mortar round can pierce the canvas of an army tent. We understand this frail place that exists during war, a foggy place somewhere between the real world and the afterlife, a place where life feels important. Even if this place is only in our heads, we can all describe what the sand looks like, how strong the scent of diesel fuel can be, and how good it feels to have a warm body an arm's length away.

With the news reporting that six U.S. soldiers die a week in Iraq, it is entirely possibile that one of our men, the men I've been living with for so long, will die. It is only a matter of time. I am also reminded that it could be me who is killed over here. Right here, in this shit-covered airplane hanger, I build my own coffin in my head. I build it because I have to; I build it because it makes me feel better knowing what it will look like, how long the sides will be, and how deep the opening will go; I build it to calm my fear and the fear of the men standing next to me; I build it out of anger, resentment, guilt. I build it because I need to; I need to come to terms with this being my coffin, this ceremony being my final farewell, and this country being the last thing I see.

I want to write it all down and give it to my fellow soldiers. I want to tell them my measurements and that I don't even really want a coffin when I die. *I want you to light me on fire and watch my body burn, much like we do when burning shit.* But I can't do that; you don't do things like that during war. Men will talk about death before war—when they're scraggly teens ready to enlist in the army and serve their country—or after war—when they're old vets sitting on creaking bar stools telling war stories—but during war we don't talk about things like building coffins or eulogies or extra dog tags. Instead we talk about women, the size of our dicks, our favorite movies, and sometimes nothing at all.

Two Toonies and a Loonie

It's funny how people hold on to things. Years after you'd left, I still think about that night you and I spent in a hotel in Winnipeg and the five words that made me fall in love for the first time.

There was no line outside the hotel liquor store. It was still early—a little after 8 p.m. You and I had waited outside a dance club for an hour before giving up and catching a taxi back to the hotel. We stopped at the liquor store. When we walked in, we noticed how empty the place was, how hollow our footsteps sounded vibrating off the liquor bottles. We rejoiced in not having to wait in line to buy a few drinks, so we took our time. We walked those aisles for ten minutes, trying to decide what to buy.

It was late-autumn in Canada, and we'd driven the four hours north through snow in order to spend a little time together. We'd been dating for nearly two months and that was our first trip together. There had been a couple of awkward silences during the drive up, the kind that signal a turning point in a relationship. It was the first time we'd been left alone together without the opportunity to flee back to our apartments and away from the other person. It was nerve-racking watching you white-knuckle the steering wheel as we drove into town, your blue eyes magnified by all the snow. I was trying to think of something new to talk about. I didn't realize then that sometimes silence is a good thing.

I grabbed a six-pack of beer—something I couldn't do back home—and walked to the counter. You grabbed a pack of wine coolers and joined me. The man behind the counter looked over the two cases of alcohol, and then he looked at us. We must have stared back at him with our young, hopeful faces, two giddy kids. He may have smiled. I don't remember.

We handed him some Canadian bills and in return he handed us three coins. "Two toonies and a loonie," he said. Loonie and toonie are slang terms for one- and two-dollar Canadian coins, but we didn't know that. We just laughed at the way the man said it, the way the double o's sounded coming from his Canadian mouth. Later, in our hotel room, we sipped our beers and repeated the phrase over and over until we tired of it. *Two toonies and a loonie. Two toonies and a loonie.* There was something funny in those five words. It may have been the snow that fell around us as we gingerly skipped across the courtyard on the way to our room, but something about those five words stuck with us like a joke that people tell over and over and over. It became out mantra for that trip—*Two toonies and a loonie.* But it also became more than that.

To anyone else, that phrase meant nothing. But to me, those words seemed much more significant. There was so much more in the way we said them, the memories they provoked, the feelings we placed alongside them. They were a snapshot of our relationship, and years later, during other trips with other boyfriends and sometimes while I was alone, I'd think about that scene, those five words, and you.

We didn't finish the alcohol that night. Instead, we each drank a single beer and then laid down together in a giant queen-sized bed. We stared in each other's eyes for an hour, quietly talking and laughing. You later said a new set of words: "I love you." And despite my better judgment, I said them back.

Vets

In the middle of October, after hearing that we'll be in Iraq another six months, we settle in deep. We've been living in the moment of the war, moving from place to place, mission to mission, never stopping long enough to push the stakes of our tents deep into the sand. We are wandering gypsies, and we like it. But when Captain Roar stands before Bravo Company and tells us that we are in for the long haul, we stare back at him and ask him what we are supposed to do. Nobody is ready to settle into a long hibernation in Iraq.

I think we finally realize that this war isn't going to be brief. Therefore, our tents become more than just tents. We build wooden half-walls to block the crisp evening wind and construct real wooden door frames to replace the curtains we use in the summer. We build rafters and crossbeams, remove the tentpoles, and lay the canvas tent-skin over the new wooden frame. We add on porches and decks, wire in lights, and build small, boxy patio chairs. In the evenings we sit on the porches, playing cards, reading, smoking, or sometimes just talking as the cool desert night settles in around us.

"She was perfectly normal when we were engaged," Jones says.

His wife wants to adopt ethnically diverse children instead of having her own. Roach and I laugh as Jones recounts the story.

"After we got married, she went crazy," he says as he fans out his cards in his hand. "I just want to know what happened to the fun, sane girl I knew when we were engaged. I want that girl back!"

Jones folds his cards and sits back in his chair. Roach and I laugh and look over at him. He looks tired just from talking about his marriage, and I can't blame him. I can't blame any of the men who vent about strained marriages.

I look through the camo netting covering the porch and out into the dark night. Camp is quiet tonight. To boost morale, the battalion has set up video conferencing for troops to talk to and see their families back home. It's our generation's equivalent of writing letters to our wives and girlfriends—instant gratification that life goes on back home. We have declined teleconferencing with our families in order to give married soldiers more time with their wives. While most of the married men are waiting their turns to sit before a television screen and look at an image of their loved ones halfway around the world, Roach, Jones, and I are playing cards and half-joking about how wars tear people apart.

"You'll call home and she'll be like, 'Do you want to talk to Ndugu?'" Roach says as he discards, "and you'll say, 'Who's Ndugu?' and she'll say, 'He's our fifteen-year-old Asian son. Nobody wants the older ones.'"

Roach and I laugh. Jones shrugs and smiles back at us.

"Yeah, it'll be straight to marriage counseling for us when I get home," he says. "I'm just afraid I'll get home and realize that she's this totally different person."

Silence. Roach clears his throat; I suppress a laugh. I look into Jones's face and see his troubles—a future he's not sure of and a situation he has no way of changing. There's nothing like the silence of a worried man. War has taken its course, and there is nothing Jones, Roach, or any of us can do about that.

I look down at my cards and feel the same cold realization surge through my body. I understand the concept of time and change. I know that when I return from this deployment, I will not be the same person I was when I left. I also understand that the people in my life will have changed. While I'm stuck in Iraq, the world around me is moving at a much quicker pace, and when I get home nothing will again line up. Everything will bump and grind, and nothing, not relationships with my parents or even close friendships I've had for years, will be the same. It feels like I'm standing on the train platform, watching each boxcar whiz right on by.

It's the feeling of being left behind.

I peer out into the dark and notice men walking back from the teleconferences. Even in the settling dark I see Rainman's swagger from a mile away. His walk is distinctive to him—short legs slowly stepping forward, knees slightly bowed, a bounce to his step as his broad shoulders lumber toward us. But even from this distance I can tell he is smiling.

I know more about Rainman's wife than any of the other Bravo Company wives. "She's forty and she's beautiful, has a gorgeous body, and she's my wife," Rainman said one night while clearing sand from his weapon. He adores her, even in times like these, when they're worlds apart. When the company announced the teleconferences, Rainman's wife told him that she was showing up in a trench coat—and only a trench coat.

Rainman steps onto the porch and leans against the railing. Roach, Jones, and I stop our game and ask about the teleconference. He isn't shy about any of the details, telling us about his wife showing him her breasts.

"Then of course she wanted tit for tat," he says, laughing.

It isn't long before we're joined by other men from the platoon, all eager to share their stories about seeing and talking to their loved ones. They are giddy and hyperactive. They talk wildly about how their wives looked, how they moved, what they said. They look like footballers talking about a well-executed play. They are happy, and watching them laugh and smile and talk about their wives, I am torn between feeling happy for them and alone, more alone than I've ever felt because I have nobody to talk this energetically about. I am single, and while my parents and friends write letters and send e-mails, I still feel alone. Even if I did have someone to teleconference with, I can't really talk about it with these men. All I can do is sit on the sidelines and watch.

"I was nervous," Newman says as a big smile spreads across his face, his aw-shucks dimples forming on his cheeks. Cole and Rainman have formed a semicircle around him. "I was just anxious. It was like warming up for a football game or something."

Cole and Rainman nod. They *are* men after a football game, each sharing an understanding of how it felt talking with their wives.

"I made the mistake of saying, 'I love you,'" Cole says as he steps back and spits tobacco juice into the sand. "She started crying right away. Then I was like, 'Let me see the belly.' She stood up, lifted her shirt, and showed me her belly. She looked like a totally different person."

I can only imagine what it's like to see your wife as a different person, or to see, for the first time, your unborn child, millions of miles away, through a thirteen-inch television screen. Cole's wife is due any day now, and as he tells the story of seeing his wife pregnant for the first time, I get an image in my head of what it must look like—how his hand must have reached for the screen, how badly he must have wanted to be able to touch his wife, feel that swelling belly, press his ear against it, and feel, for the first time, his kicking child.

"I got her to flash me," Newman says. "At first she was like, 'I'm not going to do that.' She was looking around, trying to see if anyone was watching. And I said, 'But Rainman's wife is showing up in a trench coat. Come on!' And then she did."

We all laugh. Someone tries to get Newman to tell us more, but he shakes his head, smiles, and looks down at his boots—the rest is just for him.

"You know those calls are monitored," Roach says. "So I'm sure the monitors are saying, 'All right! Morale calls for the soldiers in Iraq.'"

Roach jacks his elbow back as he imitates the monitor guys. I picture three or four middle-aged, beer-bellied, balding men—the stereotypical guys I'd imagine having such a job—sitting around high-fiving each other as Rainman's wife opens her trench coat and Newman's wife lifts up her shirt.

When we hear that we'll be in Iraq for an entire year, the mood around camp hits an all-time low. Cole and King walk around camp with long faces, imitating *Seinfeld*'s Soup Nazi by saying, "No morale for you!" Someone even suggests that Cole and King go to Demke, our supply sergeant, and request some morale, joking that maybe a new shipment of morale had arrived and Demke had forgotten to distribute it. But Demke is fresh out of morale.

Now, as men start to drift toward the tents, where they'll climb into their cots and fall asleep dreaming about their wives, the porch empties and I am left alone with the night. Even though I don't share the men's energy and excitement, I understand their need to express their feelings—the feeling of seeing one's wife as a different person, the feeling of appreciating her for who she is, all over again, and the feeling of being a father. It makes these men seem more real; it makes me appreciate and respect them more when I understand that somewhere, across land and sea, they have lives that don't involve mortar attacks, roadside bombs, and M16 rifles. They are able to take themselves out of Iraq for a moment and place themselves where life is a little more normal.

It also makes me realize that I have nobody like that in my life. I don't have a boyfriend or husband waiting back home, someone to talk to when I'm feeling down or depressed. I have parents and siblings who love me, friends who trust and support me, but I don't have that person in my life who lifts up my morale like Cole and Newman and Rainman have with their wives, and, sitting on this porch alone, that really starts to sink in.

I've never told my parents about my sexuality. For a while I thought they'd just figure it out. They'd maybe hear it from somebody in my hometown or my sister would let it slip during Christmas or Thanksgiving. But then I remembered the reasons why I joined the military and the image they have of me.

When I joined the military I was looking for my parents' respect and praise. I wanted to make them feel proud of me, like they did of my brother Brandon because he was such a good sportsman. My brother excelled at every sport he ever played. My parents would attend almost all his sporting events. Their jackets would be emblazoned with giant buttons depicting Brandon in football pads or Brandon holding a baseball bat or Brandon crouching like he was ready to pin another wrestler to the mat. They'd come home from his events bragging about his accomplishments. I'd listen to them and wish they'd say the same things about me, but they never did.

They never did because I was horrible at sports. I ran track for several years, but once I got into high school, I lost my youthful enthusiasm for it. And I lost my speed. I couldn't keep up with the other racers, and the few times my parents did come to watch me run, I let them down by coming in almost last in every race.

So I joined the military during my senior year of high school, and I finally felt like my parents were proud of me for something. During that first year, while I was living at home and driving to Rugby, North Dakota, one weekend a month for drill, every time my mother woke me up and watched me drive away from the house, I felt she was proud of me for doing something respectable and useful like participating in the army. I knew my parents were proud of me, and I never wanted them to lose that feeling. So I never told them I am gay.

Two days before Halloween, I receive a package from home. My friend Ashley has sent a box filled with Halloween candy, Mad Libs, a John Mayer CD, and, at the bottom of the box, a mullet wig.

"What's that?" Roach says as I lift the wig out of the box. The hair is wavy on top and straight in the back. I lower my head and place the brown synthetic hair tightly around my scalp. I toss my head back and look over at Roach, my top front teeth bucked out over my lower lip.

Roach bursts into laughter. The rest of my roommates look over at me. They get up and stand around my cot, asking to try it on.

"Here," Roach says, "you need these."

He hands me a pair of BCGs, the thick, brown-framed glasses the army issues to the troops. We call them Birth Control Glasses (BCGs) because nobody would have sex with someone wearing them. I place the glasses on my face, and when I look up at the rest of the men surrounding me, I have a complete Halloween costume—a nearly blind, mullet-wearing redneck.

We take the act door to door. In Elijah and Newman's tent, Rogers dons the wig and glasses, and when Elijah starts playing some eighties funk music, he dances on the wooden floor, flexing his muscles and bowing out his legs like a redneck weightlifter. Newman names it "The Mullet Muscle Dance." We take turns wearing the wig—each of us, I imagine, feeling what it's like to be somebody else for a night. We snap pictures, laugh, and even comb the wig, happy to have such a distraction.

Later in the night, we're forced to participate in a practice drill. The idea is that if an enemy is able to get inside the gate or attack Anaconda, we'll know what to do. We're lying in our tent in full battle rattle—Kevlar helmets, flak vest, canteens, ammo pouches—pointing our weapons at the door. Roach is kneeling behind his cot, propping his elbow on top of it. Rainman has this serious look on his face as he lies perfectly still near the front of the tent, waiting for a hajji to come bursting through the door.

Rogers and I are lying on the dusty floor in the middle of the tent, waiting for the squad leaders to come in and give us the "all clear."

After half an hour, we tire of wearing our entire battle rattle. We let our helmets fall to the floor and open the Velcro on our flak jackets. Rogers goes over to his cot, retrieves a CD, and places it in the boom box. Instantly, an Irish drinking song comes bursting through the speakers. Before long, we've shed all our gear and are singing and clapping along to the music. Rogers gets up and tries to do an Irish jig, his feet kicking out while his hands rest on his hips. He kicks left, then right, then grabs his M16 with both hands and thrusts it into the air as his feet kick wildly around the room.

In the middle of Iraq, in the middle of a war, in a moment we are told to take as seriously as if our lives depended on it, we are dancing to Irish music and laughing as Rogers parades around the room. Roach gets up to do the jig with Rogers. Everyone else is hooting and hollering, and I'm sure that if the Iraqis did break through the wire, none of them would ever even consider coming near our tent for fear of the maniacs inside.

I reach into one of my bags, grab the mullet wig, and hand it to Rogers. He places it on his head, and the party continues. *Here is our normal moment. This is what it feels like to escape this place.* I laugh, clap my hands, and offer the BCGs to Rogers.

A week later, Iraqis attack Anaconda's front gate, killing one soldier and wounding five, and I never again bring out the wig.

We are supposed to have Veteran's Day off, but some big-wig general finds out and makes us work.

After two days of rain and clouds, the sun finally shines some light on Iraq. We've settled into a routine of doing base projects at Anaconda. It is warm, the perfect day for working, and a gentle autumn breeze drifts in over the work site where we're pouring concrete. It is almost as if the gods are giving us a treat for Veteran's Day—one perfect day in Iraq.

I spend the entire morning cutting rebar. I lift the forty-foot unfinished steel rod onto the table and ask Roach to hold the bar in place while the rebar cutter slices the steel into foot-long, manageable pieces. The pieces fall onto one another, clinking and rolling around before falling into the dusty sand. I spend all morning doing this and thinking about being a veteran.

I don't know any veterans of foreign wars. My grandfather wasn't a vet. My father has asthma, so I'm guessing the military wouldn't have let him in. My uncle Tony served in the air force, but I know very little about what he did during his time. I don't even know where the vets hang out in my hometown—we don't have a VFW. All I know about veterans is the picture I'm given by the entertainment industry—old, nostalgic men sitting on bar stools, drinking beer at one in the afternoon, grumbling about how loud the jukebox is. That is the only picture I see. What perplexes me most is that these old vets seem comfortable with the image. Young people don't see the men who fought in World War II, the troops who defended hilltops during bitter winters in Korea, or the soldiers who lost their buddies in Vietnam. Instead, we see these old men wearing baseball caps and jackets with the word "veteran" printed in bold letters or the bumper stickers on Buicks that tell any kid tailing them that the man driving 10 mph used to be an artillery gunner in World War II.

In the afternoon, the entire battalion lines up in a formation for a Veteran's Day ceremony. The battalion commander has requested one large, mass formation: officers up front, sergeants in the middle, specialists and privates in the rear. Each soldier is an arm's length away from the next, each boot placed side by side down the line, each chest bowed out, and each head held high.

The commander speaks. The chaplain prays. Some general reminisces about old army vets. The color guard raises their flags and fires some blanks. We salute. It is all just a haze for me. Each speaker blends into the next, and by the end I have a headache. The ceremony is formulaic and too military. It is a showcase of military brass, what the men in the lower ranks call a "dog and pony show." I find myself drifting off, watching the swaying leaves or the seagulls that fly over our camp on their way to the base dump. After the ceremony, I walk back to my tent and know that I am not alone in these feelings.

Outside our tent, Lake bullshits about being a vet. Back home he used to work as a used-car salesman, a profession I imagine he excelled at. He's the perfect bullshitter. During monthly drills, he'd ramble on about the number of used cars he'd managed to talk up to naïve customers or how tame his colleagues were compared to him. I don't doubt his ability to spin a yarn. Right now, he's got a small audience assembled in between the tents, and he reenacts the scene running through his head.

"When I get home, I'm going to go to the grocery store and demand that I be first in the checkout line," Lake says. He grins at the crowd with his signature used-car salesman smile. "'I'm a veteran! I'm a veteran!' I'll yell. 'Back to the end of the line, old man!'"

The crowd laughs as Lake's finger points off to the motor pool, sending the invisible old man to the end of what we're assuming is a long line. I laugh along and wait for Lake to continue. When he gets going like this it's best to just sit back and let the scene unfold.

"Then some guy will come up and say, 'I was in World War II,'" Lake says as he shifts his weight to his right foot and steps back, "and I'll say, 'OK. I'll go behind you.'"

The scene continues in much the same fashion as Lake takes a step back with each remark:

"'I served in the Korean War.'"

"'OK. I'll go behind you.'"

"'I served in Vietnam.'"

"'Alright. Fair enough. I'll go behind you.'"

"'I served in Desert Storm.'"

"'Well, that's about equal so I'll stand *beside* you.'"

By the end the crowd has begun to disperse. People walk back to their tents, laughing as they prepare for the night. King and Cole stick around and continue to talk about how ridiculous the ceremony was and how drawn out the entire event seemed.

I sit out on the porch and watch the men. If a World War II or Vietnam War veteran had seen Lake's act, I'm sure the man would have punched him right there. Lake jokes about the war, about hearing mortar attacks, about death, about wives leaving men while we're over here, and I can't blame him. He deals with these things through humor, and while older vets may see scenes like Lake's as disrespectful, I respect Lake even more because of his candor, because comedy is his answer to war.

We laugh because we have a different idea of what it means to be veterans. Even now, as vets, the title doesn't mean the same thing it used to. We get angry after six months away from our families and start demanding privileges like teleconferences and e-mail. We fuss over the heat, complain about burning our own shit, and when we're forced to pull guard duty in the towers surrounding the base, we take books along and read during our four-hour shifts, paying little to no attention to the possibility of enemy forces crawling into our camp. I don't think we understand what it means to be veterans yet. We aren't on the front lines of this war. We aren't raiding houses in Baghdad like the Marines. We're building up bases now, repairing schools, building picnic tables, and pouring concrete, jobs people wouldn't normally associate with a war. But this war seems like such a different war from the ones we've seen in movies. We are a generation that demands instant gratification. We have the ability to instantly send e-mails during war and the opportunity to see our wives and loved ones through tele-conferences, but we want to be instant veterans. We want the respect and prestige that comes with the title, without fully understanding what being a vet means. Maybe in thirty years, when we've had time to reflect and consider how serious this war is and we're sitting around telling war stories, we'll understand our role in this war. But who's to say we'll *ever* sit around telling war stories.

As we dance around in wigs in the desert and act out grocery store veteran scenes, we demonstrate that we're too young and idealistic now to care about being called vets.

My mother has a military photo of me hanging in her living room. The photo was taken at the beginning of basic training, in the fall of 1998. The military marches you into a room, right before they put you through the rigors of running obstacle courses, shooting semi-automatic weapons, and throwing hand grenades, and snaps a picture. They paste the top half of a Class-A army uniform over your chest and a hat atop your head. They don't ask you to smile. In fact, I think they prefer that you frown. *Look tough like the army pawn you're about to become.* Besides, who smiles before going into the army?

It is the same military photo almost every army parent receives—same uniform, same American flag backdrop, same growling look. The only thing different is the face and the name. I imagine that there are millions of other mothers with nearly the same photo hanging in their living room. When I left for Iraq, my mother told me that she had moved the photo to the dining room; that way, while my family eats dinner, they can be reminded that I am in Iraq.

Walking back from the work site, I am reminded of this photo and the image my family has of me. It's the same image every American gets on Veteran's Day—the snapshot of a son or daughter serving in the U.S. military, an uncle who paid the ultimate price for his country, high school classmates who enlisted after graduation because they had nothing else to do, or the cousin whom family members talk about whenever the war is mentioned. I don't know how many times I heard the phrase "I have a (insert cousin, son, daughter or any relative here) serving in the military" as I was preparing to leave for Iraq.

In my hometown, when any member of the community asks which of the five Lemer boys I am, the common reply is: "The one in the military." Through the community newspaper and my mother's proud boasting, they know I spent two months in Fort Leonardwood, Missouri, for basic training. They know I spent another two months in Gulfport, Mississippi, learning how to be a carpenter. They read about my deployment to Kosovo in 2000. They know how I spent the hot days in Kuwait, and they've heard from my mother what kind of missions I am doing in Iraq. That is how they remember me; that is how they separate me from my four brothers.

It is this image they have of me that makes me uneasy. I am remembered solely for being in the military. While I'm still young and hope to eventually put this deployment and my military service behind me, I am reminded that thus far in my life the most significant thing I've done is serve my county. It is this thought that makes me both proud of my past and scared of the future. But then I think about the alternative. If I'm not remembered as being the son who served in the military, what will I be remembered for? Isn't it nice to be remembered for accomplishing something, for doing something like serving your country?

As I near my tent, I walk by a metal Conex box Demke uses for storage. Above the Conex are about twenty-five dirty, white, oscillating fans, posed atop stands like elegant geese poking their heads above the swamp grass. Some of the fans are gently twirling in the breeze, the blades spinning around like they're alive. When we were at BIAP, when the temperature rose to 130 degrees, these fans were our most prized possession. Now, watching them spin in the wind atop the Conex, like last year's Christmas fad, they look sad and beaten down. They were great when we needed them, but now that we have air-conditioning in our tents, we've discarded them like trash.

Seeing the fans, I can't help but think about how most people view veterans. Once a year, we march the veterans out, parading them around towns, saluting their achievements, honoring what they've done for this country. But once that day is over, once we no longer need them to remind us of why we're Americans, we forget about them; they simply become old men sitting on bar stools and complaining about loud music.

I kick my way across the sand toward my tent. For now, I'll accept my status as a new veteran. But when the time comes, I won't be an old vet sitting on a bar stool in some VFW. I also won't be the old vet stomping around town yelling about his achievements. I want to be remembered for more than just having served in the military.

At the very least, I don't want to be a discarded fan.

Out Came a Spider

In the dream I am guarding the Baghdad zoo. The night sky is starless, a blank void of darkness, and below the horizon the grass in the field looks deep blue like an ocean of softly shifting waves. Out on this ocean of grass are all the animals of the zoo. There's a shaggy-looking lion asleep near the wall that surrounds the field. A gaggle of geese is camped out nearby, weeds growing around their slender necks. There's a giraffe, a zebra, a couple of wolves, and a monkey or two. They are all asleep in the field, living together in harmony—at least for one night.

I'm in a guard tower overlooking these animals. The guard tower is in the corner of the field, a white, two-story shack with floor-to-ceiling windows. I feel like a prison guard up in that tower, looking down on everything below with disdain and distrust. It is quiet and motionless, almost too calm, and the atmosphere gives off an ominous glow. Beside me, a faceless soldier is asleep, and I feel like I am the only living thing awake in Baghdad.

The eeriness of the night gives way to fear as three figures appear along the horizon. They are nothing more than shadows, three black silhouettes slinking along the wall. They take careful steps around the animals, as if they are crooks tiptoeing around security obstacles. There are no faces, no hands, no fingers pulling at triggers. They are shadows, ghosts almost, moving across the field toward me.

In the dream, I don't think to raise my gun and fire shots at the figures. I'm too much in shock. I don't think to wake the man next to me or to use the radio to relay the information back to headquarters. Instead, all I think about doing is running. Whenever I have a bad dream I think about running. I am five years old again, and I'm running to my parents' bedroom.

I climb down from the tower and dash into the only building at the zoo, the one in the middle of the field. There is one long hallway, and I start to run down it, checking each door along the way. I look behind me, waiting for the figures to round the corner, waiting for shots to be fired. I find all the doors locked, and I panic. At the end of the hall I grab the knob of the last door. Inside is my mother's basement pantry, pitch black and damp. When I was a child, my mother sent me to the pantry to fetch jars of preserves, and I stood in the doorway shivering, afraid of the moisture and concrete and the creatures I knew lived there. I step inside.

I am damp with sweat. As I crouch down, I feel rats scatter across my boots. I cradle the rifle in my arms, point the muzzle at the door, and wait. Deep down in the pit of my stomach, I feel my muscles tighten, fear spreading through my body. I close my eyes, grip my rifle tighter, and wait for them to find me.

I wake from the zoo dream nearly screaming. I am sweating, and across the tent I hear the heater kick in and start to blow warm air. My sleeping bag has been kicked off my bed. Instead of retrieving it, I lie on my cot and stare at the ceiling, thinking about the dream and watching the condensation drip from the green canvas.

It is December 15, ten days until Christmas, and it's been raining all night. The nights have gotten cooler, and for the last two weeks we've endured sloppy rainstorms off and on. I've been in a sour mood lately, and the weather hasn't helped. Lately, I've been thinking about distancing myself from the men in my platoon. I thought it would be easy being a gay soldier and having nothing to talk about with them. I thought the other men would easily figure it out and chastise me. But nothing like that ever happened, and after living together for nearly a year I've found that I can't simply detach myself from them. If I did, *I* would be the one creating a riff in our military bond; *I* would be the one making it difficult for gay men and women to serve in the military, and that's not what I wanted. I wanted to show that being gay in the military really doesn't (and shouldn't) matter.

I eventually rise from my bed and walk to the computer and phone tent in the middle of our section of base. The tent has six phone booths in the middle of the room, and along the outer wall are fifteen computers with Internet capabilities. Inside, I sign into one of the computers. Before I pull up a browser and check the latest news headlines, I get caught up in a phone conversation taking place behind me. I hear a female soldier say, "Do you have the TV on? We've captured Saddam!" and then hang up. She then proceeds to dial a second number. She repeats the same question and statement, hangs up, and moves down her phone list, making a half-dozen calls back home to tell them about the news. As more and more people hear the news, the tent is abuzz with excitement.

The news continues to spread throughout the afternoon. There seems to be a sense of joy in the air, and back in my tent I convey this joy in my journal entry. I write: "Well, they've captured Saddam. They've finally got him. They have the tyrant in custody. It's very good news. Now the fighting may die down, things will settle, and his few followers will quit fighting us." And while I feel overjoyed at the fact that we've caught Saddam, I can't help but feel a little sorry for the former leader because I understand what it's like to live in hiding, to be forced to crawl into a hole and hide yourself away from everything you're used to. I've been forced to do that the entire deployment. I've been in my mother's old farmhouse pantry, waiting.

In the evening, just before midnight, I walk to Bravo Company's MWR tent for a bottle of water. CNN is broadcasting pictures of the hole Saddam crawled out of. I watch the camera zoom into the spider hole, and I imagine a tired, old man crouched down in the dirt, shivering and cold, wondering how it came to this. *Where has my life gone?* Saddam may have asked himself, and I nod my head because I understand.

I hear the faint sounds of boots marching across concrete. The steps are getting closer, louder, and more urgent. They stop, and then start again, growing in volume as they get another step closer to my hiding place. When they stop outside my door, I know this is the end. I know they will throw open the door and find me, a shivering soldier weeping in a hole.

I think about running. I want to run away from it all, past the day I received that phone call placing me on active duty, past the boring days in Fort Carson, past the snowballs and pantyhose and newspaper listings of the soldiers killed during the war, past the endless miles of sand in Kuwait, past the scorpions, past the Iraqis selling moonshine, past the old Iraqi documents, past the crying mothers and the millions of begging children whose voices I can't get out of my head. I want to run past it all and into the future, where I leave the military behind and live the life I've always wanted to live. But I'm tired of running. I've been running my whole life. If this deployment has taught me anything, it's that I don't always have to run. I don't need to run away every time it gets rough. When they open the pantry door, I don't try to dash out. I'm not weeping or even shivering, and

I no longer feel the fear in the pit of my stomach. I've been exposed, and instead of curling up tighter into myself, I look up at the face standing before me. I can't make out the features, so I stand, look straight into that face, and say nothing.

I am no longer afraid.

Dump Gulls

The holding area at the north gate of Anaconda Army Airbase has a kind of Auschwitz feel to it. It's about half the size of a basketball court and smells like a locker room. Dozens of Iraqi men are standing along the fence, all watching us and waving IDs. Iraqi men come here every morning looking for work, all eager eyes and grabby fingers. Recently, the army began hiring them for various jobs around base. There are work crews for painting, laundry, picking up garbage, and jobs like the one today, where we'll ask Iraqis to reinforce the fence surrounding our base so men like themselves can't get in.

The men near the front are the undependable ones. They are either men who've been deemed untrustworthy because they've failed to show up for work or are new to job details. Behind these men are a number of other Iraqis, less-eager men who are simply waiting for their U.S. supervisor to show up. These are the men Major Schull is interested in when he's walking around the holding area to look for his crew.

Major Schull is the kind of soldier who makes other soldiers nervous. He looks like a drill sergeant: bald head; thick-framed glasses covering intense, beady eyes; a booming voice that makes young troops instantly stand up straight. He doesn't wear a hat, and the morning light makes his head look large and bulbous. I watch that head bob around the holding area as he works his way through the crowd. He reminds me of a swimmer working his way through seaweed; his body swiftly dodges the dozens of hands that reach for his skin.

It is half past seven, early morning, a week after Christmas. Before we arrived at the holding area, Major Schull stood before us puffing on a cigar and saying, "This isn't a difficult job. Just watch them." *Just watch them.*

Those were the words of this deployment. I'd been watching people for months. But there was something ominous in those words, some kind of warning Major Schull knew we needed. All I could think was, *How hard can it be watching a handful of miserable Iraqis?*

Major Schull is looking for a man named Deebo, his work crew leader. While he looks for Deebo, I step closer to the fence and scan the faces of the men. They remind me of the children I met at the soccer stadium in Baghdad, children who've grown up but still must resort to begging. I notice a young Iraqi man, no older than me, wearing headphones and smiling.

"What are you listening to?" I ask.

The holding-area fence comes up to our waists, and from behind the fence the man takes off his headphones and hands them to me. I put on the headphones and listen to whiny sitar music and a harsh, male Arabic voice. I have trouble finding the beat, but I smile back at the man when I hand back the headphones.

"Mee-sta, do you have a misses?" he asks.

I laugh and shake my head. They can be so direct, just like children.

"Mee-sta, I have two wives, one baby, no money," he says as he counts down with his fingers. "Please, Mee-sta."

The man folds his hands together and proceeds to beg me to hire him. I don't have the heart to tell him that I don't have that kind of power. Instead, I point at Major Schull, who is still looking for Deebo. The man turns and walks away.

I watch another major approach the holding facility. He gazes into the crowd of faces, all eager men holding IDs. He points at a man near the front, and the Iraqi worker moves through the gate of the holding area and stands near the major. The major then proceeds to choose a few more Iraqi workers in a similar fashion, as if he's choosing teammates for a game of baseball or pets from a litter of puppies. The whole process seems so degrading and childlike that I feel bad just watching it. I want to walk up to Major Schull and say, *Which ones do you like? You can have whichever ones you want. Just pick them and let's get out of here.*

Deebo finally shows up. He is a short, pudgy man wearing a dirty, tan-colored shirt and sweatpants the color of peaches. He doesn't look particularly strong, or even very trustworthy, but I imagine Major Schull picked him because he knew some English and was good at supervising other workers. Around Deebo are a dozen other men, some young, some middle-aged, all in dirty clothes and gloves. But they are smiling. As the workers climb into the backs of Hummers, I notice the similarities between

Deebo and another worker, a short, round man wearing a blue trench coat and tan slacks. I'm convinced they're brothers.

The men are divided up into three teams. My team is working near tower 46. When we get to our work site, Deebo's brother and six other men start applying concertina wire along the top of the perimeter fence. Deebo's brother is in charge, and I do nothing but sit back and watch the men work. *Just watch them.*

The workers spend most of the morning securing concertina wire to the top of the perimeter fence between towers 46 and 47. Four of the men use a ladder to climb over the fence and work from outside the base, while Deebo's brother and another man, a tall young kid with a sandy mustache and a handsome, freckled face, work inside. They work without disruption for most of the morning.

Around noon they start asking about lunch, and I don't know what to tell them. I was only told to watch; I know nothing about lunch. One of the workers outside the fence finds three orange gourds, large and squash-like, and he throws them to Deebo's brother. They spend fifteen minutes breaking the gourds open, only to find them rotten. They turn to the stem of the plant. Deebo's brother strips the stem like it's celery and chews on the stalk. He strips the stalk even further and hands pieces around to the rest of the workers.

I watch in fascination. The crew has stopped working and is crouching on the ground, all chewing on pieces of stem. They look like Neanderthals posed like that, men so primitive and simple that they don't even find their actions bizarre. This is part of their lives. They are surviving. They are acting like any of us would, put in that situation. We don't recognize it because we've become spoiled in Iraq. Gone are days of MREs and mornings without showers. We have everything we need in Iraq now, and it's hard to remember a time when we didn't have these luxuries, when *we* looked like Neanderthals crouching in this country.

The workers catch me staring at them, but they don't seem to mind. They're used to it. I try to look away but I can't. The phrase returns to my head: *Just watch them.*

So I do.

Christmas came and went in Iraq. The base command made attempts at cheering up the soldiers. They shipped in lobster and steak for a Christmas feast, and prepared a banquet table full of food from back home. They decorated the chow hall with garland, ribbons, and mistletoe, pumped out carols from a couple of loudspeakers, and even had an ice sculpture of Santa—half red, half white—dripping all over the floor. There were sweet potatoes, ice cream, people wearing Santa hats. One of the guys in Bravo Company received a Santa outfit in the mail and walked around our tents holding his fake gut and chuckling like a drunken fool. There were even carolers, a group of soldiers who rode around base in a sleigh, filling the night with fake cheer and merriment.

I wasn't fooled. It was my first Christmas away from home, and I did everything I could not to think about it. Instead of listening to the caroling and sitting in the chow hall sipping cider and reminiscing about holiday traditions, I accepted a $30 bribe from Viv to take his guard-duty shift. I sat in a guard tower along the base perimeter, watching birds flitter above the reedy marsh just past the wire, and imagined I was back home, ten years old. It was spring, and I was watching my father work a field from a second-story window of our farmhouse.

But just as I was about to forget about Christmas, something reminded me that there was no getting away from the holiday. In the middle of the guard shift, I watched a tractor slowly pull into view. A middle-aged Iraqi man was driving it, and next to him were his two wives, wrapped in maroon garments. The tractor was pulling a flatbed trailer where three children sat silently watching us. These were our own private carolers.

"What's this, a sleigh ride?" said the other soldier in the tower.

I watched the trailer slowly move through the marsh, the children watching us the entire time. I thought I saw one of the children, a little girl, open her mouth, as if she were about to sing, but then I realized that I was imagining things. That was what I wanted to see. I wanted to see these young children singing to us, maybe a song of gratitude for helping them get rid of Saddam. But the children just stared back at us, a mix of longing and jealousy in their eyes.

The staff sergeant in charge of the guard towers arrived. He brought hot meals from the chow hall, two steaming plates of meat and potatoes. Eating the food and watching the trailer disappear, I felt sorry for those children. Even in Iraq, a country we don't like and where we don't belong, we had everything we needed. By December we had hot meals (and good meals at that), regular mail, access to phones and the Internet, a regularly stocked PX. I am reminded of one of Saddam's son's palaces outside BIAP. I had to drive a major out to the palace one evening while we were stationed at BIAP. While the major met with other military officials, I sat near the man-made pond, watching the water ripple and flow, and examining the architecture of the mansion on the other side of it. I watched that mansion as I imagined Iraqis did, fascinated and angered by their leader. I dipped my foot into the water, skipped a pebble across the surface, and wondered how Saddam and his family could have lived in such manufactured elegance when the people of Iraq had so little.

Thinking about those children in the sleigh, I couldn't help but wonder if the Iraqi people look at us the same way they used to look at Saddam.

Over the radio I get a message instructing me to take my team of workers to the dump.

The dump takes up the whole northeast corner of the base. When we first arrived at Anaconda Army Airbase, the dump was nothing more than a mound of discarded parts, old lumber, and broken bottles. By December, it has expanded into a massive maze of pits, heaps of trash, smoke, and ash. As units start preparing to cycle home, they discard anything they can't take with them: worn oscillating fans, televisions, tires, old uniforms, broken folding chairs, even letters sent from churches and old ladies back home. In no time the dump has become a treasure trove of wasted and unwanted items.

When we arrive at the dump site, the military police are standing along the fence, yelling at a group of Iraqi kids. Part of the fence is missing, and the sand below the wire has been cleared away so someone could slide right under. A few yards from the fence I notice a fan sticks up from a pile of trash and a string of garland from the Christmas decorations. Above, dozens of birds circle the dump. They're dump gulls—nasty, rotten birds with beady, black eyes and hooked beaks, the kind who feed off decay and trash. They aren't the beautiful sea gulls that sail above the water on greeting cards and over beaches. No, there is no grace to these birds. They swoop and dive into the dump, and sift through the trash with their pointed beaks. I look up and notice that the dump is full of gulls, some perched on piles of trash, others circling above, waiting to swoop down and capture something and fly it into Iraq. It almost looks like a bizarre beach scene, where on the other side of all this trash is a white sandy beach and crystal-clear water.

Major Schull stands back from the hole in the fence, watching. An unlit cigar hangs from his lips. He reaches into his pockets and pulls out a lighter shaped like a cell phone. When he clicks the button on the lighter, a flame appears, and the phone chimes a tiny ring. The lighter seems out of place in Major Schull's chubby hands. It seems like something a rebellious teenager would use rather than an army major, and I want to tell him this.

"Here's the deal," he says, eying his new cigar as he puffs away. "We need to get this new layer of fence up so these bastards can't get back in."

Major Schull continues to stare at the hole in the fence while he addresses us. He tells us that an Iraqi kid cut the outside layer of concertina wire, lifted up the inside layer, and crawled through to retrieve some trash. A soldier in a nearby guard tower shot the kid in the leg. This incident posed a problem because the Iraqi people had noticed how our dump has grown. They know how wasteful we are, and they've begun to take advantage of it. Iraqi men have begun hiring children—young kids small enough to crawl under the perimeter wire—to retrieve trash from our dump.

Major Schull has thrown me for a loop. I expected him to be flipping out right now, running back and forth in front of the hole, cursing at the children who've made his life a little bit harder. Instead, he's completely calm, smoking a cigar, and pondering how to proceed. He takes a long drag and looks out over the dump. Smoke billows from one of the piles of garbage and drifts into the blue sky. I know what's coming. In his mind, Major Schull is thinking, *Assemble the troops.*

"Fall in," Major Schull bellows.

I watch as Major Schull's hand-picked workers form three ranks in front of him. Deebo stands at the head of the first rank, his chest pushed out. Behind Deebo are his brother and my team of workers. I watch Major Schull instruct the group. He's treating the men as if they are soldiers even though most of them have no idea what he is saying.

Major Schull begins with his signature line.

"Here's the deal. First, I need third squad . . ."

"Third team, Mee-sta?" Deebo interrupts.

"Yes, third team," Major Schull says, a little irritated. "I need third squad to go over the wire to repair the hole. Take pliers and tie wire."

Major Schull pauses to take a drag from his cigar.

"Then, second squad will take shovels and pile dirt at the bottom of the fence, where those bastards are getting through."

I try to hold back a laugh as Major Schull is explaining the project. Most of the workers look confused and have a hard time following his detailed plans. Plus, he's just insulted their children by calling them bastards, which may or may not have registered with them. It's hard to know what the Iraqi men are thinking, but I look between Major Schull and the men, and wonder how much is sinking in. Do the Iraqis understand this pompous man smoking a cigar? More importantly, does Major Schull understand anything about these men?

"Then," Major Schull continues, "Deebo, you take first squad and start laying out the new inside layer of wire. Alright? Any questions?"

There are none, and Major Schull nods his head.

"Then let's get to work."

The Iraqi workers start the patchwork project, but they fuck it up. Major Schull wants the workers to pull the concertina wire tight, so it isn't in large loops like they're used to, but the workers can't figure this out. In a split second I watch Major Schull go from calm and collected to angry and agitated. He starts yelling at the workers. He pushes a couple of the men out of the way and starts showing them how it is done. When this happens, I can't help but smile because this is the Major Schull I expected when I met him this morning. This is the kind of guy I pegged him to be, and this act proves why.

While Major Schull argues with his team, I watch the dump gulls fight over scraps. The birds are darting between piles of garbage and nibbling on whatever they can find. I watch them jump from point to point, like rats. Rats with wings. They squawk at each other, at the garbage, at us, and flap their wings to scare off other birds. I watch in amazement, much like I watched the Iraqis chew on the gourd stems, trying to pull myself away.

Toward the end of the day, around three in the afternoon, Major Schull pulls Deebo aside and tells him that the workers can't take any garbage from the dump. *Nothing*, he says, then gets into his Hummer and drives away. Deebo and the other workers watch him leave, and when he's gone, the workers stop working and start digging through the dump. They come up with handfuls of discarded trash. One man has three Christmas wreaths around one arm and a couple of old rubber tires around the other. Another worker has found a round container of powdered Gatorade, still half full. He opens the lid, dips one finger inside, and tastes the powder. A third man finds a cardboard box with twenty-four empty Mountain Dew cans and decides he has to have them. He also finds a picture some soldier threw into the dump. Every single one of the workers comes back from scavenging the dump with a smile on his face, as if this were his luckiest day.

The workers began making piles of the trash. The other soldiers and I start telling them to stop. We try to get each worker to understand that they can't take trash from the site, that Major Schull said nobody leaves the site with garbage. The workers pretend to understand; they know what we're saying. They pretend to turn and walk back to the dump, but once we turn our backs they run toward the truck with their trash, like children deceiving a parent.

We eventually have to lecture each worker like he is a child, getting right in his face and saying, *No trash! No trash!* until they understand and drop whatever it is they have acquired. I let the other soldiers do this; I just don't have the heart. Watching the men take their treasures back to the dump, I again think about why I'm in this country—to help the people of Iraq. As I watch the other soldiers lecture the workers, I wonder what has happened in Iraq. Are these men not human? Do they not want the same things we do—food, shelter, a set of arms to hold us close, a place to lay our heads? I don't have it in me to tell these men that they cannot have these things we've discarded, the stuff nobody wants. The adage *One man's junk is another man's treasure* comes to mind, but it's so much more than that. When a man must beg for another's trash, you have to wonder how it ever got to this.

Some of the other men start to laugh at the workers and the stuff they've pulled from the dump. It is easy for them to laugh. We have so much waiting for us back home. But this is all these men have, a few random opportunities to make their lives better. Most of them won't ever leave this country. They'll be working here for years, every few days trying to sneak trash away from our dump, trying to build something for themselves out of what we don't want. They are like the dump gulls, constantly picking at the scraps and trash others have left behind. As long as there's trash, there'll be people sneaking in to steal it.

We eventually have to trick the workers into letting go of their trash. They've loaded the back of one of the trucks with garbage. We instruct them to stand near the fence, while one of the soldiers drives the truck around a pile of rubbish. The soldier dumps everything in the truck, and returns with an empty and clean truck. In doing this, the workers finally get our point.

At the end of the day, as we're loading the workers into the truck, three low-flying military helicopters pass over the dump. The choppers make the dump gulls take flight. I watch the birds fly in circles above the dump and think about what went on here today. There's a divide between us and the Iraqi people. We're two different groups of people without a solid understanding of each other, and until we figure out some way to communicate, some way to see eye to eye, there will always be conflict over here. The Iraqi workers know it; Major Schull knows it; and the soldiers who've spent all day watching the workers know it.

I watch the gulls circle above the garbage and smoke. They circle over the holding cell at the north gate, where men will meet again in the morning.

They fly over our tents, where soldiers shuffle cards and start packing for our trip home. They fly over the chow hall, over basketball games, over old Iraqi documents written in dusty Arabic, over Hummers, bonfires, memorial and re-enlistment ceremonies, burning shit, stray dogs, boxing matches. They make circles above the soldiers—soldiers with laptops, soldiers with guns, soldiers with memories, secrets, lost desires. They circle over the airport strip, where in a few more months we'll load ourselves into a C-130 and fly home, never to return to this land.

Epilogue

Of all the days I spent in Iraq, it is those last few weeks that I recall most vividly now.

We weren't working any missions. Our replacements had arrived, and we'd finished handing over our missions to them. We didn't have to tear down our tents; they were staying in Iraq. We were all packed and ready to leave, just waiting for our flight out and dreaming about home.

We sat around our tents watching movies and playing cards. Trangsrud and Tuna were teaching Tyge how to play pinochle. Fly was twisting Tyge's GI Joes into different sexual positions. Ivy was swearing at the deer hunting game on his laptop. Viv was serenading us on guitar with one of his original tunes or telling us (for the fifth time) his story about having sex with his ex-girlfriend for five hours straight ("My dick was so raw after that!"). Every now and then we'd hear people hooting and hollering, and we'd go outside to find the first sergeant or Captain Roar duct-taped to a pole. During movies the guys sat around the television screen commenting on the women: *Look at the titties on her* or *Check out those jugs*. We all knew we were going home so we went wild.

We sat around the tent like men who'd accomplished something. We had had our war and were now ready to return home. We were ready to embrace our loved ones, greet our friends, shake hands with our neighbors, and tell our stories. There was something comforting about those last few lazy weeks in Iraq, something so unthreatening we almost forgot where we were.

One day in late February 2004, Trangsrud and Tuna came back from the chow hall and asked if I'd been outside yet. I hadn't. *Well, go look*, they said. When I got close to the door, I noticed a bright glow between the frame and the tent. I pushed open the door and noticed that the sky was orange—a bright, vivid tangerine. The clouds had trapped the sunlight in, catching and holding it between the sand and the sky, making the whole place glow. It was as if I'd stepped out onto what I imagined Mars to look like. I walked out beyond the tent, my arms outstretched, my head tilted back, trying to figure it out. Trangsrud and Tuna stepped out behind me, and soon others were walking around the tents, staring up at the sky. We'd been in Iraq for almost a year, and the country had never looked like that. We were seeing something new, and for a while we just stood outside, bewildered and speechless, our heads tipped back in amazement as we tried—once again—to figure out what was going on in Iraq.

We flew home on March 8, 2004—Anaconda Army Airbase to Spain; Spain to Fort Carson, Colorado. We got off the plane and shook hands with a number of different officials—most of whom we didn't even know or recognize. We handed over our weapons, which, for some of us, was hard. To prove that we were in fact in America, they handed us lunch— a McDonald's cheeseburger, Coke, and a chocolate chip cookie. They then bussed us over to the barracks where the battalion had beer waiting. Everything moved so quickly. We were home, but it hadn't yet sunk in. It all seemed so new—raw and unfamiliar.

On our second night back a group of us from the platoon went to a restaurant in Colorado Springs to celebrate our return. We ordered "two for one" drinks and ate huge meals. We got a little tipsy and started telling tales from Iraq. At one point Rogers said, "I feel more cocky now that I've been to war, like war has hardened me or something." We all looked at him with big, glossy eyes and agreed. We were indeed cockier than when we arrived. We felt like we'd completed something grand and returned to tell the tale. I looked into the other soldiers' eyes and saw different people. They weren't the same men who'd left North Dakota a year earlier. I didn't know what it was, but I could see it in all the soldiers who returned from the war. It was there, behind their pupils—a piece of the war we'd carry with us forever. Even though we weren't on the front lines of the war or helping Marines pull down statues of Saddam, we were there; we had a part in something bigger than ourselves. For most of us, that was all we needed.

Later, as we wandered half-drunk through a mall, Rogers stopped to point at a couple of young children.

"I love American kids," he slurred. "They don't ask for anything. There's no 'Mee-sta, Mee-sta! Give me food!'"

We stopped next to him, nodded our heads in agreement, and started to escort him forward. He was right. It was nice not to be approached by a crowd of children everywhere you went. But we'd gotten used to that kind of attention, so when we returned it was a bit of a shock to see everything back to normal. We took in everything as if seeing for the first time. Those kids—the ones Rogers pointed out in the mall—they were no longer silent children. Instead, we'd always be reminded of the way Iraqi children said the word "mister" and how unabashedly they begged. The houses were different, the streets somehow strange and unfamiliar. Shadows weren't the same; loud noise made us jump. We were always afraid someone was just around the corner, waiting to take us out. It was all changed. Everything. We were looking at a whole new world.

Rogers liked to call our year in Iraq "The Lost Year," a seemingly fitting epithet to the year we wandered around the desert.

When we were in Iraq, people pasted up posters for lost items all over the walls of the chow hall. Once I saw a poster for a lost M4 rifle and grenade launcher, and chuckled to myself. The poster described the weapon, listed the SNS number, and gave a phone number to call in case anyone found it. I never understood how anyone could leave their weapon behind, especially after carrying it around for so many months. My weapon had become a part of me—my third arm. I never got to fire it in Iraq, but it was always there, slung across my back or over my shoulder. I knew how to take it apart, how it fit back together, where the sand liked to collect, where the metal liked to shine. When I turned it in to the armory at Fort Carson, I had a hard time letting go.

In February, near the end of our time in Iraq, the posters became an annoyance. They were everywhere. Lost weapons. Lost wallets. Lost boonie hats. A lost cat named Skippy. I wanted to paste up my own lost poster:

LOST

One year of my life
If found, ask where it's been, scold it for running off,
and send it back to SPC Lemer.

I could talk about what was lost in Iraq until I was blue in the face, but what good would it do? What would change knowing that my childhood innocence and naïveté about the world was sucked from me while in Iraq? When it came down to it, I was lucky. There were people who lost far more than I did: legs, arms, wives, girlfriends, lives.

What I regret most are the lost relationships. In July 2004 I drove to Wahpeton to turn in my gear and sign the papers releasing me from the military. I had lunch with Rainman, who told me about his vacation with his wife and how she was more beautiful than ever to him. Several months later, Fly sent me an e-mail when his first child was born. King, Rogers, and Trangsrud moved into a house across the street from my apartment in Fargo. I feared they would show up on my doorstep, a case of beer in hand, wanting to get drunk and talk about Iraq, but they never did. Part of me wanted them to show up, so I could have someone to talk to about the war, but by the time I was ready to talk, they'd moved out and moved on. I had dinner with Tuna, his wife, and a handful of other men from the platoon. We sat around the table, silently staring at each other. We didn't know what to talk about outside the military, and we parted ways promising to keep in touch, knowing we never would.

After those first few months back, I stopped seeing people from my platoon around town, and I started to sever ties with everything and every-one related to my military experience. At a gay bar in Moorhead, I ran into a woman I knew from my military company. She didn't recognize me, and I had to explain to her how we knew each other. We exchanged phone numbers, and she left me voice messages every so often, seeing if I wanted to do something—grab a drink, go out for a night of dancing. I never returned her calls. She reminded me of my time in the military, and I wanted a clean break from it all.

But I couldn't stash away everything about the military; some things stuck with me for years. The one thing the deployment gave me, the thing that I took away from it, was self-respect. I was no longer scared about being a gay man in a world that didn't accept me. I'd spent seven years as part of an organization that didn't acknowledge or understand my lifestyle, and I survived just fine. The "last rodeo" was hard, but I wouldn't call it lost. In fact, that year in Iraq gave me more perspective on who I was than any year prior or any year since. For me it was the kind of thing I needed to turn my life around, to point me in the right direction, to confirm the feelings I had about being the man I wanted to be.

And Jeremy was a big part of that.

Once, at a restaurant in Fargo, I was approached by a soldier from my platoon whom I had hardly known. We hadn't talked much during the deployment, but he came up to me, inquired about how I was doing, and asked if I'd heard about Cole. I hadn't. He then told me how Cole was involved in an accident at his job. He was hospitalized with a concussion and when he woke up he didn't remember anything about the deployment; he had forgotten ever being in Iraq.

While I couldn't imagine not remembering being in Iraq, I knew one day I'd start to slowly forget about the war. As each year goes by, I forget more and more about those moments during the war—especially the small ones like waiting out the heat inside concrete bunkers in Kuwait or the long silence after Newman told us about the dead mechanic.

And just like the war, my memories of Jeremy have also faded. All I have left is a handful of events, the ones I replayed in my mind while in Iraq. I never told anyone in my platoon about Jeremy, but I wanted to. There were times when I imagined myself letting it slip over a meal in the chow hall or while we were cleaning our rifles, but I never had the courage to say anything. Instead, I kept my head down, listened but rarely spoke, and, in the nighttime, remembered what it was like to be with him, and to be young and in love.

In February 2006, while at a red light in Mankato, Minnesota, I found myself stopped next to a soldier on his way to drill weekend. It was a warm afternoon, and the soldier had his window halfway down, music blaring from the speakers. He took a swig of mouthwash and wiped his mouth on his sleeve. He wore a black beret and a camouflage jacket. On his shoulder was the backwards American flag patch, a symbol that he'd been deployed overseas.

For a moment, I thought I recognized the soldier. He could have been in my unit or in Iraq the same time I was. I wanted to roll down my passenger side window, lean over, and ask him if he was headed to drill. I wanted to talk to him as a peer—another soldier—familiar with his situation. It had been several years since I'd talked to anyone in my platoon, and every now and then I'd find myself wanting to talk with someone who knew what it was like to still find sand on my uniforms, years after leaving Iraq, someone who remembers how the stars looked over Kuwait, and how distinct the smell of diesel fuel and burning shit could be. I wanted to talk to the ones who stayed in the military, the ones like Bobby who labored through the rest of their enlistment, waiting for another deployment call. I wanted to talk to the ones who got out, like I did, so I could ask them if they received a letter from Major General Michael J. Haugen saying that the National Guard wanted me "back on their team" and offering me a prior service enlistment bonus of up to $15,000. I wanted to ask them if they held onto that letter, as I did, if they ever thought about getting back in. Mostly, I wanted to talk to someone who understood why I couldn't stop thinking about the war.

I didn't roll down the window. I couldn't. I was no longer a soldier. I took my finger off the window switch and looked ahead. The light turned green and the soldier sped away, his *Army of One* bumper sticker reminding me that I could never go back.

Acknowledgments

There are many people who helped make this book a reality. First, I would like to thank Raphael Kadushin and the staff at the University of Wisconsin Press for believing in my story. I would also like to thank the men and women of the North Dakota Army National Guard, who took me along on an experience that changed my life. Thank you to Alicia Strnad and Lin Enger, early readers of my stories. Thanks to Richard Robbins, Candance Black, Terry Davis, Roger Sheffer, Diana Joseph, Richard Terrill, and anyone who read, commented on, and supported my writing while I was at Minnesota State University–Mankato. Thank you to Beka Ongstad for making me laugh and think, even from afar. Thank you to Ashley Marek, Amy Dalrymple, Teri Finneman, Ann Johnson, Niki Johnson, Jessica Benjamin, Catherine Hooper, Natalie Stowe, Heather Rounds, Lynda Majarian, Amanda Dyslin, Jeremy Leiferman, Kyle Mestad, and Pippi Mayfield for your friendship and support. Finally, I would like to thank my family for always supporting me as a writer. Thank you to my mother for being such a good sport and to my father for teaching me the lessons needed in life.

LIVING OUT

Gay and Lesbian Autobiographies

David Bergman, Joan Larkin, and Raphael Kadushin
SERIES EDITORS

In My Father's Arms: A True Story of Incest
Walter A. de Milly III

Midlife Queer: Autobiography of a Decade, 1971–1981
Martin Duberman

The Man Who Would Marry Susan Sontag:
And Other Intimate Literary Portraits of the Bohemian Era
Edward Field

Body, Remember: A Memoir
Kenny Fries

Travels in a Gay Nation: Portraits of LGBTQ Americans
Philip Gambone

Widescreen Dreams: Growing Up Gay at the Movies
Patrick E. Horrigan

The End of Being Known: A Memoir
Michael Klein

The Last Deployment: How a Gay, Hammer-Swinging
Twentysomething Survived a Year in Iraq
Bronson Lemer

Eminent Maricones: Arenas, Lorca, Puig, and Me
Jaime Manrique

Body Blows: Six Performances
Tim Miller

1001 Beds: Performances, Essays, and Travels
Tim Miller

Cleopatra's Wedding Present: Travels through Syria
Robert Tewdwr Moss

Taboo
Boyer Rickel

Secret Places: My Life in New York and New Guinea
Tobias Schneebaum

Wild Man
Tobias Schneebaum

Sex Talks to Girls: A Memoir
Maureen Seaton

Outbound: Finding a Man, Sailing an Ocean
William Storandt